# Projects in the Computing

Mike Holcombe, Andy Stratton, Sally Fincher
and Gary Griffiths (Eds.)

# Projects in the Computing Curriculum

**Proceedings of the Project 98 Workshop, Sheffield 1998**

 Springer

Mike Holcombe
Department of Computer Science, University of Sheffield, Sheffield, S1 4DP

Andy Stratton
Department of Computer Science University of Sheffield, Sheffield, S1 4DP

Sally Fincher
Kent University, Canterbury, CT2 7NF

Gary Griffiths
School of Computing and Mathematics, Teeside University,
Middlesborough, TS1 3BA

ISBN 1-85233-010-4 Springer-Verlag Berlin Heidelberg New York

British Library Cataloguing in Publication Data
Projects in the computing curriculum : proceedings of the
   Project 98 workshop, Sheffield 1998
   1.Computer science - Study and teaching (Higher) - Great
   Britain - Congresses 2.Computers - Study and teaching
   (Higher) - Great Britain - Congresses
   1.Holcombe, W. M. L. (W. Michael L.)
   004'.0711'41
   ISBN 1852330104

Library of Congress Cataloging-in-Publication Data
A catalog record for this book is available from the Library of Congress

Typesetting: Camera ready by editors
Printed and bound at the Athenæum Press Ltd., Gateshead, Tyne & Wear
34/3830-543210 Printed on acid-free paper

# FOREWORD

Dr Peter Milton, Director of Programme Review, Quality Assurance Agency

I am grateful to the authors for giving me the opportunity to write this foreword, mainly because it represents the first occasion that the Fund for the Development of Teaching and Learning (FDTL) has led directly to a publication such as this. In my former capacity as Director of Quality Assessment at the Higher Education Funding Council for England (HEFCE), I chaired the FDTL Committee during 1996/7 and am delighted to see the projects which were selected so painstakingly leading to successful outcomes.

Assessment of the quality of higher education (HE) was introduced in 1993 and was intended to improve public information about what was on offer in British universities and colleges, as well as to assist in the enhancement of educational opportunities for students. This was part of a larger agenda in which educational quality and the standards achieved by students have come under increasing scrutiny, with a long-term objective of linking funding allocations to the quality of the provision.

It was in this context that the FDTL Initiative was launched in 1995 to support projects aimed at stimulating developments in teaching and learning and to encourage the dissemination of good practice across the HE sector. Good practice is identified through the process of quality assessment and bids for funding can only be made by those institutions which have demonstrated high quality provision. To date, the programme includes 63 projects drawn from 23 subject areas.

The 44 projects funded in the first phase, of which this project in Computer Science is one, started in October 1996 and cover the 15 subjects assessed between Summer 1993 and Spring 1995. Phase two, comprising 19 projects drawn from a further eight subjects, commenced in October 1997. The Initiative is funded by the HEFCE and by the Department of Education Northern Ireland (DENI), with just under £14m allocated for the four-year period 1996-2000, and is co-ordinated by HEFCE staff in conjunction with the Centre for Higher Education Practice at the Open University. All institutions which have been awarded grants are themselves making contributions towards the projects by releasing staff and resources and through overhead costs.

Phase one projects are entering their second year of activity, with dissemination of outcomes taking many forms. These include training events, the production of teaching and learning materials, the construction and maintenance of websites and e-mail discussion groups, newsletters, conferences and workshops. Future dissemination will be even more innovative, particularly in terms of exploiting the natural links between different projects in the same subject areas. It is with pleasure, therefore, that I commend the material contained herein to you.

# PREFACE

Computer Science is a practical subject. We teach the underlying theory of course, but it is by putting the theory into practice that one really learns how to design and build quality systems. Thus much of a student's effort is focused on practical work. In many cases this practical work is fairly constrained, often a specific task or problem is set and the solutions to these are of a fairly predictable nature. The real challenge appears when the problem is of an open ended nature and the student or students have to explore many different issues on the way to constructing a solution. The role of projects in the computing curriculum is therefore of great importance. The Project'98 workshop, from which this volume has evolved, was held to look at current experiences and ideas about the many and varied types of University projects.

What is a project? It could be a large piece of work carried out by an individual student over perhaps two semesters, perhaps in the last or penultimate year of study and often research-oriented. Equally, it could be a first year group project where a small group of students are beginning to experience the problems and issues related to teamwork in the context of a simple software development problem. In the papers in this volume we will meet a broad cross-section of project styles. In each case the project consists of an extended piece of work involving several weeks effort. In many cases each student or team is investigating a different problem or issue and in other cases there is a single problem and the teams compete to find a solution.

In all these cases, particularly where the project is somewhat open ended, there are concerns about assessing the work fairly and reliably. There is much to be learnt here, as well as in the processes whereby the teacher manages the project process and the extent to which students share this responsibility.

The academic community is also being told by industrial colleagues that their educational provision is not entirely relevant to industry's needs. Projects can provide a mechanism for overcoming some of these worries and help students to develop many of the skills and understanding needed to apply computing technology in an effective way in the world of work.

In an age where quality assurance issues in education are a major concern the development of innovative project based learning can seem to be a high risk undertaking. The setting of realistic and defensible objectives has to be undertaken and this can seem daunting. Yet many examples of staff developing exciting and effective practices can be found, some of them in this volume.

We must not, however, forget the student dimension. Without their enthusiasm none of this is possible. One unique feature of this book is that it has contributions from students. In one case the student examined the way group allocation might affect project outcomes, the other contribution (from a group of students) describes the work of the prototype company that they set up. We would have liked to have received more student contributions and perhaps, if there is another volume like this, this will come to pass.

We hope that this volume will provide some ideas and experiences that can be used by others in developing their use of projects in the computing curriculum in the attempt to achieve many of our educational objectives.

Some of the issues addressed include:

* managing project work;
* assessing project work;
* industrial projects;
* large group projects;
* individual projects.

# ACKNOWLEDGEMENTS

This book originated with the Project'98 Workshop held at the University of Sheffield in April 1998. It was organised by three of the educational development projects funded by the Higher Education Funding Council for England under its Fund for the Development of Teaching and Learning. These three projects all share a focus on the teaching and learning of computer science and software engineering through project work.

We would like to thank all those involved in the organisation of the workshop and the Programme Committee for all the work they did in making the Workshop such a success. In particular we must thank Marie Willett for making sure that everything ran so smoothly.

# PROGRAMME COMMITTEE

Mike Holcombe (Sheffield University)
Andy Stratton (Sheffield University)
Sally Fincher (Kent University)
Gary Griffiths (Teesside University)
Dan Simpson (Brighton University)
Andrew McGettrick (Strathclyde University)
Alan Jones (Teesside University)
Gordon Davies (Open University)
John Slater (Kent University)
Neil Willis (Leeds Metropolitan University)
Bernard Suffrin (Oxford University)
Steve Madddock (Sheffield University)
Tony Cowling (Sheffield University)

# CONTENTS

## PART 1 Professional Issues and Projects

## PART 2 Group Projects

## PART 3 New Directions

# PART 4 Negotiation

# PART 5 Managing Projects

# POSTER

# STUDENT POSTERS

# INTRODUCTION

The first part of the book is concerned with the teaching of a variety of professional issues. It is becoming increasingly important, as the computing industry develops into a professional, accredited and regulated activity that universities address these issues. In his paper on teaching ethics, G Brown tackles the difficult and challenging task of trying to persuade a generally sceptical audience that ethics are important and can impact upon many practical professional aspects of life as a software engineer. By asking students to keep a personal diary and to record their thoughts on ethical issues that arise in their daily lives he hopes to achieve a more direct and personal involvement with students in a way that case studies may not.

The paper by M Petre and S Fincher looks at a collaborative project involving a number of universities in the management and organisation of project work in the curriculum. The Effective Projectwork in Computer Science (EPCOS) programme seeks to identify good practice in this area and to attempt to evaluate and help to transfer this experience to other departments. Aspects such as outcomes, allocation, management models, assessment, negotiation, integration with the curriculum and large teams are examined.

The focus of L Neal's paper is the learning of professional issues through organised group projects. Here the groups of students look at a scenario describing a plausible problem which has a number of ethical and legal dimensions. The students investigate and discuss the issues and write a group report and give a presentation.

In part two we examine more general group projects. The first paper describes a group project for second year students which involves solving problems for industrial clients. The paper, by A Stratton, M Holcombe and P Croll also explores the problem of running such projects in an era of increasing class sizes.

The use of an Internet web site to provides a strong motivation for students to focus their group projects on. V King explores some of the issues of enthusing students through the use of such a virtual workspace. A number of promising experiences are reported.

Knowledge based systems is the technology considered by M Lee, A Harrison and A Sammes. Here group projects are used in the development of significant expert systems with a wide variety of knowledge domains. Experiences and observations on the running of these projects are described.

The Professional Skills at Teesside project is described in the paper be G Griffiths and M Lockyer. The purpose of the project is to provide supporting materials in the areas of group projects, live projects, professional skills, supervised work experience and student support and monitoring. The paper describes the activities of the project and offers some conclusions.

Part three looks at some new directions and reflections on project work.

The idea of senior students setting up their own software company and trading with real clients is considered by M Holcombe and A Stratton. This course, although only recently introduced, has been a successful experiment and the paper describes the background and some of the responses from the students on it.

R Boyle's paper poses a number of important questions about the purpose of project work. The non-technical outcomes, skills and experiences are often as important as the technical knowledge gained. The paper concludes with some proposals to ensure that these non-technical aspects are considered in the planning of project work.

The next part focuses on negotiation.

Most projects involve some degree of negotiation even if it is of an informal type during the course of a meeting between students and supervisers. M Birtle's paper looks at the process of addressing negotiation in an explicit fashion. A framework for negotiated learning in team projects is proposed together with some suggestions for implementing this within a university course.

B Morris looks at some of the problems associated with organising individual projects for large classes. The idea of a learning coach who coordinates and motivates the students as they develop their project from idea to fruition is explained.

In part five the issues of managing and organising projects is considered. R Cooper and R Welland describe the approach of their university in using technology to assist in a variety of aspects of the process. The use of suitable web pages is shown to be of value in this respect.

The views of an industrial consultant who is responsible for managing group projects provides an interesting alternative to the usual academic perspective. S Price has been managing student groups directly for a number of years and his application of industrial attitudes to the process have a number of educational benefits.

Finally we hear about the perceptions of the students actually doing the projects. P Capon describes the results of a survey carried out amongst project stuents and looks at the differences between some of the perceptions of the students and those of their teachers, particularly relating to the assessment of the project.

The book ends with some posters describing a number of aspects of project work.

L Wright looks at the experiences of teaching a large class and concludes that the planning of a "cyber cafe" makes an interesting and useful activity for orienting a group project around.

Two posters submitted by students complete this part. K Thorn examined some of the psychological issues in the process of group formation as part of a project in cognitive psychology. Some interesting information is obtained from surveys and analysed. The VICI company is a software house set up by a group of fourth year students which is trading on a number of fronts, software development, consultancy and training. Some further details of the company's activities are described.

# PART 1

## Professional Issues and Projects

# Teaching Professional Ethics to Software Engineers

Guy J. Brown

Department of Computer Science, University of Sheffield,
Sheffield, United Kingdom

## 1 Introduction

Like all people, software engineers face ethical dilemmas in their working lives. Friction may occur between deeply-held values, such as conflicts between honesty and respecting privacy, or between loyalty to one's employer and avoiding harm to others. There is good reason, therefore, to ensure that students of software engineering are equipped with the skills needed to resolve such conflicts. Of course, the same may be said of students entering other professions, such as medicine, law or civil engineering. However, software engineering currently faces a number of challenges that set it apart from the other professions, and which make the need for effective ethical education particularly pressing.

One compelling reason for ethical education of software engineers is that they wield tremendous power. A surgeon performing an operation has responsibility for a single life; a software engineer writing the control system for an aircraft has responsibility for hundreds. Furthermore, increasing amounts of financial and personal information are held in computer databases, giving those in the computing professions unprecedented opportunities to steal or invade privacy. Technological changes are occurring so rapidly that enforcement institutions cannot keep pace with their social and legal implications; ultimately, we must rely on the ethical standards of individuals.

Computer technology also transforms and aggravates some old ethical problems, and raises others that are quite new [1]. Concerns about the privacy of surface post have been transformed by the advent of electronic mail; theft of intellectual property has been aggravated by the digital storage of text, audio and video; and the distribution of material with political, sexual or racist content on the internet is posing novel ethical problems.

Additionally, the tendency for those working in computer-related disciplines to be ethically 'detached' is well documented. Computer abusers often believe that they can rationalise their acts; those who gain unauthorised access to computer systems claim that weaknesses in computer networks are being pointed out, or that harm is done only to an organisation (which can more easily be rationalised) and not to an individual [2]. This attitude also extends to academics, many of whom are implicated in computer misuse (particularly software theft); as a result, students receive ambiguous signals about computer ethics [3]. There is also a tendency to disregard the human element when debating ethical aspects of computer technology [4]. Common statements such as 'computers cause unemployment' imply that technology is an autonomous force and therefore deny a basic fact – that all ethical issues arise through human agency.

Despite these important issues, technical innovations in software engineering are proceeding far in advance of our understanding of the ethical and social implications of computer technology. Medical ethics, legal ethics and business ethics are all established fields of academic study, but the field of computer ethics is still in its infancy. Indeed, courses in professional ethics are regarded by many staff in science and engineering departments as time wasted on vacuous philosophical discussion, which would be better spent on the rigorous study of technical topics. Worse still, many faculty regard courses on ethics as 'easy', and may even perceive them as contributing to the lowering of academic standards [5]. Given this attitude amongst faculty, it is not surprising that students also perceive such courses to be a 'soft option'. Further, many faculty in science and engineering departments consider that since ethics is not a 'technical' subject it can be taught by anyone regardless of experience.

In summary, there seem to be compelling reasons for providing undergraduate students in software engineering with an effective ethical education. Currently, however, software engineering education is dominated by technical issues, and skills in ethical reasoning are poorly addressed (concerns that software engineering education is too 'technicist' have also been expressed by [6] and [7], amongst others). As a result, students of software engineering graduate with little understanding of the ethical implications of software development, and are often poorly equipped to uphold the standards of behaviour demanded by professional organisations and the general public.

## 2 Values in Professional Practice and Higher Education

Professional bodies such as the British Computer Society (BCS) and the Association for Computing Machinery (ACM) have responded to the need for ethical education of software engineers in two ways. Firstly, they have introduced codes of ethics which formally state the values that are important to the software engineering profession as a whole, together with codes of conduct which state the required standard of professional behaviour [8], [9]. Historically, professions such as medicine and law have established codes of conduct in order to demonstrate that they can control their membership (and therefore avoid external regulation). Codes of conduct have particular significance for these professions, since physicians and lawyers who transgress the codes can be prevented from practicing. However, an individual need not be a member of the BCS or ACM to be regarded as a professional software engineer (indeed, many practicing software engineers are not affiliated with either organisation). Hence, although the BCS and ACM are able to ensure that their *members* are accountable for unethical behaviour, they have limited influence on ethical standards in the software engineering profession as a whole.

The second response of the professional bodies has been to encourage the inclusion of professional ethics in the curricula of software engineering degree courses. This has been achieved both by publishing recommendations for curriculum design [10], [7] and by imposing constraints on the content of accredited courses. Inevitably, courses on professional ethics that meet the BCS and ACM requirements tend to stress the importance of professional codes of conduct. As such, they place more emphasis on the collective moral stance of the profession rather than upon individual moral decisions. One could argue, then, that even with the inclusion of such courses in the software engineering curriculum, students still do not acquire the intellectual tools needed for ethical decision making in a professional context.

While professional bodies are attempting to establish a consensus on the values that are important to the software engineering profession, a similar debate is currently taking place in higher education. In much the same way that the software engineering profession is under increasing public scrutiny, so higher education is facing increased expectations from students, parents, employers, government and the professions. As a result, universities are being asked to re-examine long-established practices, and to enunciate the aims and objectives of teaching and learning in unambiguous terms; an example is the Higher Education Quality Council (HEQC) 'graduateness' project, which is attempting to clarify the core properties that characterise a graduate [11]. Value questions are playing a central role in this process; just as professional software engineers have debated their values in order to establish a code of conduct, so the values that underlie teaching and learning in higher education are now being questioned.

Value issues are also being debated in relation to pre-university schooling. Hyland [12] argues that the pressures of the National Curriculum have led to a neglect of moral education at school level, and that this deficiency is paralleled in post-16 education due to the influence of the National Council for Vocational Qualifications (NCVQ). In the competence-based education and training model espoused by the NCVQ, moral education is principally intended to ensure that prospective workers have the values required by employers. Hyland argues that, as a result, values are treated within a framework that is technicist, uncritical and morally impoverished; the analogy with software engineering education in the universities is clear.

In the remainder of this paper, we address a number of value questions that arise in the teaching of professional ethics to students of software engineering. Our study is motivated both by a desire to develop an effective ethical education for students of software engineering, and to investigate wider value issues in higher education. Ethical decisions are intimately connected with values; hence, a course on professional ethics provides a particularly intriguing vehicle for investigating values in teaching and learning. Furthermore, a course in professional ethics provides a context in which the values of the teacher and the values of the student are more openly debated than in most teaching environments.

# 3 Teaching Professional Ethics to Software Engineers

A number of courses in professional ethics for software engineers have been described in the literature. Many of these emphasize the use of case studies, which may be real-life examples [13], or fictional writing that is intended to illustrate a particular aspect of ethical conflict [14], [15]. Group discussion is another commonly used approach for teaching professional ethics. For example, Wong [16] suggests that student groups should discuss a particular topic (such as privacy, employee monitoring, responsibility for software errors and so on), and then report a summary of their discussion to the whole class (see also [17]).

These approaches recognise that effective teaching of professional ethics demands a different approach to the formal lecture presentations which so dominate teaching in science and engineering. However, the most common approach – analysis of case studies – treats ethical dilemmas simply as a problem-solving exercise. As a result, students may see work in professional ethics as being no more than an abstract intellectual exercise.

We believe that what is missing from the teaching of professional ethics is an *experiential element*. Like all philosophical enquiry, ethical enquiry in the context of professional practice can only be fully appreciated by personal involvement. Moral dilemmas encountered through the analysis of case studies do not engage the student in the same way as a real moral dilemma; they do not convey its subjectivity, nor its complexity.

Collier [18] has argued forcefully for the role of an experiential element in the learning of moral judgement. He makes an important connection between depth of understanding and depth of emotional experience. Strong and sustained feelings for a close relative convey a much greater understanding of that person than one feels for a casual acquaintance; for the same reason, students should have more than a superficial engagement with ethical issues:

> There would appear to be an urgent need ... for education systems to include programmes which prepare students for recognising, and learning to think critically about, subjective perceptions and value questions. To develop such insight, in a form which influences one's active professional judgement, the usual lecture courses are inadequate; the learning must have an experiential element and indeed 'existential' basis; it must be 'felt in the bones'. The existential dimension required in the exploration and analysis of value issues will only be secured if students become personally involved in the study of the motivation and morality of human situations.
>
> (Collier [18], page 287)

We propose that such an experiential element can be achieved by encouraging students to reflect upon their own practice as university students. Practice as a student is training for practice as a member of a profession. In both contexts, an individual has responsibilities that may be placed in conflict; to teachers, sponsors and other students; or to clients, employers and the profession. Moreover, university life is a source of real ethical dilemmas that provide a rich resource for ethics teaching. Of course, simply existing in the university environment and facing day-to-day ethical problems is not sufficient; it is widely recognised that in order to make effective use of first-hand experience it is necessary to reflect upon it [19].

# 4 A Portfolio Assessment in Professional Ethics

In an effort to enhance the experiential dimension of ethics teaching, a portfolio assessment was devised as part of a course in professional ethics taught to second-year undergraduate and postgraduate students of software engineering. The portfolio consisted of three components; written responses to fictional case studies, a personal diary and a critical evaluation of the portfolio's contents.

The personal diary was conceived as a means by which students could reflect on their own practice (see also [20], [17]). Whereas case studies concern the fortunes of fictional characters, a diary communicates personally experienced emotions. We hoped, therefore, that reflection upon ethical dilemmas arising in student life might provide a strong experiential dimension to the portfolio. Students were asked to write about specific incidents in their lives as software engineering students which raised ethical questions. Additionally, it was suggested that the diary might contain reflections upon material in other modules that raised ethical issues, or upon newspaper articles or television programmes that raised ethical issues and were related to information technology. Given that the diaries might contain 'private' writing, students were given an assurance that the confidentiality of their diaries would be respected.

The portfolio assessment suggested a number of research issues, which were addressed as part of an ongoing action-research study. Our working hypothesis was that the diary element of the portfolio assessment would enhance the experiential element of the professional ethics course. More specifically, we expected the diary to evoke a greater felt response than case studies, and for this to enhance the student's learning experience. Clearly, the diary would only enhance the experiential element of the professional ethics course if students used it to record and debate their 'true feelings'. However, such a true record may be compromised by factors such as an inability to express complex thoughts and feelings, or concerns about privacy. The role of these factors in our course, if any, was therefore an important research issue.

Data was gathered from interviews with twenty students on the professional ethics course. Additional evidence was obtained from questionnaires, my research diary, and from documents that formed part of the student's portfolio assessments. In the process of this study, the issue of *authenticity* emerged as an important theme; by authentic, we mean an action or response that genuinely reflects the values and value priorities of an individual. In the following sections, the theme of authenticity is followed as a common thread through aspects of the learning, teaching and assessment of professional ethics.

# 5 Authenticity in Learning

Evidence from the interviews suggested that many students were unable to identify closely with the predicaments described in the case studies. Some interviewees stated that they could not relate to the situations that the characters were in, and expressed a detachment between their own feelings and those of the case study characters:

> It was fairly detached, because from the scenario you've already given us a background of what that person is like ... and therefore you still have to answer it in the way that he would be like ... what you have to do is transpose yourself onto them, and use their reasoning rather than your own.

This quote suggests that the students' responses to the case studies could have been an expression of the implied values of a fictional character, rather than an expression of their own values (in other words, the reader was thinking 'what should this character do next?' rather than 'what would I do next if I was in this character's position?'). Why might the authenticity of the answers to the case studies be compromised in this way?

One possibility is that the dilemmas described in the case studies took place in an unfamiliar context. The case studies were adapted from [14], which focuses on the ethical problems facing managers and company decision-makers in the computer industry. Several interviewees stated that they found it hard to identify with the dilemmas facing the characters, because they had little understanding of the commercial backdrop. Additionally, many of the interviewees failed to identify with the case studies simply because they didn't concern emotive subjects:

> Nothing that happens with computers these days is really particularly unusual ... most of the ethical issues have more or less been cleared up some time ago, or at least have been debated to the point where I no longer bother to think about them too much. This does seem to be a subject in which morality is low down on the list of requirements ... it seems to be part of the culture, or maybe its just part of the mind set of people who enjoy computer programming.

As we have already noted, the ethically detached 'mind set' of those working in computer-related disciplines is widely recognised [21], [22], [23], [16]. It appears, therefore, that case study-based teaching of professional ethics in the domain of computer science is hindered by an intriguing paradox; we argue that the teaching of professional ethics should contain a strong experiential element (students should 'feel it in their bones'), and yet case studies based purely on computer science issues appear to evoke very little emotional response.

Another reason for the failure of students to identify with the case studies was suggested by the following interviewee, who was asked how closely he related to the scenario characters:

> Not at all, mainly because they're fictional. If they were real characters I'd feel far more for them than people who've been completely made up and fictional ... what happens to them doesn't particularly matter. If I'd known that they were real people and you were writing about something that actually happened, I'd have identified with them a great deal more.

This quote suggests another perspective on the issue of authenticity; case studies that are presented purely as fiction may be insufficient to stimulate serious personal reflection. In short, if we require an authentic response from the reader, the stimulus must be perceived as a factual account.

We now consider the diary component of the portfolio. Evidence from the interviews confirmed that students used the diary as a medium for recording and reflecting upon significant personal events. Indeed, for some students the diary writings were cathartic; they presented an opportunity for debating unresolved issues which were causing anxiety. For example, one student wrote several diary entries about his decision to leave a part-time job, expressing regret that he had let down his employer at a time when they were short-staffed. Another student used a diary entry to reflect upon her decision not to inform an employer that had mistakenly overpaid her.

The aim of the diary was to engage students in genuine reflection upon their values and value priorities. In some cases, however, the authenticity of the diary entries may have been compromised because students didn't understand its purpose as a mechanism for reflection; some diaries were rather superficial commentaries on news stories or other events, rather than subjective, personal writing. An entry in my research diary, made in the second week of the professional ethics course, also suggests that there was some uncertainty about the diary:

> A lot of students have asked about the diary this week. The commonest problem seems to be that they simply don't know what to write about. Some seem to relish the opportunity to talk about their personal experience, others seem less sure - 'nothing has happened which raises an ethical issue'. One asked about the confidentiality of what he was writing, concerned that I would 'turn him in'. Another student joked that the main purpose of the diary was to provide me with something 'juicy' to read.

This entry in my research diary also suggests concerns about privacy. Although students were reassured of the confidentiality of their diary entries, many were reluctant to write about their thoughts and feelings. Again, this has implications for the authenticity of their writing; students should not be expected to reveal what may be intimate personal experiences unless they have complete trust in the tutor and are certain of confidentiality. More than half of the interviewees expressed concerns about privacy, and many of these opted to write predominantly about newspaper articles rather than their own personal experience. Another reason why the authenticity of the diary entries may have been compromised is because students found it hard to express in writing what may have been rather complex and subtle experiences (see also [5]). Several interviewees alluded to this problem.

The notion of 'authenticity' was further investigated by asking interviewees whether they considered their diary entries to be a 'true record' of events that occurred in the semester. The majority of interviewees agreed that this was the case. Interestingly, a higher number responded positively to a questionnaire statement 'the diary was an accurate account of incidents occurring in my life during the semester', suggesting that some students made a distinction between a 'true' record and an 'accurate' one. What, then, did interviewees understand by the term 'true record'? Investigation of this issue raised some interesting perspectives, which again have a bearing on the notion of an authentic account. One interviewee suggested that the diary was motivated or constrained by the requirements of the assessment:

> I didn't recognise a lot of ethical situations which came along
> during the day. Unless you instantly recognise those and think
> about them later, I don't think [the diary] is a true representation
> of what happens, because you're forcing yourself to write about
> things that might not be ... you know ... ethical issues.

Our notion of an authentic account implies a subjective and personal piece of writing which reflects the values and value priorities of the author. For this interviewee the diary entries were not authentic because they were neither completely subjective nor completely personal; indeed, the interviewees suggest that they were written through an unnaturally intense process of self-analysis ('forcing yourself to write').

Many interviewees associated a 'true record' with one that was factual, rather than fictional. The issue of a fictional account was investigated further in the interviews, because it was anticipated that students might write fictional diary entries for a number of reasons (concerns over privacy, a lack of personal events to discuss, or perhaps a tendency to elaborate). This line of investigation was suggested by a diary entry submitted by a student in the year before the current study, which explicitly raised the issue of fictional writing:

> A computer science student was asked by her lecturer to submit
> some material outlining incidents which had raised ethical issues
> during the semester. She looked at the portfolio of her work as the
> hand-in date loomed closer. It was pathetically thin. Fear gripped
> her heart as she began to wonder if this assignment would be less
> than perfect. Surely she could fabricate a few entries and make up
> a few events? As long as they sounded realistic then the lecturer

would never know. The student thought and she thought some more. She didn't know what to do.

(Extract from student portfolio)

In fact, we found no evidence that the writing of fictional accounts was widespread; only 10% of students responded negatively to the questionnaire statement 'the diary was an accurate account of incidents occurring in my life during the autumn semester'. Additionally, the interviews indicated that most students who responded negatively to this statement did so because they wrote mostly about news stories or because they moved events in time, not because they wrote fictional accounts. The interviews revealed that fictional writing was an emotive issue for students, who often associated the term 'fiction' with deceit and fabrication. Several students indicated that they probably could have written fictional entries in their diaries, but that it would have felt dishonest:

> It wouldn't have made much difference, but I wouldn't have felt happy doing it ... I'd rather do it truthfully ... whoever marked it wouldn't know if it had happened or not ... but I wouldn't feel comfortable, I'd just like to put what really happened down, otherwise its not a true diary, just a piece of fiction.

In this quote, the interviewee suggests that writing fictional diary entries 'wouldn't have made much difference'. Is this really the case? More specifically, we should ask whether the fictional basis of a diary entry invalidates its authenticity; in other words, does writing an account of a fictional dilemma still engage the author in a consideration of his own values? On first consideration, we might assume that writing a fictional diary entry is no better than analysing a fictional case study of the kind discussed above. However, there is a difference. All fiction is autobiographical in some sense: the author identifies with the characters that he creates in some way, even though he may not be totally identified with any one of them. Hence, even writing fictional diary entries may encourage students to reflect upon their own values. Indeed, it has been suggested that fictional writing provides a powerful mechanism for enquiry into professional practice [24].

That said, it seems likely that the emotional response to a hypothetical dilemma that is conceived by oneself is likely to be less intense than the reaction to an unanticipated real-life situation. Several interviewees expressed similar concerns when asked about the implications of writing fictional diary entries:

> It wouldn't have the same kind of emotional content really, would it? If something's actually happened to you, you'd have a far more personal opinion of it than if you'd made up an event ... it wouldn't be a personal event, it would be another scenario.

In summary, we have identified a number of factors which may have compromised the authenticity of student's diary entries; some students did not fully understand the diary as a mechanism for personal reflection, while others had concerns regarding the privacy of their diaries. Many students found it difficult to express complex thoughts and feelings in words. Additionally, some interviewees suggested that the diary engaged them in an unnaturally intense process of self-analysis which went beyond personal reflection; they were 'forcing themselves to think things'.

# 6 Authenticity in Teaching

The emphasis of our course on professional ethics was on critical enquiry and self-awareness; traditional values were analysed without attempting to subvert them (the purpose of ethical inquiry is, after all, to ensure that such values are not accepted uncritically). Even so, 'indoctrination' may occur even when a tutor has no conscious intention to do so; teachers speak from a position of authority on technical issues, and hence students may also gain the impression that the teacher's views on ethical issues are the 'right' ones.

In fact, we found little evidence in the interview transcriptions to suggest that indoctrination should be a concern. On the contrary, several students commented that the lecture material was presented in a rather 'neutral' way:

> I didn't notice very many of your own opinions ... I didn't realise until now that there weren't.

> I thought that the way [the scenarios] were written was very clever, in that you couldn't really find out what your opinion was ... I suppose in one way that was why they were sometimes quite hard, because you might see a question where you think 'it's obvious what he wants me to write here' but you couldn't really see that at all.

These quotes imply that a course on professional ethics can be taught in a 'value neutral' manner. Is it really possible to conceal one's values when teaching professional ethics (or, indeed, any subject), and if so, is it desirable to do so?

It is widely recognised that indoctrination is an important and difficult issue in the teaching of ethics [5]. So, should a teacher try to present an impression of complete neutrality? Surely, such an approach would not be authentic. Actions in teaching are only legitimate if they genuinely reflect one's own values; one cannot defend decisions and opinions if they are not genuine. We would prefer, therefore, that teachers state their ethical position and allow students to question it. However, should this mean that any opinion is acceptable? For example, if a teacher of a course in professional ethics genuinely believes that an illegal act is morally acceptable, should he express this opinion? Such an action might be regarded as incompatible with the role of a professional educator, yet to say otherwise would not be authentic.

In short, our findings suggest a conflict between professional roles and personal values in teaching. This conflict arose several times during the professional ethics course. On one occasion I was confronted with the issue during a tutorial discussion; the corresponding entry in my research diary suggests that this was a rather uncomfortable experience:

> During the tutorial today, one of the MSc students brought up the subject of software theft. He told me that he had considered copying Microsoft Word from a friend, until he heard that it was possible to buy it at a discounted price through the University. He also said that the lecture material we had covered on copyright law had made him think twice, although I suspect that he was just telling me this because he thought it was what I wanted to hear. At the end of our conversation, he asked 'anyway, can you honestly say that you have never copied software yourself?'. I mumbled for a while, but basically avoided giving him an answer.
>
> (Extract from my research diary)

The issue of this conflict also arose during the interviews, and was made particularly clearly by one interviewee when asked about the influence that the lectures had on his diary entries:

> I'm not sure whether what you were saying is what should be, or whether its the feeling within yourself. It might be something like 'this is the course and I have to teach it', but you as an individual don't think so ... I think that 90% of the time, its just someone who's paid money to teach something from a book. They might be advocating something to you, but they have a different agenda.

The conflict between role and person in teaching has previously been noted by Buchmann [25]. She contends that teachers are bound by obligations to fulfil their role. One obligation is to students, to take an interest in their learning, but there are also obligations to more remote agents; professional bodies, university policy makers and the discipline itself. Further, she claims that the requirement for authenticity in teaching should not remove the obligations associated with the teacher's role; a proper regard for authenticity in teaching should involve making authentic choices within a framework constrained by externally imposed standards.

Buchmann's argument suggests that it is neither authentic nor desirable for teachers to conceal their values. Perhaps we should question, though, whether concealing one's values is possible at all. Some interviewees suggested that they detected very few of my opinions during the lectures, but does this mean that the course was taught in a 'value neutral' manner? Even if my own values were not openly discussed during the presentation of the course material, they influenced the selection of that material and the emphasis that I placed on different topics. Churchill [26] makes a similar observation:

> Even when we are not teaching ethics (perhaps especially then), moral values are taught. Values are embedded in teaching styles and strategies and in the general environment of the classroom, laboratory, or hospital ward ... It is in this sense that values are not only present, but central in teaching. Moral values are taught – like it or not – unless one artificially (and inaccurately) confines the term 'teaching' to the transmission of formalised units of knowledge.
>
> (Churchill [26], pages 301-302)

Education is never value-free; indeed, values such as the basing of arguments on evidence and logic are central to academic culture. Nevertheless, the finding that some students considered my course on professional ethics to be taught in a 'value-neutral' manner remains an unsettling one; on reflection, it seems clear that I was reluctant to admit my ethical position on some issues.

# 7 Authenticity in Assessment

The notion of an authentic assessment has been discussed by a number of authors [27], [28]. Wiggins [29] suggests some principles that are necessary for authentic assessment. He proposes that criteria for success in the assessment should be publicly known, and that the assessment should be dynamic (in other words, it should capture change over time). Additionally, the scoring should include an element of self-assessment, should allow students to identify their strengths and weaknesses, and should allow them to demonstrate what they do well. Finally, he suggests that authentic assessments should encourage the integration of skills and knowledge acquired from different sources, and should promote pride in ownership.

The assessment of our professional ethics course satisfied many of these requirements. Students were asked to compile a portfolio of diary entries and commentaries on fictional scenarios, together with a critical evaluation of the portfolio which discussed its strengths and weaknesses. The portfolio therefore contained an element of self-assessment, and involved the integration of knowledge from different sources (deciding what evidence to include in the portfolio may also be regarded as a form of self-assessment). Further, the assessment was dynamic; tasks were completed at regular intervals throughout the semester, and students were asked to comment on the changes in their ethical reasoning over time. The purpose of the assessment was clearly stated to the students, and the criteria by which it was assessed were carefully documented and distributed at the start of the course.

However, evidence from the interview transcriptions suggests that the concept of a portfolio assessment (or, indeed, any kind of assessment) as 'authentic' is problematic when considered from the perspective of the teacher. Authentic assessment is knowing what you want your students to know; in other words, the assessment clearly communicates a requirement for a certain kind of behaviour that the tutor considers desirable. In some sense, then, an authentic assessment embodies the values of the teacher who devises it. Equally, the assessment only satisfies its goal if it elicits the required behaviour from the student. In the context of the professional ethics course, the goal of the assessment was to engage students in a discussion of their own values and value priorities. The success of our assessment therefore rests on the authentic communication of values by two agents: the teacher (whose values shape the form of the assessment) and the student (whose values shape the form of the portfolio). Did the assessment encourage students to consider their own values, and to openly communicate them in the portfolio?

In fact, we have already presented evidence which suggests that the contents of many portfolios did not genuinely reflect the values of the author. For example, for many interviewees there was a conceptual gap between a personal diary and the diary kept for the course. One indication of this was the tendency of some students to dismiss minor incidents or incidents not directly concerned with the field of computer science, which might otherwise have been recorded in a personal diary. Some students didn't record events in their diaries because of concerns about privacy. Additionally, many students indicated that because the diary was assessed, they took much more care in writing it that they otherwise would.

In summary, our findings suggest that an assessment which satisfies the criteria for authenticity may not be entirely successful from the perspective of the teacher, because it may not elicit an authentic response from the student. Furthermore, our study exposes a central irony which challenges the notion of an authentic assessment: students invest little effort in a piece of work that is not assessed, but assessing a piece of work fundamentally changes the way in which students approach it.

# 8 Authenticity and Professional Decision Making

Students were introduced to two techniques for the analysis of ethical dilemmas; moral philosopy and professional codes of ethics (specifically, the codes of the British Computer Society and the Association for Computing Machinery). The questionnaire and evidence from student portfolios both indicated that most students found the moral philosophy more helpful than the professional codes when analysing fictional ethical dilemmas. For example, only 50% of students completing a questionnaire agreed that the professional codes were a great help in analysing fictional scenarios, but 85% agreed that the moral philosophy was a great help. Evidence from the portfolios suggested that most students found the professional codes easier to understand and apply, but that they gained greater insight through the consideration of moral philosophy. One student outlined the reasons for his preference in the critical evaluation of his portfolio:

> One area where the moral philosophy certainly did help was in evaluating the scenarios. The various techniques helped to provide a framework around which to probe and evaluate the situations. They helped to point out areas which were worth discussing in detail, even if none of them in the end actually

formed much of a basis for my opinions of the scenarios.

The codes of the BSC and ACM were in comparison almost totally useless in looking at the scenarios. The terms and recommendations that they suggest are so vague that they couldn't be used as a basis for making absolute decisions about any of the situations which I evaluated. At the same time the codes also do not seem to be general enough to provide a moral framework for making decisions either.

Another student made the following observation:

> The ethical codes are just someone else's attempt to relate moral philosophy to computer science, which is what I was trying to do in the scenarios and diary entries myself.
>
> (Extract from student portfolio)

These quotes are interesting because they suggest a conflict between professional values and personal values, an issue that we have already discussed in the context of teaching practice. Indeed, other commentators have criticised professional ethical codes precisely because they imply a segregation of personal and professional values [30]. For example, the guidelines for the ACM code of ethics state that they should 'serve as a basis for ethical decision making in the conduct of professional work' [8]. Should one's own values have no influence on the decisions that are made in a professional context?

Again, we can consider this issue from the perspective of authenticity. To make ethical decisions solely on the basis of a professional code is not authentic; it does not truly reflect ones own values and value priorities. As Buchmann [25] has noted in the context of teaching practice, authentic choices must be made within a framework constrained by externally imposed standards (in this case, professional codes of ethics). Some evidence has been presented that the students in our study were sensitive to this issue. Our findings should be of concern to policy makers in professional computing organisations, who see ethical codes as a key element in acquiring professional status for software engineers and computer scientists.

## 9 Concluding Remarks

In this paper, we have argued that there is a pressing need for ethical education of students entering the software engineering profession. Work in professional ethics cannot be treated simply as a problem solving exercise; it should contain an experiential element. To this end, a research study has been described in which case studies and a diary were investigated as mechanisms for engaging students in authentic reflection upon their values and value priorities. Our findings suggest that the diary proved more effective in this regard than the case study approach.

The cycle of action-research requires that planning and implementation of research initiatives should lead to changes in practice. In the light of our findings, it is clear that the case studies employed in the portfolio assessment should be rewritten. Too many of these currently focus on the circumstances of companies, rather than individuals, and concern contexts which are unfamiliar to students. The failure of computer science issues to evoke a strong emotional response is a harder problem to address. However, in the course of our study we did identify issues that were emotive for some students (e.g., invasion of privacy, development of military technology) and those that were not (e.g., software piracy, computer fraud).

A course on professional ethics is an interesting context in which to investigate wider value issues in higher education. We have argued that professional software engineers face some novel ethical problems, but they also face dilemmas that are common to all professions, including teaching; the conflict between role and person that emerged in our study is just one example. Similarly, wider concerns in higher education have implications for the teaching of professional ethics. For example, the current debates on 'transferable skills' [31] and 'graduateness' [11] raise questions for the teaching techniques described here. The experiential methods described in this chapter address ethical analysis within the context of professional work; are the skills in ethical reasoning acquired through this process also 'transferable' to other social contexts? Experiential methods may prove ineffective for software engineering education if they are too closely tied to specific ethical problems in professional practice, because technical and ethical aspects of the field are changing so rapidly. Indeed, perhaps the only thing that we can say with certainty about the future of computer technology is that it will raise new and challenging ethical dilemmas. We must ensure that students of software engineering are equipped to meet this challenge.

## References

1.  Maner W. Unique ethical problems in information technology. In: Bynum T, Rogerson S (eds) Global Information Ethics. Opragen Publications, 1996.
2.  Samuelson P. Can hackers be sued for damages caused by computer viruses? Comm ACM 1989: 32: 666-669.
3.  Slater D. New crop of IS pros on shaky ground. Computerworld 1991: 25: 90.
4.  Laudon KC. Ethical concepts and information technology. Comm ACM 1995: 38: 33-39.
5.  Callahan D, Bok S. The teaching of ethics in higher education. The Hastings Centre (Institute for Society, Ethics and Life Sciences), New York, 1980.
6.  Morrison PR, Forester T. Teaching computer ethics and the social context of computing. Australian Comp J 1990: 22: 36-42.
7.  Huff C, Martin CD. Computing consequences: A framework for teaching ethical computing. Comm ACM 1995: 38: 75-84.
8.  Anderson RE, Johnson DG, Gotterbarn D, Perrolle J. Using the new ACM code of ethics in decision making. Comm ACM 1993: 36: 98-107.
9.  BCS. The new BCS code of conduct. Comp Bull 1992: 4: 6-7.
10. Turner J. Computing curricula 1991: A summary of the ACM/IEEE joint curriculum task force report. Comm ACM 1991: 34: 69-84.

11. HEQC. Assessment in higher education and the role of 'graduateness'. Higher Education Quality Council, London, 1997.

12. Hyland T. Morality, work and employment: towards a values dimension in vocational education and training. J Moral Ed 1995: 24: 445-456.

13. Chaney LH, Simon JC. Strategies for teaching computer ethics. J Comp Infor Syst 1994: 2: 19-22.

14. Kallman EA, Grillo JP. Ethical decision making and information technology: An introduction with cases. McGraw-Hill, New York, 1993.

15. Gotterbarn D. Computer ethics activities for use in introductory computer science courses. Working paper, Department of Computer Science, East Tennessee State University, 1997.

16. Wong EYW. How should we teach computer ethics? A short study done in Hong Kong. Computers and Education 1995: 25: 179-191.

17. Martin CD, Holz HJ. Integrating social impact and ethics issues across the computer science curriculum. In: Aitkin R (ed) Information Processing 92 Volume II: Education and Society, Elsevier Science Publishers, 1992.

18. Collier KG. Learning moral judgement in higher education. Stud in Higher Ed 1993: 18: 287-297.

19. Kolb DA. Experiential learning: experience as a source of learning and development. Prentice Hall, Englewood Cliffs, NJ, 1984.

20. Barger-Lux M. Exploring ethical issues in health care with students: course development and teaching strategy. J of Med Tech 1984: 1: 916-919.

21. Forcht K. A diploma can't ensure ethics. Computerworld 1991: 25: 25.

22. Im JH, Van Epps PD. Software piracy and software security measures in business schools. Infor Man 1992: 23: 193-203.

23. Leventhal LM, Instone KE, Chilson, DW. Another view of computer science ethics: patterns of responses amongst computer science students. J Syst Soft 1992: 17: 49-60.

24. Rowland S. The power of silence: an enquiry through fictional writing. Brit Ed J 1991: 17: 95-111.

25. Buchmann M. Role over person: morality and authenticity in teaching. Teachers College Record 1986: 87: 529-543.

26. Churchill LR. The teaching of ethics and moral values in teaching: some contemporary confusions. J Higher Ed 1982: 53: 296-306.

27. Mitchell R. What is 'authentic assessment'? Portfolio: The Newsletter of Arts PROPEL (December 13). Harvard University, Cambridge, MA, 1989.

28. Collins A. Portfolios for science education: issues in purpose, structure and authenticity. Sci Ed 1992: 76: 451-463.

29. Wiggins G. A true test: toward more authentic and equitable assessment. Phi Delta Kappan, 1989: 703-713.

30. Luegenbiehl HC. Computer professionals: moral autonomy and a code of ethics. J Syst Soft 1992: 17: 61-68.

31. Griffin A. Transferring learning in higher education: problems and possibilities. In: Barnett R (ed), Academic Community: Discourse or Discord? Jessica Kingsley, London, 1992.

# Using Other People's Experience of Project Work: Realising Fitness for Purpose

Marian Petre
Centre for Informatics Education Research, Open University
Milton Keynes, England
and
Sally Fincher
Computing Laboratory, University of Kent at Canterbury
Canterbury, Kent, England

## 1. Introduction

Project work is an integral part of all accredited UK Computer Science undergraduate degree programmes. The Engineering Council requires all courses leading to Chartered Engineer to "embody and integrate theoretical, practical and project work". The British Computer Society (BCS) and the Institute of Electrical Engineers (IEE), the relevant professional accrediting bodies, emphasise this learning mechanism. Moreover, experience of projectwork is becoming commercially and industrially crucial.

Yet managing project work is problematic, because Computer Science (CS) projects are: **expensive**, demanding considerable supervision as well as technical resources; **complex**, marrying design, human communication, human-computer interaction, and technology to satisfy objectives ranging from consolidation of technical skills through provoking insight into organizational practice, teamwork and professional issues, to inculcating academic discipline and presentation skills; **continually demanding** set in the context of a rapidly changing technology which affects technical objectives and demands ever-evolving skills in both students and supervisors.

In a young and changing discipline, some aspect of project work is questioned in almost every institution. However, the body of literature on the dynamics and personal skills involved in project work in general does not address many of the issues raised by Computer Science's peculiar mix of social, technical, and technological components. There is comparatively little literature which is CS-specific [1].

Project EPCoS (Effective Projectwork in Computer Science) addresses this, aiming:

to identify, make explicit and systematise existing practices in Computer Science student project methods and techniques in order to make existing knowledge and experience — and especially existing good practice — readily accessible;

to realise techniques for transferring project work practices between institutions; and

to execute and evaluate such transfers.

This paper describes the work-in-progress of Project EPCoS, outlining the structure of the project and setting out its major activities; presenting the conceptual framework for dissemination, projectwork context, and transfer of practice which has emerged to support its examination of projectwork; and discussing the work-to-date on the "catalogue" of projectwork experiences.

## 2. Project EPCoS: Focus, phases and activities

Project EPCoS is funded by the Higher Education Funding Council of England's (HEFCE's) Fund for Development of Teaching and Learning (FDTL) programme over three years (1996-1999). The core members of the EPCoS consortium are the Computer Science Departments of the Universities of Exeter, Imperial College, Kent, Leeds, Manchester, Southampton, Teesside and York, and the Centre for Informatics Education Research at the Open University (CIER) and the Computer Science Discipline Network (CSDN). Thus, the consortium represents the full spectrum of university institutions — large/small, rural/metropolitan, "old"/"new" — and takes full advantage of its diversity in expertise and its recognised teaching excellence.

EPCoS aims to provide resources and insights for CS academics who are interested in projectwork and in assessing, changing or improving the current projectwork practices within their curriculum. EPCoS has three phases, roughly corresponding to the three years of the project: *Data collection:* The first phase of work (to April 1998) has been to solicit, collect and collate project work experiences from universities throughout the UK (aiming for input from all of them). *Transfer bundle preparation:* The second phase (in progress) is to prepare "bundles", fully-documented examples of good practice ready for transfer. *Transfer and evaluation:* The third phase (to come) is to execute and evaluate the transfer of bundles between partner institutions, in order to examine the processes by which practices are transferred between institutional contexts, in order to identify effective models of that process.

This paper presents work-to-date and so focuses on the activities of Phase 1.

EPCoS is working towards three categories of product:

Discourse (All phases): We aim to encourage productive discourse about project work within the CS academic community and in this way to consolidate a practitioner constituency. We engage in discussion (with the concomitant sharing of information) via electronic media, and we hold face-to-face events such as workshops, to encourage mutual dissemination of information about projectwork within the discipline. By using these methods and media, we seek insight about subtle factors that affect success in applying practices, in order to develop better methods for transfer.

Catalogue of practice (Phase 1): We are engaged in systematic, large-scale collection of projectwork practices (based on a common template) from all UK CS departments. This template-based data is collated in three forms: an "Archive" which includes all data collected; a "Catalogue" which encompasses detailed case studies, examples of use, and supplementary materials in a conceptual framework; and an "Atlas", a tabular form which allows easy identification of patterns of practice.

Transfer experience (Phases 2 and 3): It appears that transfer of practice between institutions (possibly even within institutions) is rare and is almost always based on chance factors such as personality and opportunity. EPCoS is trying to make it easier to adopt practices from elsewhere, not just by making it easier to find out what other institutions are doing that may be of interest, but also by examining how transfer can be actively managed. The consortium is examining various models of transfer both analytically and practically. Each partner is creating a "transfer product": a package of material that embodies effective practice and that has been generalized and documented to assist take-up by another institution. Each partner will subsequently adopt some practice from another institution and will evaluate the experience of transfer.

The project examines eight axes of practice within projectwork: technical outcomes, allocation, management models, assessment issues, negotiated learning contracts, large team projects, integrating project and curriculum, and non-technical issues. These axes cover 'knotty problems' in projectwork: issues for which members of the consortium and their colleagues in other universities are still seeking 'best practice' — and hence for which transfer of practice is likely to be beneficial.

# 3. Key Project Concepts

Over the first year of the project, in the normal intellectual way, we have developed a variety of concepts which are key to our understanding of the subject. These developed as the data collection proceeded and the analysis commenced; however, with such a large and geographically-distributed consortium there was a particular need to articulate these developing ideas so that all members were working with a shared understanding of the goals and processes. The conceptual frameworks for dissemination, projectwork context, and transfer of practice not only reflect the current state of the project but also provide a basis for reflecting on projectwork practice.

## 3.1 Levels of dissemination

The EPCoS activities are closely allied to a three-tier dissemination strategy espoused by the project:

Disseminating *awareness*, so that other interested parties can involve themselves at an early stage;

Disseminating *knowledge* to a level at which the rationale and methodologies used can be understood, extracted and adapted to local conditions;

Disseminating the *use* of the results to change practice.

Of course, these three levels can be applied at different scales, and the activities to which we apply them may overlap. Indeed, in terms of dissemination concepts, they may interlock. For example, considering Project EPCoS as an integrated, time-delimited project, we disseminate awareness of our work through mailing lists, workshops and conferences (such as Project '98). However, considering EPCoS primarily as a data collection effort, we may be disseminating *awareness* of the data within a broader dissemination of *knowledge* of Project EPCoS activity overall. Activities aimed at encouraging discourse disseminate both awareness and knowledge of projectwork issues and awareness of the EPCoS project *per se*. All our activities and products are closely allied to this strategy and will be discussed in this paper with reference to it.

## 3.2 Projectwork context — educational frameworks

Our principle categorisation involves three constructs: practices, contexts, and practitioners: *Practices* are created by practitioners and situated within contexts; *Contexts* contain practices and impose constraints; *Practitioners* are the creators of practice. The cultural consensus of practitioners in a context constructs the meaning of the practice.

It is axiomatic that practice varies enormously from one institution to another. Yet, to fulfil the aims of the project, it was necessary to find some way to abstract the fundamental aspects of provision from their presentation in a local context. We needed a methodology to factor out the differences of presentation and isolate — and accentuate — the underlying characteristics, in order to facilitate comparison. To this end we devised a standard template for data collection. The template is derived from an analysis of how educators describe their practices to each other, and what information they use to characterise their project work. It covers aspects of scale, context, learning objectives, project structure, assessment basis and mechanisms, history and evolution of practices, parameters pertaining to group projects, and self-assessment of the experience with the particular 'instance' of project work.

This template recognises that practice is composed of a number of elements within an educational framework. Any element may be satisfied by a number of different teaching and learning mechanisms (for example the element "project guidelines" may be provided in a number of satisfactory ways), but all elements of practice fit together into an educational framework. The framework itself may differ between instances and institutions (e.g., a project instance devised for an MSc course is unlikely to be appropriate for lower-level undergraduate courses), and so the template can be construed as a "meta-framework" whereby all possibilities are encompassed, and it is the selection (and completion) of certain combinations of elements which indicates the educational framework within which the instance is situated.

In this way, practices are captured and made comparable, transcending the purely local. Characterizing the educational framework is a way of recognising — and addressing — the particular needs which drive change in a given situation. Just providing the database of projectwork instances (i.e., giving access to other people's experience) would be enough to facilitate *change*. But establishing the educational framework is required in order to facilitate effective *transfer*. How other experiences may be used, what constrains their adoption, depends on the other constructs we have identified.

## 3.3 Context and constraints: fitness for purpose

For successful transfer to take place, either the practice must be context-independent, or the original and target contexts must be compatible. These requirements mean that we must be able to describe context in a way that exposes the features which affect transfer. The purpose of the data collection is not only to catalogue the status and variety of CS projectwork, but also to serve as a guide for the transfer of practice between institutions. Consequently, the data collection must capture the contexts in which practices are situated. For the purposes of comparability, the template data is sufficient. A candidate piece of practice can be identified by matching elements (within an educational framework) to need. However, identification and selection does not guarantee transferability; at best it is the first step toward it.

To adopt a practice from another institution (or context), it is necessary not only to know what it is, but also on what it depends. For example, the assessment methods of a particular example of projectwork might be inseparable from the specific deliverables required. We call this sort of relationship a **critical dependency**: one piece of practice cannot be taken without the other.

Alternatively, a piece of practice may not completely dependent on another but should (due to institutional or historical circumstance or due to deliberate and specific design) be taken together with other parts of the practice. For example, the group allocation methods used might be tightly connected to the scale of the project. We call this sort of relationship a **critical adjacency**: whilst each piece of practice can be taken individually, they were closely related in their originating context and should be viewed together.

The uncovering of these adjacencies and dependencies requires good local knowledge and is time-consuming and sometimes troublesome; this is especially so when instances are "home grown" and aspects that evolved over time now appear to be inter-woven and inter-dependent. The unpicking and uncovering of these adjacencies and dependencies is one of the major benefits of EPCoS later-phase products, which address *dissemination of use*. This benefit accrues to EPCoS because of the luxury of our position. Within a normal academic life, whilst there is time and space to notice and comprehend local pedagogic problems, and possibly there is time to search for some better alternative, there is but seldom time to search for constraints and eliminate (or recognise and adopt) them. Yet this is the reality of fitness for purpose. To identify only the *need* is to identify only half the problem. If the *context* in which the "problem" is not examined and the *constraints* on the chosen replacement practice are not identified, then the chances of a fit being found — and found to work — are small.

Thus we can see that consideration of context and constraints provides a package that encompasses "fitness for purpose", and once such a package is fully identified in this way, it can be transferred. However, the vehicle of transfer is always (and only) practitioners.

## 3.4 Practitioners: transfer models and process

Because an examination of the *process* of transfer of pedagogic practice is an aim of the project, we need to examine (and characterise) the ways in which transfer occurs. EPCoS has not invented the idea of practice transferring from one institution (or context) to another. However, from observational and anecdotal enquiry, we believe that there are few ways in which transfer "occurs naturally". In order to share these concepts, we have developed a series of metaphoric models which are easy to comprehend and discuss. (Of course, like all metaphors, they are not precise, and will break down when probed. Nevertheless, we have found them useful.)

We have identified three main ways in which transfer "naturally occurs": charismatic embedding, piecemeal accretion, and coveting.

**Charismatic embedding** is a process which happens when individuals move between institutions and take practice with them. The practice may be of their own invention, or it may be something that they have become accustomed to, and so introduce it in their new setting. The key factor is that the impetus is from a single individual. The success of this sort of transfer would seem to depend not so much on the quality of the element being transferred as the personality and status of the individual who imports it. [2]

The second method we have termed **piecemeal accretion**. This is characterised by individuals taking fragments of practice from elsewhere and bolting them into their own, local framework. The distinction between these two is in the granularity and the scale of the transfer. The former is liable to involve larger and more coherent pieces of practice used on a larger scale (for example structures of courses) which are visible at a departmental level; the latter will more likely be a small piece of practice which can be incorporated by one person into his or her own teaching, without involving any changes which would require departmental (or other QA) approval. An example of this would be the use of "asking anonymous questions" mechanisms [3].

In both of these models, the concepts of constraint are not explicit, because the mechanisms are embedded in an individual's intimate knowledge of the local situation. The constraints are subsumed in "knowing what will work", and there is no need for them to be examined explicitly. In the third naturally occurring model, **coveting,** this is not the case. Coveting is exemplified by individuals who have developed something for their own purposes which they are subsequently convinced to export [4]. The unifying characteristic of these transfers is that the impetus comes not from the originator but from the receiver. The originators in no way set out to make an exportable product and do not set themselves up to offer these to a wider market. Nevertheless, their practice or product is discovered and solicited by others (accretors or embedders). At this point the originator becomes involved in adjusting the product to the needs of the new environment. The receiver not only locates, but also creates the demand for, the product; indeed, in saying, "I want one like yours" the receiver creates the recognition of it as a product at all.

In the context of EPCoS' more formal requirements for transfer, it seems unlikely that these will be appropriate models. However, we recognise that they are familiar methods, which may become vehicles for other transfer models. We shall try to observe whether this is the case in the evaluation cycle of our own transfers.

We believe the following constructs will be relevant metaphors and models for our activity. At the heart of each metaphor is the question of where the responsibility for examining constraints lies:

First is the metaphor of **surgeon**. In this model the surgeon deals with a donor (which might possess any piece of appropriate practice in any institutional context) and a recipient. The surgeon is responsible for making sure the proposed practice is compatible with the recipient context by examining the constraints in *both* parties. The donor provides the essential element of practice, but plays no role in the exchange. (The surgeon must try not to kill either patient.)

Second is the metaphor of **vendor,** who stands between **supplier** and **buyer**. Here the responsibilities are shifted. The vendor packages the practice of the supplier (the original context of the practice selected for transfer) in such a way as to either make it largely context-independent, or to identify explicitly the constraints which it requires (providing a label of ingredients, as it were). The vendor does not examine the constraints of the buyer's context, but expects the buyer to be aware of them and to take account of them in selecting an appropriate product for adoption. (The vendor-buyer half of this process can be compared to the existing practice of piecemeal accretion; in the accretion models, it is the accretors who take the practice "as found" or themselves adapt it for their local conditions.) What a vendor has to offer is a **bundle** of material, which may come from one source or many sources, but which is extracted as far as possible from any critical adjacencies and dependencies.

These key project concepts — a three-tier dissemination strategy; constructs of practitioner, practice and context; and metaphoric models of the transfer process — are all brought to bear on the resources being produced by project EPCoS. The first of these products is The Catalogue.

## 4. The Catalogue

The primary vehicles for the dissemination of our findings in Phase 1 (the state of the project to date) are: the **Archive:** the complete Web database of projectwork instances, with links to any supplementary material, either electronic or paper-based; the **Atlas:** an abstraction of the data Archive, and a subsidiary component of the Catalog; and the **Catalogue:** a representative collection of projectwork practices produced in comparable form and set in a conceptual framework.

The EPCoS project is working to map the range of project-based learning practices and to generate insights into what characterizes the contexts in which particular techniques are effective.

All three resources are based on systematically-collected data organized in accordance with a template. The template is derived from an analysis of how educators describe their practices to each other, and what information they use to characterize their project work. It covers aspects of scale, context, learning objectives, project management structure, assessment basis and mechanisms, history and evolution of practices, parameters pertaining to group projects, and self-assessment of the experience with the particular 'instance' of project work.

The Archive is simply a Web database of all of the data collected, giving pointers to any supplementary material (e.g., project notes, assessment schemes, instructions to students, course booklets, etc.) provided by the contributing institutions. The Archive is augmented by simple and adaptable (i.e., unassuming) search, select and sort tools, including: simple **selection** tools which will abstract material by 'instance' or by template question (across every instance in the database); a simple keyword **search** mechanism, so that answers to template questions can be extracted by topic or theme; a **profiling** tool: enquirers can fill in an on-line form which allows them to request a shortlist of instances which display certain characteristics.

The Atlas is an encapsulation of the template data in tabular form. This form assists familiarity with the shape of the data and provides at-a-glance comparability between practices. Whilst a useful overview tool, this form of data presentation is attended by two cautions. First, any encapsulation involves abstraction (i.e., selection and simplification), and the symbols we employ neither capture nor convey the richness and complexity of the original data. Second, the Atlas is only concerned with the template-based material and does not (indeed, cannot) encompass the diversity of our additional qualitative evidence. Hence we conceive the Atlas as a preliminary tool, serving *dissemination of awareness.* — of the data resources we have collected and collated (and hence acts is a vehicle for dissemination of awareness of itself *and* of the data Archive on the Web).

The Catalogue provides a quality of information that serves *dissemination for knowledge*. The Catalogue contains and extends the Atlas; it draws representative examples from the full data Archive in order to illustrate the range of projectwork practice in CS. The aim of the Catalogue is to bring the instances to life by associating them with project "war stories" which add vividness and provide human perspective — and to situate the material in a conceptual framework to support reflection. Hence, the Catalogue material encompasses in-depth case studies of standard, unusual or innovative practices, illustrated with anecdotes of frequently-occurring situations. This evidential and anecdotal material is supplemented by short, reflective essays.

Because examples in the catalogue are all presented in template form, the Catalogue provides comparability of practice by its very form, making it is straightforward to pick out and compare particular aspects of many examples. It facilitates access by cross-referencing the Atlas data (where practicable and appropriate) and hence the raw Archive data. In assembling a body of authentic examples, EPCoS aims to provide a resource that enables extrapolation and synthesis of new techniques. We hope to present enough contextual detail to enable the CS academic to recognise and "know" the instances presented and thus engage with the material and draw insights from it — and simple, effective access to make exploration and comparison feasible. The resources are designed to be readily accessible to CS educators, who may use them to generate generalizations, to identify emergent patterns, to 'make sense' and 'make meaning' from an otherwise apparently disparate set of anecdotes.

The concept of dissemination for knowledge is what *realises* fitness-for-purpose. An examination of the usage we anticipate for the Catalogue will outline how this knowledge might be achieved.

## 4.1 Catalogue Usage

We have designed the Catalogue (and its component parts) with a view to the knowledge users will need in order to use the material efficiently and effectively. We envisage two main categories of use: "finding fits" and "added value".

### 4.1.1 Finding Fits

An obvious use of the catalogue is to find similar practices which are confirmatory to those adopted at one's own institution. This is neither a small nor a belittling use; there is value in locating local practice as normative. However, any survey is always time-dependent, and it would be dangerous to assume that this would remain a positive use of necessarily coeval material. The value of the statement "we are doing just the same as they were in 1998" or even " we are doing just the same as *we* were in 1998" will lessen with every passing year. However, the complementary practice of finding *mis-fits* may remain viable over a longer period.

The practice of finding mis-fits is of a different order from that of finding fits; its purpose is not to confirm normality, but to confirm (and preserve) distinction — which is generally perceived to be better and/or beneficial practice. This habit is not confined by the boundaries of time, for practice can be justified to be distinct against fundamental pedagogic values which alter less over time than other factors such as specific personnel, funding or student demand. The statements "we are doing things differently than they were in 1998" and even more significantly "we are doing things differently than we were in 1998" are not confirmatory of practice, but of progress; neither is so easily grasped without the benchmark the Catalogue provides.

### 4.1.2 Added Value

EPCoS aims to add value to the pedagogic practices and climate of the discipline. If our endeavour added nothing to the disciplinary debate that cannot be gathered by talking with and soliciting the opinions of colleagues, then it would be endeavour spectacularly wasted. However, we believe that our activity adds much, particularly with regard to dissemination for knowledge. First, and most obviously, EPCoS adds new data, not in the sense of inventing or discovering new materials, but in the sense of revealing the space of possibilities. The act of gathering materials in a standardised and comparable way creates dimensions, which were previously unavailable to the practitioner.

Scale: Colleagues have twofold value in one's assessment of practice: first, one gauges them against how much they are sympathetic to one's own pedagogic ideals and outlook; second, one values them for the breadth and range of their experience. We believe that any CS academic would be hard-pressed to locate a quantity of practice and experience comparable to that contained in the Catalogue from within their own network of professional colleagues.

Detail: The level of detail we have captured is an equally unusual resource within personal compass. Pedagogic information in particular is difficult to locate. There are several potential explanations for why this should be so, which may act independently or in concert. Teaching remains a fundamentally private activity, concealed behind the classroom door. It may be difficult to press friends and colleagues for sufficiently detailed descriptions of practice without appearing to be stealing or poaching their ideas. This becomes especially problematic if there is a local climate where teaching is neither a rewarded nor highly regarded activity. Further, there may be institutional-level prohibitions about what may or may not be published to "outsiders".

Variety: Finally, it is axiomatic that friends and colleagues tend to be drawn from similar areas. In this way it is difficult to find material which is truly different or unusual. Although local practice may not be satisfactory, it is often difficult to 'get out of the box' of existing thinking. The Catalogue assists academics by providing a wide range of materials and practice, from every kind of institutional perspective.

Characterising: As noted above, one turns to colleagues for more than facts, experience and knowledge, in eliciting examples of practice. One gains also from the way in which they conceptualise the area of pedagogic activity and support reflection on existing practice. The Catalogue can help to develop an awareness of areas of common concern by identifying (and promoting in discourse) the ideas which inform the presentation. These ideas concern the necessity of identifying parameters of constraint; identifying what characterises success and failure — and which parameters distinguish between them. Additionally, the framework of the Catalogue uniquely affords the opportunity of identifying patterns of practice — indeed, forming abstractions over collections of similar practice, so that 'best practice' may emerge as a composite.

In order to serve our own usage of the Catalogue and Atlas for this sort of reflection, the EPCoS consortium has drafted 'selection profiles' based on the template categories: ranges of values for selected criteria which can be used in conjunction with the Atlas as filters for project instances of interest. The profiles are of two varieties:

General good practice criteria: These are broad criteria used to decide if a project instance constitutes good practice in general, i.e., these criteria are used to identify exemplary project instances.

Aspect interest criteria: These are used to decide if a project instance is of interest under a special topic' (i.e., one of the eight axes of practice). They help identify projects, which are of interest in particular aspects, whether or not they are of interest in other regards. The ranges of values for these criteria are often designed to exclude standard practice and highlight novel approaches.

The exercise of creating selection profiles and using them to try to characterise the factors that come into play in different aspects of projectwork contributes to the evolution of the conceptual framework.

If fitness-for-purpose can be realised by using the Catalogue, it cannot be separated from the other products of the EPCoS project, nor actualised without a consideration of the third-tier (dissemination for use) tools and products. It is this level of material, we believe, that changes the concept of fitness-for-purpose from a passive to an active consideration.

# 5. Towards Transfer: Dissemination for use

The latter half of EPCoS activity focuses on the transfer products (the "bundles"), process and experiences. By encapsulating projectwork techniques for use and by characterising effective models of transfer, these support *dissemination for use*.

The transfer bundles and experiences will be evaluated in terms of two varieties of criteria:

General evaluation criteria: Criteria which will be applied project-wide to evaluate bundles and transfer experiences in terms of general parameters 'good practice'. Derived from discussion and consensus within the consortium about the key parameters, they are intended to provide a basis for drawing generalizations across all the transfer experiences.

Experience evaluation criteria: Criteria by which the particular bundles and transfer experiences will be evaluated in terms of the objectives of the specific partner's special topic. Their specification goes hand-in-hand with the specification of the bundles.

The aim of the evaluation is to draw out the lessons of the experiences, so that they can contribute to future transfers. Of course, the evaluation criteria themselves form a product which enables the consideration of material for transfer.

# 6. Summary

The value of the EPCoS project — from its activities of data gathering, analysing and systemising to its experiences of transfer practice, evaluation and experience to the presentation of its dissemination "products" in a conceptually robust framework — is in providing enough richness to allow practitioners to match experience to context: to assess and realise fitness for purpose.

**References**

1. Knudsen M, Vinther T (eds): Project Work in University Studies, Roskilde University, Denmark, September 1997.
2. Lundberg, W article to misc.business.facilitators, 13 June 1997.
3. Barnes D. Students Asking Questions: Facilitating Questioning Aids Understanding and Enhances Software Engineering Skills. In: ACM SIGCSE Bulletin, 29(4), pp38-41, December 1997.
4. Latham JT. Managing Coursework: Wringing the Stone or Cracking the Nut?. In: Alexander S, Magee P (eds). 3rd Annual Conference on the Teaching of Computing: Computing Curriculum Development and Delivery pp 122-131, Centre for Teaching Computing, Dublin City University, August 1995.

# Using Group Project Work to Enhance the Learning of Professional Issues

L. R. Neal

Department of Computer Science, Brunel University, Uxbridge, UK, UB8 3PH

## Abstract

This paper addresses an approach taken with large numbers of honours computing students studying the professional issues that are expected to be included in accredited information systems engineering courses. The students work in groups to complete two major projects. The first task is to prepare a report and recommendations for action on problems posed by a chosen scenario. Each scenario involves a range of issues and requires the in-depth investigation of a number of areas in order to be able to compose a report of sufficient depth. The second task is to prepare a presentation on a chosen topic which is subject to peer assessment. In this paper the organisation of the group activity is described together with the assessment procedures.

## 1.    Introduction

As putative professionals, it is incumbent on computing students to become aware of the wider issues affecting the computing profession beyond the purely technical. Many disasters and troubles in the computing world have come about in the past through a lack of professionalism in the people involved. Academic staff in the Department are keen to produce graduates who have not only a good grasp of the issues but who are also prepared to act in a professional manner. From a more mundane perspective, it is also to a student's advantage, when interviewed, to be able to show awareness of the issues, particularly when competing for jobs with equally qualified and experienced applicants. The increasing responsibility given to students, to organise and work in groups on investigations largely chosen by themselves, develops a mature approach to problem solving. The contexts and issues studied prepare students for an effective role in any future employment.

It is accepted that Professional Issues should be addressed in computing courses seeking professional accreditation [1], [2], [3]. The area covers a wide range of topics such as Computer Contracts, Intellectual Property Rights, Health and Safety at Work, Software Safety, Computer Misuse, and Data Protection. Even one of these topics such as Computer Misuse,[4], can cover a vast amount of material e.g. computer fraud, unauthorised access, alteration and removal, hacking, viruses, Internet security, cryptography, etc., each of which could be regarded as worthy of individual study. Some areas may imply a knowledge of the law beyond that can be reasonably expected of computing students. Whilst not requiring computing students to become legal experts, all should develop an awareness of the issues to the level that they recognise when to call on further professional help as outlined by Bainbridge [5]. Also it is important that students become aware of professional codes of conduct and practice [6], [7].

## 2. The Professional Issues Module

### 2.1 Module Scope

All major computing courses at Brunel University include a second level module devoted to Professional Issues. These issues are of particular concern to potential graduates in computing as nearly all will be looking for careers as computer professionals. Successful graduates from the course satisfy the education requirements for membership of the British Computer Society and also for chartered engineer status through the Engineering Council. Part of being a professional is to be aware of issues beyond the purely technical.

Six general areas are investigated, namely

- Safety Issues
- Intellectual Property Rights
- Contracts
- Computer Misuse
- Data Protection and Privacy
- Professionalism

Associated areas such as finance and business organisation are covered in other modules.

### 2.2 Module Objectives

By the end of the module, participants should, firstly, be able to discuss, from a basis of sound knowledge and understanding, the major factors affecting professional behaviour in each of the major topic areas, and secondly, have developed the necessary skills to keep up to date with developments in each of the areas. In carrying out the activities of the module, participants will have had the opportunity to develop their skills in

- carrying out investigations
- project management
- group activity
- reporting
- presentation

# 3. Module Content

Three mechanisms are used to enable students to study the material in depth - namely a major response to a scenario, a presentation on a particular topic and preparation for an individual examination on factual knowledge. The first two activities are treated as major projects based on group activity, with the students accepting the responsibility for managing and completing the work.

## 3.1 The Scenario

A number of scenarios have been prepared that attempt to present a real life situation. Each scenario covers four to five issues across the areas delineated above. Working in groups, students are expected to produce a major report taking the stance of a consultant called in to advise on the situation. An example scenario is given in Appendix 1. One vital task is to identify which areas are of relevance to the scenario in question. A group will be only in a position to do this after each area has been assimilated in sufficient depth for its relevance to be determined. It must be emphasised that this is a group activity. Whilst good individual effort is called for, all decisions and results must be agreed through a group consensus.

## 3.2 The Group Presentation

When seeking permanent employment, students need to become aware that part of second round of many recruitment procedures is for them to have to make a presentation before the interviewing panel. Building on the student's experience in their previous level 1 studies, the work here provides another opportunity to practise this difficult skill.

A list of forty topics is published and each group is expected to prepare a presentation on one of these topics. These are specialised areas that require investigatory work beyond course texts. A 20 minute presentation is given by each group towards the end of the semester. This is followed by a short discussion period. As well as covering the basics, groups are expected to have found out some real life examples and case studies concerning the issues addressed. They are expected to produce a summary for the other groups to include reference pointers to the material that they have researched. The lecturer in charge takes this summary into account when making a provisional assessment for the presentation.

The other groups assess the presentation and this peer assessment is taken into account in determining the final mark. This assessment will address the quality of the work presented beyond just presentation skills. Criteria for each grade is determined. This indicates that a pass grade will be given for a minimally satisfactory performance where other people's ideas have been put across successfully. An A grade should reflect first class work that "you (the student) would have been proud to present yourself". There should be mastery of the material covered and a good synthesis of the problems encountered.

## 3.3    Factual Examination

Basic factual knowledge is assessed on an individual basis through a multiple choice paper with questions based on the set text for the module. This a one hour paper taken under normal examination conditions. Students are expected to gain a broad knowledge of each of the areas as well as following particular issues in more depth. All questions on the paper are compulsory and each question can have one, two or three correct answers. Initial external examiner's worries about a multiple choice paper at level 2 have been satisfactorily resolved with an negative adjustment for incorrect answers.

# 4.    Group Activity

## 4.1    Group Organisation

Students are put into arbitrary groups of six and advice is given on working together. This strategy is debatable but it is pointed out that in future employment one rarely has the choice of one's working partners. It will be up to the group to organise itself to carry out both the investigation and the presentation. Groups must meet regularly, at least twice each week, but sufficiently often to carry out the activity.

Each group must appoint members to appropriate roles for supervising the work e.g. a manager for each project, librarian, group contact, meetings secretary, etc., as well as deciding who is going to make any particular contribution. While some members of the group may prefer to put more effort into preparing the presentation and others into researching material and preparing the scenario reports, it is expected that all should contribute to both activities. Monitoring of activity is through the group reports as described in the next subsection and section 5 of the paper.

One of the main aims of this module is to reinforce an awareness of the need for everybody to behave in a responsible and professional manner. It is the responsibility of the group to accommodate individuals in the process and it is the responsibility of each individual to make a positive contribution to the team. For example, agreeing a time for the group to meet and being on-time for such meetings; agreeing a plan of action with time scales and producing results for the group accordingly.

Each group report must be signed off by all members of the group. Any problems encountered in carrying out the process should be reported through a nominated contact person to the lecturer in charge of the module. The final report should contain an evaluation section covering how the process went and what has been learnt from the activity (of working together). Any individual can submit a supplement to the report if a major disagreement occurs, but every effort must have been made to work together. This includes individuals who would regard themselves as being hampered by others. It will not be an advantage for an individual to have gone their own way and produced a brilliant report if s/he has not contributed to the group as a whole.

## 4.2    Monitoring of Activity

Groups meet regularly from the second week of the semester onwards and appoint members to appropriate roles for the carrying out of the work. Groups are encouraged to identify the appropriate issues for their scenario and to carry out general investigation of each area either individually or in pairs. Two reports are required (see below) that describe the on-going activity. Towards the end of the period, each group synthesises the material so that a coherent final report can be submitted. These reports must have appended the formal minutes of all group meetings indicating attendance and apologies for absence.

Contact is maintained through a nominated member of each group. The lecturer in charge holds a regular weekly meeting with these contact persons to monitor the progress of the groups. Feedback on the reports and response any other queries is given through e-mail messages. A single copy of any material for distribution is given to the group contact who then distributes it to his/her group members. A detailed study guide is distributed with initial pointers to where the investigation for a particular area can commence. For the last session this material has been available on the web (see section 6). Apart from the introductory session, the lecturer in charge does not attempt to lecture on any of the topics. However, a series of guest lectures are given from eminent people to stimulate interest. Talks have been given by the head of Scotland Yard's computer crime squad as well as experts on Internet security, computer law and software theft. Professionalism is covered by representatives from the Engineering Council and the British Computer Society.

Quality control of the activity is through the normal Departmental procedures. The examination paper is reviewed both internally and externally. The exam results and all reports are subject to internal review and all assessment material is available to the external examiner who attends the level 2 examination board.

## 4.3     Mechanism for Sharing Knowledge.

Each of the investigations will need addressing from many different aspects. It is suggested that each member of the group take responsibility for one major area. Each should carry out some in-depth reading/study in the area and bring this knowledge back to share with the group. This is an efficient way of covering a wide area of study. The group can then decide the relevance of the material to the investigation in hand. Students are advised not to get upset if the group decides their area has little relevance to the particular scenario chosen. It does not mean that area is not important more generally.

# 5.     Group Reports

## 5.1     First Report

At the end of the third week of the semester, each group submits a short report containing a list and responsibilities of the roles taken, and an outline action plan for carrying out the initial investigations. An individual student may take on more than one role, but an equal work load should be aimed at amongst the members of a group. This report should not include the results of any investigations. It is intended to ensure that groups have met and have organised themselves to carry out effective work. The report should have appended to it the minutes of each group meeting held so far, including the attendance.

## 5.2     Second Report

A short progress report is submitted at the end of the seventh week of the semester. This should summarise progress and achievements to date. The purpose of this report is to indicate that all students are active and that substantive investigatory work is being carried out. The detail of these investigations should not be included but some indication of the activity through a summary of each area should be given, together with the sources of the material. Again, minutes of all group meetings should be appended.

## 5.3    Final Report

Each group must submit a major report concerning their investigation. This will form the major component in the assessment of this part of the module.    The report should conform to the house style of the Department and be of good quality. As well as the major report on the investigation findings, the report should have a final evaluation section.    This should address the process of carrying out the activity, including what has been learnt from working as a team throughout the period.    The report should have appended to it the minutes of each group meeting held since the second report, including the attendance.

The assumption throughout is that group has organised itself so that each member has made an equal contribution to the activity.    If this has not proved to be the case then the evaluation section should indicate this together with an agreed weighting for the contribution.    It is important that all members of the group should sign off the report as an agreed submission from the group as a whole.    An individual who feels aggrieved by the group report has the right to submit his/her own report on the activity.    The lecturer in charge attempts to resolve disputes through interviews before making a final judgement.

## 5.4    Presentation Summary

Each group must submit a executive summary of their presentation, including references to sources. Copies will be distributed to other groups.

# 6.    Resources

Extensive web-based material has been prepared to guide students through the learning process.    This can be accessed through the web link

http://www.brunel.ac.uk/~csstlrn/

This material includes guidance on working together in groups, as well as on preparing presentations and a methodology for investigating scenarios.

In staff time there is a price to pay in running the module in this fashion compared to conventional lectures.    The scenarios need constructing and up-dating and considerable monitoring of the activity is necessary.    Arrangements have to be made for three to four guest lecturers a session.    The lecturer in charge makes himself available for one timetabled hour a week to meet with individuals or groups with problems.    In addition, running 28 groups in the current session has involved about one and a half hours a day over four days a week spent in responding to e-mails and in further individual sessions giving out advice and dealing with problems. It is not always clear who is actually taking the module. Maintaining correct class and group lists, sorting out the contribution of part-time and repeating students is time consuming. The time needed to construct a good multiple choice paper is costly but this bears fruit in the subsequent ease of marking.


# 7.    Assessment

The basic assumption made is that groups will organise themselves to ensure that all members make an equal contribution to the work. However, an individual's marks can be modified according to the contribution s/he makes. The assumption is monitored in two ways. The first mechanism used is to require that all reports have the minutes appended of all the group meetings held. Unexplained absence is questioned at the regular meetings of the lecturer in charge with the group contacts. The second mechanism is to have an evaluation section in the final report in which groups can report on lack of effort and/or a redistribution of the marks if certain members have put in effort over the odds.

A contribution of individual assessment is made through a one hour multiple choice examination at the end of the module that examines basic factual information from the course text.


## 7.1    Assessment of Group Investigation Component

| | |
|---|---|
| Process | 10 marks |
| Report on main investigation | 40 marks |

A basic group process mark will be adjusted for individuals according to their contribution to the activity. The process mark is based on evidence from: - good first and second reports, support of group activity, evaluation section of the final report, attendance at group meetings and presentations, submission of presentation summary

The following areas are judged to assess the major final report on the scenario investigation - coverage of topic, up-to-date illustrations, synthesis of discovered material, reasoned arguments setting out pros and cons of each case.

## 7.2    Assessment of Group Presentation

For the presentations, each group is invited to assess the other groups and this peer assessment is taken into account in determining the group mark. The assessment will address the quality of the work presented rather than just the skills of the presenters.

- Content (basic coverage)                          10 marks
- Content (depth and relevant examples)             10 marks
- Organisation and presentation of material          5 marks

## 7.3    Individual Assessment

Individual assessment is through a multiple choice written paper. The material used is mainly from the set text which covers all of the areas encompassed by the module as listed in section 2.1  In addition a few questions are added arising from the special guest lectures for that session. A typical question is

Which condition(s) must be satisfied before an action for breach of confidence can succeed ?

| | |
|---|---|
| a | that there was confidential information involved |
| b | that the information was disclosed in circumstances giving rise to an obligation of confidence |
| c | information has to have been actually used or disclosed |
| d | that the recipients were aware that the information was confidential |

Note that there can be more than one correct answer !

## 7.4    Overall Assessment for the Professional Issues Module

The assessment will be based on achievement in three areas:  the group investigation, the group presentation, and an individual written examination. The following weighting of components is used

- group investigation         50 marks
- group presentation          25 marks
- written paper               25 marks

# 8.    Results

The module has run over three sessions with over 90 groups.  All but a small number of the groups functioned well with several enthusing about the experience. Some examples of the student response are given in Appendix 2.  There were a number of initial problems as groups clarified what was expected from them, but effort at that stage paid dividends.  A few students did not like group work, feeling that they would be held back by 'weaker' colleagues.  One group per session has had major personality problems, finally split into two.  A further group, made up of repeating students, seemed to fizzle out and were required to put in individual reports.  A third group had problems as their 'leader' seemed to take on too much of a dictatorial stance.  With four other groups, individuals did not appear to have made an proper contribution.  However, based on the evaluations made by the groups, the way of working seems to have been successful and in each session four or five of the groups have put in really excellent reports, researching areas beyond the current knowledge of the lecturer in charge.

# 9.    Conclusions

It is believed that the procedures described provide a framework for group activity that can be used effectively for student learning.  The activity requires students to work together in teams in order to achieve an acceptable result.   It gives individuals responsibility for their own learning experiences.  It allows students to address areas beyond the technical that employers say they regard as important, enhancing skills needed in future employment as well as providing a wide coverage of the professional issues relevant to their field of study.   The approach is more demanding from the lecturer's viewpoint but the positive response from the students is worth the extra effort.

# References

1.    Bott F. et al.  Professional Issues in Software Engineering.  2nd edition, UCL press, 1995

2.    Myers C.  Professional Awareness in Software Engineering.  McGraw-Hill, 1995

3.    Neal L.  Essential Components of First Degree Courses in Computing: Professional Issues.  1st European Workshop on Industry/University Co-

Operation in the Field of Computing. Dublin City University, March 1998.   http://www.ctc.dcu.ie/themework/

4.      Elbra T.  A Practical Guide to the Computer Misuse Act 1990.  NCC Blackwell, 1990

5.      Bainbridge D.  Introduction to Computer Law.  2nd ed.  Pitman Publishing, 1993

6.      Anderson R.  The ACM Code of Ethics: History, Process and Implications. in Huff C and Finholt T eds, Social Issues in Computing. McGraw Hill, 1994

7.      British Computer Society.  BCS Code of Conduct, BCS Code of Practice. Obtainable via the BCS web pages  http://www.bcs.org.uk/

# Appendix 1

## Scenario 2 (after T. Cornish)

Middleshire NHS Trust have out-sourced all of their IT services to Marwick Software Services Ltd. and have done so for the past five years. These services encompass the day to day maintenance and support of all the Middleshire NHS Trust computer systems, including the Medical Expert Systems software, containing safety critical data.   However Marwick Software Services Ltd. discovered that 14 days notice of termination of their existing support and maintenance contract is being considered after a number of incidents.  These include: breach of medical confidence; use of pirated software and the general misuse of the system for 'personal sexual stimulation'.  You have had an informal and unsuccessful meeting with the Senior Software Engineer of Marwick concerning the above matter.  After the meeting you receive an anonymous e-mail stating that alterations to the code of the medical expert systems software have been made.  You are informed that these changes will take effect in 15 days if the threat of termination of the contract is not revoked.  Many other NHS sites signed long-term contracts with Marwick earlier this year.

You are the newly appointed Senior Executive in the NHS Trust responsible for IT.  Your son is in intensive care receiving highly specialised treatment for a very rare disorder.   The doctors are dependant upon one of the specialised expert systems for this treatment.  You are a computer professional, a member of the BCS and a chartered engineer.  You are required to report to your CEO on the above, with   your   comprehensive   evaluation   of   the   situation   together   with recommendations for a successful conclusion to the problem.

# Appendix 2

## Student Response

Students PE, TF, BP, RR, AW, FZ          Group 8

" . . . . Not everything worked well. Getting meeting times that we all could attend was difficult - keeping track of where everybody was problematical, as everybody went their own way - not allowing too much time before a report should be handed in. These were not large problems with the group, but small areas that can be improved upon. . . . Overall, we performed well as a group, and worked pretty well together."

Students WJ, AM, NK, NK, NS, AT          Group 24

" . . . . As a group we felt that we worked well. We obviously had a few disagreements, especially towards the end of the project; people were getting quite stressed by this stage of the semester, and the problem that there were two or three other deadlines for other modules very close by. We finished all of the course work to the best of our abilities and it was all handed in on the time that was requested by the study guide. . . Overall we feel that the module was a success and that we did learn a lot about how to deal with people who you don't really know very well."

Students DB, OL, FM, AP, EP, BT          Group 28

" . . . What has been learnt ? This was discussed by the whole group . . . we say generally we have all enjoyed working together. Even though we all had our ups and downs we learnt to support and encourage each other. We have learnt about the importance of communication, saying what is on our minds, accepting suggestions, working together for one goal and in one accord.

DB (group leader):- 'I have learnt to be responsible, how to go about independent research and how to communicate with group members.'

OL (group co-ordinator):- 'I have learnt to be open-minded. I could confidently put forward my ideas to the group.'

BT (group secretary):-    'I have learnt that even the most boring jobs are very important.'        "

Students  RN, SH, OH, JB, PE, NS        Group 7

". . . We feel that we have worked together very effectively as a team.  In particular the group has benefited from two of its members having just returned from industrial placement.  We feel very pleased with the way in which our group has experienced a free flowing exchange of ideas in its meetings and the members all have great respect for other's opinions, knowledge and experiences.  This is perhaps the single most important factor which has enabled us to complete the project to what we feel is a satisfactorily high standard."

# PART 2
## Group Projects

# Improving the quality of Software Engineering courses through University Based Industrial Projects.

Andrew Stratton, Mike Holcombe, Peter Croll

*Department of Computer Science, University of Sheffield,
Regent Court, Sheffield, S1 4DP, U.K.*

*A.Stratton@shef.ac.uk,
M.Holcombe@dcs.shef.ac.uk,
P.Croll@dcs.shef.ac.uk*

Through the use of University Based Industrial Projects, students at Sheffield University have been gaining the advantages of industrial contact, while still studying full time. This paper discusses the experience gained, within the Department of Computer Science, from running Industrial projects and other initiatives, focusing specifically on a second year project called the 'Software Hut'. A set of guidelines, and good practice, derived from over ten years experience, are described and discussed. The implications of changes in client requirements and the effect of increasing class size are considered and possible solutions are proposed.

## 1 Introduction

The problem that University graduates can be unsuited to the requirements of Industry has been focused on by many sources, recently this has included HM Government [1], SARTOR [2] and The Times [3]. This problem has previously been addressed by including a placement year, during which students go out and work in industry. Placements are a good way for students to gain experience of working practice in industry and commerce. However, some problems of placements include the need to find a large number of relevant jobs for students, the increase in study time by a year and the difficulty of assessing the quality of placements. Student motivation can also be affected when students do not see an increase in their job opportunities or an improvement in the standard of their first job.

In recent years, as with most Computer Science departments, a second area of concern has arisen - student numbers have increased to the point where some courses are unable to run without modifications to the way in which they are run. With Industrial projects, this could create a problem finding sufficient, and suitable, clients for students to work for.

Finally, many of the past industrial initiatives within the department have used industrial clients whose requirements are related to the more traditional computerisation of manual tasks. There appears to be a decrease in the number of clients with these 'traditional' requirements. More and more clients seem to have already solved the 'easy' problems and are now encountering more sophisticated problems. Current initiatives within the department need to consider the implications of a change in the pool of industrial clients.

The objectives of this paper are to summarise ways to improve the industrial experience obtained by students, to evaluate methods of coping with a growing number of students (without a loss in quality) and to gain a greater understanding of how the market of industrial clients is changing.

The paper concludes with a general validation of industrial projects, with several caveats towards methods of implementing such projects.

The next section gives an overview of industrial related courses and initiatives within the department.

## 2 Industrial Project courses and initiatives

Since 1985, a large number of industrially oriented opportunities have been developed within the Computer Science department. The purpose of these initiatives has been for students to acquire real world skills relevant to software engineering and computer science. The initiatives have received widespread commendation from industrial collaborators and employers, since they provide real and highly relevant experiences for students in the reality of software development projects in industry and commerce.

## 2.1 Overview

The industrial project courses and initiatives include the 1st year "Crossover"

| | Year 1 | | Year 2 | | Year 3 | Year 4 |
|---|---|---|---|---|---|---|
| *Semester* | *1* | *2* | *1* | *2* | *1 and 2* | *1 and 2* |
| *Course* | | | | | | |
| MEng in Software Engineering[1] | | Crossover Project | | Software Hut Project | Individual Project[2] | Software Company |
| BSc Computer Science | | Crossover Project | | *Software Hut Project[3]* | Individual Project[2] | *Computer Solutions Company[4]* |
| BSc Dual Honours | | Crossover Project | | *Software Hut Project[3]* | Individual Project[2] | |
| MSc | Maxi Project[5] | | | | | |

Dissertation[6]

[1] Not all students are allowed, or maybe wish, to study for the full 4 years; some students will leave after 3 years (with a maximum of a BEng or BSc)
[2] May be industrially linked
[3] Optional course for this degree
[4] It is intended to run a 4 year, MComp, degree incorporating an industrially linked course in the fourth year
[5] Runs over both semesters
[6] MSc dissertations run over the summer, and may be Industrially linked; this year, two MSc students will be running the software company as part of their dissertations.

Figure 1. Available Industrial linked initiatives for Degrees in the department.

project, the 2nd year Software Hut Project, $3^{rd}$ year individual projects, the $4^{th}$ year Software Company, the MSc "Maxi" Project and MSc dissertations. The relationship between the courses, degrees and their chronological order can be seen in Figure 1.

All the above initiatives, apart from the MSc dissertation, run at the same time as other modules.

This paper is mainly concerned with the Software Hut project. However, background details of the other initiatives shows how the Software Hut fits in with other industrially relevant courses. In particular, the Crossover, in the first year, sets the scene for the Software Hut; it is likely that the students would find the Software Hut much harder without this experience

- The $1^{st}$ year Crossover project. The Crossover project is a first year team project undertaken by all Software Engineering, Computer Science and dual students in the Department. The course aims are to highlight practical issues that face software development teams in commercial organisations, to gain experience of software lifecycle stages, to apply methods and techniques for design, implementation and testing of software, and to provide practical experience of project management, quality issues and team work. The students work in teams under the supervision of a member of academic staff and develop a number of projects through different stages. The activity emphasises teamwork, management, documentation and quality control.

  The project was praised in the HEFCE Teaching Quality Assessment Review of the Computer Science assessment programme, [4]. The report quoted, 'At one University, during the first year of the honours degree course, an innovative "Crossover" project combines personal support for students with a group project on software development. Each group works on the project with a technical tutor for a defined period and then hands the material and documentation on to another group, thereby simulating a real industrial project. The technical tutor functions as a personal tutor for each student in the group .....'. The Crossover project is described further in [5].

- The $2^{nd}$ year ($3^{rd}$ year for some related degrees) Software Hut Project. This is described in the next section.

- 3rd year Individual projects. The individual projects that all third year students are required to do brought forth the following comment from HEFCE [6]; "The student achievement in this part of the degree is excellent. The emphasis on projects with a strong design element and often involving an industrially posed problem imparts a strong vocational flavour to the courses.".

- Maxi Project. This is an MSc Course which involves a real client and a professional software project manager; thus separating the distinct roles of client, manager and lecturer, as described in [7].

- MEng Software Company. This course runs through both semesters, and involves students forming and running companies that offer IT consultancy and software development services to outside organisations. The emphasis of the work is on learning how small IT companies are created and managed, the legal and financial frameworks with which such companies operate, the practical management of the companies and their successful trading.

  Students can choose to involve themselves in researching market opportunities for software products, carrying out IT audits on behalf of local organisations and preparing appropriate IT strategies, acting as software/computing consultants to local organisations, developing software for clients, maintaining software for clients. Students also keep company records, prepare company reports as well as developing analysis and design reports and other consultancy reports for clients; see [8] for further details.

In previous years, second year students carried out real consultancy exercises; initially within the University, and later with local companies. The students played the role of IT consultants and assessed a company's business, the scope for applying information technology in the company and produced a properly researched and costed proposal for the implementation of an IT strategy for the company. The purpose of the project was to introduce computing students to a real consultancy exercise, to help them to develop their professional skills, to expose them to some of the real problems faced by industry and to challenge them to find practical and cost-effective solutions. The students responded well to the challenge and most commented that this was one of the most exciting activities of their student career. However, when the department changed to semesters, the time available for the project was lost, and the project was integrated into the Software Hut Project.

# 3 The Software Hut Project, 1985 to 1997

The Practical Software Engineering course, COM221, is a core 2$^{nd}$ year course for students studying towards BEng/MEng in Software Engineering or, optionally, for BSc in Computer Science. A few 3$^{rd}$ year students from related degrees also choose the course as an option. The course is partly taught, having a total of 20 hours of lectures, and partly by a practical project, with 10 contact hours, between groups of students and real Industrial clients. The project (which accounts for 60% of the total course assessment) is called the *Software Hut Project*. The other 40% of the total course assessment is by exam; the questions relate to taught aspects as well as asking students to refer to the Software Hut project for examples.

The Software Hut project started in 1985 and has evolved over the years. Up till this year, each project was held in the first semester and only had one industrial client. The projects for the past few years have included:

- A Unit Trust Price Predictor
- A Help Desk Support System
- A Mortgage Comparator
- A Metal Fabrication Cost System

The project started in October and was finished by the end of the first semester, with 12 weeks allocated to the project.

At the beginning of the project, students form themselves into groups of five or six, including a Group Leader; groups of four were avoided due to problems if a student dropped out. Any students not in a group would be placed in one. Problems with allocating groups are usually minor, since the students have already worked together within their tutorial groups (size 5 or 6) on the Crossover project, and tend to work in the same groups on the Software Hut.

A key feature of the Software Hut is that it draws on the experience of the Crossover project in the previous year, see [5]. This experience appears to assist the students understanding of what is required of them.

During the first two or three weeks, the client gives presentations, up to one hour, to the students concerning their requirements. This is a time when all members of a group have face to face contact with the client. After the initial presentations, i.e. week 4 onwards, only the group leader of each group will meet the client, until the demonstrations near the end of the project. With increased numbers last year, this avoided the client meeting 60 students each week, meeting 12 instead. Each group leader has a 5 or 10 minute discussion with the client once a week from weeks 4 to 12. Some clients are also willing to be contacted by telephone, fax and/or email; the clients are advised by the lecturers to allocate specific times at which they can be contacted.

In the later weeks, the group leader demonstrates prototypes to the client for feedback; the students are encouraged to use a 4GL. Access and Visual Basic are a popular choice for their implementations, since they suit evolutionary prototyping. Finally, at the end of the project, the students submit two separate hand ins. The first hand in is the product, including installation documentation and user guide. The second hand in is a design report, containing the requirements, analysis, design, testing, etc. The product is given to the client, who is also given a simple marking sheet to fill in for each product; an example marking scheme is in Table 1.

|  |  | Grade(1 - 5)[7] |
|---|---|---|
| **User manual** | Comprehensiveness |  |
|  | Understandability |  |
|  | Presentation |  |

| | | |
|---|---|---|
| **Software** | Installation |  |
|  | Functionality |  |
|  | Ease of use |  |
|  | Robustness (doesn't crash) |  |
|  | Printout quality |  |
|  | Correctness |  |

Table 1. Example Client marking scheme for Software Hut Project

The client takes the products away, and uses them on their own system for, typically, a couple of weeks. The client marks count for half the marks for the project. The client also needs to pick a winner, and possibly a runner up. After

---

[7] Grade 1 = poor,......5 = excellent

the project has finished, the client presents the winning prize, or prizes, (worth £300 for the winning group last year) and the group and client have their photo taken for a local paper.

The design report is assessed by the lecturers separately and is worth the other half of the marks for the project.

The students appear to enjoy the experience; one student's view of the Software Hut is given in Appendix A.

After the product is delivered, the client is granted use of the product, but waives the right to maintenance (thought it is hoped to offer maintenance through the MEng Software Company in future years); the University retains the Intellectual Property Rights for student's work.

## 3.1    Locating Good Clients

One of the main challenges of the Software Hut is locating suitable clients for the course. Based on experience in the department between 1985 and 1997, there are various attributes that are desirable in clients.

- Ideally clients should have little or no experience of computers. One of the most important skills that the students learn, is to identify a customer's requirements. If the client is computer literate, or even worse – programming literate, then the students can easily get wrapped up in discussions over operating systems and programming languages. Since the purpose is to satisfy customer requirements, this communication avoids the real issues.

- Clients should have a need to improve their current **manual** system. One of the main reasons for preferring a manual system is to avoid complexity problems inherent in re-engineering part, or all, of a computer system. The division of system evolution, into 'old' manual system and 'new' computer system, is also easier for the students to comprehend. The current system is easier to investigate, since manual methods are inherently visible, as opposed to computing methods, which must be documented to become visible (and understandable).

- The client should be located relatively close to the department; some students visit the clients, which has often proved beneficial. This also reduces the likelihood of clients turning up late, having their car clamped, or even just getting lost on the way.

- The client should have a good understanding and experience of the system to be investigated. When a client is unsure of the requirements of the system, the students have no chance of recognising the need to communicate with the customer; they might produce a perfectly acceptable system, but without gaining the requirements in a professional way.

- The client should be keen. If the client isn't really interested, then this will infect the students. The client shouldn't just be responding to the offer of free software.

- The client should give a prize. The clients are encouraged to offer a first prize of about £300 to the best group. This is worth £50 or £60 per student, and provides a real incentive to do those few extra hours of work – the hours that really improve the product. When the prize is presented, a local newspaper is invited to take pictures and report the prize.

- Always insist that the clients visit the department before agreeing to use them as clients. If the client wants the lecturers to visit them, then they probably don't have enough time to become involved. The client will have to meet the students in the department, anyway, when the course starts.

- The client needs to be able to run the produced software. The main problem here is the availability of software development tools. At Sheffield, the students are expected to use Access 95 and Visual Basic 5; this implies a Windows 95 or NT machine. Fortunately operating system variance has not been a problem this year since none of the clients are using Windows 3.1.

- There should be a possible commercial product. This encourages the students to feel that their product is saleable, and has a future worth beyond being delivered to the client.

- Never have the lecturers as clients. In the right situation, this makes sense, but with the focus on industrial contact, an academic is neither regarded in the correct light (by the students) nor is able to act realistically as an industrial client. This also applies, though less so, to clients within the University; the students are likely to regard a university client as being internal and less professional, compared to an industrial client.

The above attributes were useful in composing invitation letters for mailing/faxing to potential clients, as well as guiding meetings with clients. Some of the attributes that were important in the past are becoming less important, as clients requirements change and evolve, and as the course itself changes due to increasing student numbers and timing.

## 4   Recent Changes to the Software Hut project

Since last year, a number of changes have taken place in the timing and resource requirements of the software hut. The first change was the move from semester 1 to semester 2. In general this has been a useful change; students are back in the habit of studying before the course starts, as well as having an extra semesters experience behind them. However, the change to semester 2 has made the timing of finding clients more awkward. The ideal time to contact clients is up to 3 months before the project starts. However, since semester 2 starts on the $8^{th}$ of February, the Christmas holiday gets in the way; November and December seem too early for clients to be thinking about next year. Therefore, this year, potential clients were contacted before Christmas and after $1^{st}$ January, with only 5 weeks before the course started.

Last year there was a problem with 'requirements creep'; this occurred when the client continued to change the requirements throughout the project. Due to this, only two groups produced software to a completed standard. The client was quite happy with the situation, giving first and runner up group prizes, and employing a graduate from the department to implement a full product, with all the additional requirements. However, this put a lot of pressure on the students, so this year the students will be handing a requirements specification in week 6; this is intended to solidify the agreement between client and students. The hope is that this will prevent requirement creep, or at least identify earlier that a creep is happening.

Finally, as with most Computer Science departments, student numbers have increased. There are now too many students for the software hut project to run in the same way as previous years. This year there are a total of 94 students, in 18 groups; this is impossible for one client (in retrospect, last year, with 12 groups, was too many for one client). Therefore either one or two more clients are needed every year; this year there are three clients, with 6 groups allocated to each client. First of all, it was necessary to summarise what has categorised good clients in the past.

## 4.1 Multiple Clients

This year, more clients have been needed than in previous years. Unlike last year, where there was one client and 12 groups, this year there are 3 clients with 6 groups for each client. In order to gain more clients, a more proactive approach has been taken to identify and contact potential clients. The informal methods have continued, such as asking known contacts in industry whether they were interested. Two new approaches, to the department, have been tried - 'cold calling' and advertising.

### 4.1.1     Cold calling

Cold calling was achieved by searching for local companies using Electronic Yellow Pages [9]. This allowed a search for businesses by location (down to the first part of the postcode, e.g. S1) and business type. The results gave the business name, address and telephone number. Each business was then contacted by phone, and asked if they would be interested. A total of 44 businesses were contacted; 11 asked for further information to be faxed to them.

The business types searched were: Business consultants, telecommunication consultants, joinery manufacturers, machine blade manufacturers and merchants, furniture manufacturers and designers, china and glassware retailers, tax advisers, tool and steel manufacturers, stainless steel manufacturers, silversmiths, financial advisers, investment consultants, stockbrokers and market makers, chartered and certified accountants, information services, stone masons and steel stockholders.

The replies were as shown in the Figure 2 and Table 2.

| | |
|---|---|
| Send me a fax | 11 |
| Satisfied with current computer system | 11 |
| Don't need a computer | 6 |
| We're too small | 5 |
| Based non locally | 4 |
| Not interested | 3 |
| Not used in our trade | 2 |
| Obscure operating system | 1 |
| Would need maintenance | 1 |

Table 2. Replies to 'Cold Calling' by businesses

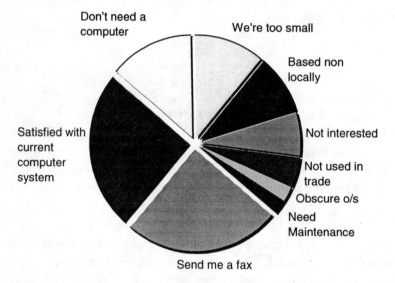

Figure 2. Replies to 'Cold Calling' by businesses

From the figures above, it can be seen that about a quarter of businesses entertained the prospect of becoming involved in a software hut project; three of these, i.e. less than one in fourteen contacted, actually visited the department. Another quarter of the businesses were happy with their current computer systems. Another quarter saw no need for a computer system and/or considered themselves too small a business to be interested.

The time spent on cold calling was approximately 10 minutes per call; therefore about 8 hours (or one working day) effort produced one client.

Three of the potential clients came to visit the department, to discuss their requirements; a china and glassware retailer, a stockbroker and an information service. The retailer has become one of the s/w hut clients (more detail is given later). The stockbroker was asked to let us know their decision, but didn't do so – and after being rung up, stated that they had become too busy to be a client. The information service client was very interested in becoming involved in a project, but the client was not allowed to proceed further by her superior. However, the client may be able to become involved next year.

The two 'unsuccessful' clients, i.e. those who did not proceed to become Software Hut clients, are of great importance to others interested in industrial projects. Setting up meetings with these clients was, ultimately, wasteful on time and resources. With little time left before the projects started, this might have been disastrous. Fortunately, contact had also been made with other potential clients.

Based on experience of cold calling clients who couldn't become involved in the project, two undesirable attributes can be identified of clients; clients who are low down in the company (i.e. clients who cannot sign cheques and/or allocate person power) and busy clients.

### 4.1.2      Informal Contacts

In past years, many clients have come from informal contacts – where one or other of the s/w hut lecturers has a contact who is keen to have a project implemented. This year, two contacts were interested in becoming clients. However, neither became successful clients. One client, once again, was unable to spare the time to become involved (and as with the stockbroker, had to be rung to discover this fact). The other client proved to have an unsuitable project. Though neither client became involved in the software hut, both companies that the clients work for are now becoming involved with the MEng Software Company, as described in [8].

Informal contacts have previously been a successful way of contacting clients. This years situation, where no clients came from informal contacts, may be just chance, due to concentration on other methods of gaining clients, or due to changes in clients requirements. Currently there is not enough evidence available to support any of these, or other, conclusions.

### 4.1.3 Advertising

The Sheffield Chamber of Commerce produces a monthly newsletter, the *Opportunities Bulletin* that is sent out free to businesses within the area. A short, 350 word, invitation to clients was placed in the bulletin at the beginning of January.

The invitation was a much more efficient method of finding clients than cold calling; five companies contacted the department with interest in becoming software hut clients. Of these, three were unsuitable, due to time constraints or unsuitability to the software hut project (these clients are being considered for other industrial initiatives). However, two clients were suitable; one client was a nightclub marketing director and the other the managing director of a surgical instrument manufacturer. Both clients have become software hut clients and appear, at the time of writing, to be good clients. A summary of all three clients is given in Appendix B.

Advertising was a suprisingly successful and efficient way of locating clients; it only took about one hour to compose a letter and send it to the chamber of commerce. There was an initial concern that the department wouldn't be able to cope with demand; this proved not to be so (maybe a few years ago the situation might have been different). The department will be continuing to use advertising for locating clients in the future; this also promotes the department's profile as being relevant to industry.

### 4.1.4 Coping with multiple clients

This year, more than one client was available for students to choose, so a method of allocating groups and clients had to be chosen.

Firstly the students were given details of the clients and told that they would have to form in to groups of 5 (or exceptionally 6). The details of the clients were essentially an overview, and did not contain nearly as much information as in Appendix B. The reason for giving a precise of the client information was mainly to decrease the turnaround time between presenting the information to the students, and their choice of client. The brief details included the clients names (which are kept out of this paper for reasons of confidentiality), the type of business, a one line problem description, an assessment of the difficulty and any differences to the product requirements that might help influence the students decision. Specifically, the students were told that:

- The china and glassware retailer was a more traditional project, with the best defined scope, the least risky project, but would require a quality product, involving the most rigorous testing.
- The nightclub required a usable product, but had a less well defined scope.
- The surgical instrument manufacturer required a prototype system, thus indicating a different level of testing, was offering a £150 runner up prize (all clients offered a first prize), but included some non-trivial technical problems that would need to be overcome for the project to be successful. The students were advised that this was the most risky project, but also that it had the greatest scope for excellence.

The students were also told the method by which they would be allocated groups, and told that there would be no opportunity to change client later.

The students formed themselves into groups, with occasional encouragement from the lecturers. In all, 17 groups of 5 (or 6) were formed, and a spare group of 2 (this group was later allocated 3 extra students who were unable to make the meeting).

In deciding on a method for allocating groups, it was intended initially to pick groups and clients randomly. However, on reflection a variety of options were considered:

1. **Allocate randomly**

    This option had its appeal, particularly due to the speed with which projects could be allocated. However, it would not allow any student choice, which could create problems later.

2. **Get groups to bid for projects to the clients**

Though probably more realistic in some ways, this option was seen as delaying the start of the project for too long, as well as involving more of the clients time than was strictly necessary.

3. **Allow students to vote for 1$^{st}$ and 2$^{nd}$ choice**

    On the surface an attractive option, but it would have to be combined with another option to decide on the order of the allocation.

4. **Allow students to 'bet' on different clients**

    Discounted, as it appeared too complex to explain and implement.

5. **Use a first come first served policy**

    This option was seen to encourage quick response without much thought, and could easily have resulted in students changing their minds before a client was fully allocated.

A combination of option 3 and option 1 was used, i.e. it was decide to offer a choice of clients, but then to allocate clients, from the students choices, in a random order.

The groups were given slips to indicate group membership, including identifying the group leader by writing them down first, and indicating their preferred 1$^{st}$ and 2$^{nd}$ choice of client. They were told that no guarantees could be made about getting any client they wanted, and that the final decision was irreversible. The projects were allocated randomly, by shuffling the slips. As the slips were picked out, the 1$^{st}$ choice was allocated if no more than 6 groups had been allocated to that client, otherwise the 2$^{nd}$ choice was allocated (or ultimately the 3$^{rd}$ choice!). There was something of a bingo atmosphere as the groups were allocated on the board. Suprisingly, all but one group were allocated their 1$^{st}$ choice. The surgical instrument manufacturer was slightly more popular, and the china retailer slightly less popular.

The allocation method worked almost flawlessly; the department expects to use the same method next year.

Unlike previous years, the marks for the project can this year contribute 60% towards the course marks, or optionally 100%; the students are being offered the option of whether to take the exam. If students are satisfied with the project mark (and have not failed), then they will have the option to accept their project mark as contributing 100% of the course marks, and therefore not attending the exam.

Another difference from last year was the need to have three academics, one allocated to each client. Currently the two lecturers and a PhD student have been allocated to a client each. The intention is to rotate the academics, to avoid one clients groups gaining a perceived advantage of other groups. It may be unfair to place such responsibility on a PhD student, in which case, the department will need to allocate only lecturers as clients (either by using more lecturers, or allocating different times in the week).

## 4.2    Client Meetings

Each potential client was invited to visit the department, to meet the lecturers and FDTL staff involved, as soon as feasible after showing interest in the software hut project. The meeting would start with the client describing their business, current situation and the problem; sometimes there was a choice of problems.

For the department, there are a number of key items that needed to be found out from this initial meeting (if not already found out from previous communication):

1. Who the clients student contact would be
2. What experience the contact had of the current system
3. How busy the contact was
4. Whether other contacts were available
5. Whether a prize was available
6. What computing knowledge the contact had
7. Details of what the project might entail, including whether any solution exists
8. The current and projected computing facilities that the system would run on

There are also a number of items that needed to be made clear to clients:

1. Details of the timetable and other aspects of the project, i.e. the time when the students would meet the clients, the number of meetings and the need to give 2 or 3 presentations
2. User documentation and screen shots from previous projects (with the previous clients name removed) are shown as examples of the quality the client can expect from the students.

3. The client is informed that the department keeps their name confidential (aside from the prize giving) as a matter of course
4. The usefulness of the Crossover project experience is explained
5. IPR (Intellectual Property Rights) issues are explained
6. A sample of previous years user assessment form are shown to the client
7. The topics of previous projects are given
8. The prize is explained

Sometimes, when the lecturers are uncertain whether the problem has a solution, or to just draw out the clients thinking about the problem, it has been useful to investigate the possible solutions to the problem. Once the lecturers are confident that a solution exists, then the investigation into solutions ends. The clients are asked to ignore any suggestions by the lecturers, since the students offer an opportunity to have multiple suggestions investigated (and students can always be encouraged in a certain direction).

Finally, the lectures usually indicate whether the department is interested, and ask the client to let them know if they are interested in going ahead with the project. If the client hasn't contacted them within a week, then a lecturer rings up to clarify the situation.

These items have evolved from a number of meetings with clients, all of which involved much more interaction than shown. One vital aspect is the visit by the clients; even though the meeting could have been performed by phone, the department has found the initial meetings to be invaluable for informal communication.

# 5 Conclusions

Industrial Software Projects, of which the Software Hut Project is one example, have been shown to be a vital part of the degree structure in the department. The project offers experience of real industrial work, including client contact, team work, time management, etc. The students are given responsibility as contractors to a real client, and appear to enjoy the process. For the lecturers, the project offers a reality that a synthesized project could not offer, as well as containing all the richness of real projects. The additional requirements, of the lecturers, are the need to contact and select clients. The guidelines within this paper, and summary of experience, have proved useful for running industrial projects. In particular, advertising appears to be a promising new area to use in obtaining clients.

Industrial projects have a few cautionary elements, mainly concerned with locating suitable clients, watching out for requirements creep and stressing time management to students.

The Software Hut project has also been shown to scale up well with increasing numbers of students, with relatively little change. The essential changes are to include at least one more client than the minimum required (in case a client drops out before the project starts), allow time to contact clients, offer a non-reversible choice to students and ensure that groups include at least one more member than the minimum required.

An initial sampling of clients, within the region of the department, indicates that businesses either have a computer system already, or don't want one. Every client, that became a software hut client, already had a computer system in place. This indicates an evolution in clients; clients who have no computing experience are unlikely to be found.

Finally, a diversity of industrial projects, at different levels and times throughout the year, are invaluable; potential clients can usually be found a suitable industrial initiative from those available.

# References

1. HM Government. Report on the National Committee on Higher Education. H.M.Stationary Office, 1997
2. SARTOR. Engineering Council, Standards and routes to registration. 1997
3. The Times. Nice Degree, shame it's irrelevant. Interface, October 15, 1997
4. HEFCE. Higher Education Funding Council Report on the provision of Computer Science. 1995
5. Holcombe M. The "Crossover" software engineering project. Engineering Professors Bulletin, September, 1994, pp 3-5
6. HEFCE. Quality Assessment Report. The University of Sheffield, Computer Science, 1994

7.   Holcombe M, Lafferty HH.  Using Computer professionals for Managing Student Software Projects.  In: Bateman D, Hopkins T (ed) Proceedings of the Conference on Developments in the Teaching of Computer Science. University of Kent at Canterbury, 1992

8.   Holcombe M, Stratton A.  VICI: Experiences and proposals for Student run Software Companies.  Submitted to Project'98.  University of Sheffield, April 1998

9.   Electronic Yellow Pages.  http://www.eyp.co.uk/.  December, 1997

# Appendix A. Student View of the Software Hut Project.

I undertook the Software hut project two years ago as part of my degree course.  The [2nd year] course was very different from the other courses that we had been previously taught.  COM 221 focused very much on teamwork and for most of us, it was our first contact with industrial consultancy and software development.

Interacting with someone from outside the department, as if we would in industry, proved an incredibly useful learning experience and also gave us a chance to apply the software engineering skills that we had learned in lectures.  We could see how the waterfall models and Z specifications that we had been taught fitted in a real software-engineering context, experiencing the problems and processes first-hand.

Our contact in the company met with us to describe his requirements and it was interesting to see how our frequent meetings developed; from requirements capturing, delivering and testing.  The entire experience of getting a feel for how the client/engineer interaction worked and developed was a very useful one.  At each stage of delivery, we would present the developing product and receive encouraging advice from the client and the guiding lecturers.

Overall, the project was a very useful experience of applying knowledge that we had learned in a realistic environment.  We witnessed the processes that software engineering went through in the context of industry and has given me personally a much better appreciation for the subject.  Of course as well as the benefits of the project, we also witnessed some of the problems too, the lessons of which are just as valuable.

Since we were working to a deadline (end of semester), our time was severely restricted. We had to read and liase with the client enough such that we understood exactly what was required. This was difficult in itself as the requirements changed quite frequently. We used prototyping to get a quick idea of what was needed; this identified the interface required. The main problem was that of completely understanding the problem domain and writing a competent and usable program in the timeframe. Producing the specification in Z and then a suitable design was most time consuming, even when the tasks were delegated amongst the group. We did not have enough time to test the system formally, although our main aim was to get a working version by the deadline.

The software hut project has been a great experience, from participating in team-working and discovering the pressures, to witnessing the software lifecycle in operation (not just on whiteboards and texts!). The course has been vital in widening my appreciation for the software engineering industry in general. Most courses do not give you this contact with the outside world and tend to teach you the basics of their course in academic isolation – COM 221 was an interesting and very welcome change.

*Dan Khan, MEng Software Engineering Undergraduate, 25th June 1997.*

# Appendix B. Summary of Clients and Projects

Details of each client and their project are given below.

## B.1    China and glassware retailer

There were two contacts for this client, both of whom worked on the salary calculations; one had extensive experience of the system, the other had less contact, but was higher up in the company.

The client has a total of 20 shops and retail warehouses distributed around the U.K. They employ a large number of part time staff, who tend to work irregular hours (though they usually have a planned number of hours per day, they often deviate from the plan). Each site keeps monthly timesheets recording hours put in each day by each employee. About a week before pay day, the sheets are collated, a projection is made for each employee for the remaining days before pay day, and the sheets are sent to the central office. At the central office, all the data from the sheets has to be collated and typed in to a standard payroll package.

The first problem was that this typing was intensive, taking up several employees time. The second problem is that employees may leave the company after the sheets are sent in, but still be paid until the end of the month.

The client was looking for a system to reduce the send in period and reduce typing.

One important limitation was that it was not feasible to buy 20 personal computers, one for each site. This was mainly due to the expense (twenty PCs is about £20k to £40k) plus the inexperienced nature of the staff in the sites (training was also infeasible, since staff turnover can be high).

Another limitation was that the current payroll system must not be replaced, since it is capable of handling all their other requirements (and is in use for other aspects of the business).

## B.2   Nightclub

The client contact for the nightclub is the marketing director.

The nightclub was looking for a system to predict the costs of events, based on financial models derived from previous events. At the time, the client used a combination of manual and spreadsheet models, with the spreadsheets being recreated from scratch every time a new event cost was forecast.

The event forecasting is dependent on a variety of factors. Each event has a number of fixed costs, such as administrative overhead, lighting, heating, etc., and a number of variable costs, such as bar staff, complimentary drink costs, etc. The revenue is calculated based on income from ticket sales and bar sales. To further complicate the calculation, different nights of the week will attract different types of customer, who will sometimes pay different prices for tickets (students pay reduced entry) and spend differing amounts at the bar (this can be deduced from the bar take from different events). The client gathers all this information, including the potential customers (e.g. 20% students, 20% nurses) to predict whether an event will be profitable; the price of the tickets is one of the main outputs of the prediction.

The client had, for some time, been combining financial models for prediction and the data used, from scratch, every time an event prediction was made. The client was seeking to separate the consistent aspects of the prediction from the variable aspects, in order to produce more accurate and efficient predictions of event costs and income.

## B.3    Surgical instrument manufacturer

There were two clients for this company, the Managing director and a recent graduate working in the graphical design department.

The client currently has a database of all hospitals across the U.K., with details of their size, location, hospital funding (i.e. NHS, private), etc. The client recently combined this information, of over five hundred sites, on a map of the U.K., showing the location of the hospitals, size and funding type.

The map has been useful in visualising the large amount of data involved, so the client proposed that the project be a prototype system, investigating the integration of a hospital database and a visual map. The concept is that, through a local area map (i.e. a cut down from the eventual full U.K. map) different hospitals can be selected to bring up the relevant database details. The database can also be searched to create new versions of the map, that indicate different aspects of the hospitals, such as time since a salesman visited, value of instruments sold, etc.

# Using Virtual Workspaces to Promote HND Group Project Success

Virginia King
Computer Science, Coventry University

### Abstract

This paper describes the current development of an Internet website to support students conducting group projects for HND Computing and HND Business Information Technology. This work is still in progress and is being documented in order to raise awareness of this approach as a means of supporting computing project students, and to draw comments from readers to assist future development. The author can be contacted by electronic mail as V.C.King@coventry.ac.uk.

The problems with motivating this group of students prior to the introduction of the website are described, as are the anticipated benefits for these and other computing project students. The use of the website as a resource centre, as a common room and as a virtual study for each group are considered, together with its potential for inter-group quality assurance activities and communication with external clients. The role of this initiative within Coventry University's Teaching, Learning and Assessment Taskforce is also covered.

## 1 Introduction

At Coventry University we have made use of the Internet to develop a virtual workspace to support HND Computing and HND Business Information Technology group projects. Students on these courses had an excellent success rate in the past. The few students who failed their projects were those who had effectively withdrawn from the whole course and who therefore failed all modules. These cases still occur, but the course team is particularly concerned about a phenomenon which was first observed in academic year 1996/7: whole project groups who performed very poorly on the project throughout the year and finally failed or scraped a pass whilst believing that their performance was adequate. These failures coincided with a rise in the number of students taking the projects module (fifty or sixty per year at the Coventry site compared with around forty previously), and with a rise in the number of first year module failures that the students carry into year two.

These students are active users of email and the Internet and spend many hours every week using computers for social purposes and for entertainment. They are studying computing or IT and have a high level of competence in the use of software and hardware, and yet they fall far below the expected level of achievement in their projects.

This initiative is based on the hypothesis that students would improve their level of success in their project, if they perceived project work as having social and skill benefits. By using a website to inform students privately of their progress, setting up a facility for sharing documents and ideas between groups, allocating an area to each group where they can lodge completed documents, and making each group project visible on the Internet, it is hoped that students will improve both the quality and timeliness of their project work.

Coventry University has set up a Teaching Learning and Assessment Taskforce (TLAA) to sponsor a set of projects which will raise awareness and use of computer mediated learning and of other forms of resource-based learning. The development described in this paper has been selected for sponsorship by the TLAA Taskforce because of its focus on HND students (a group often overlooked), and because of the great potential within the University for the use of virtual workspaces to promote group learning and cooperation where module populations are large, diverse or physically separated.

Although this development is still at an early stage, the approach may be of use to other institutions interested in promoting the success of computing students who are conducting individual or group projects at diploma, degree or even masters level.

## 2 Planning Stages for the Virtual Workspace

This development has been planned according to the evolutionary process model [1]. That is, it has been divided into four six-month-long phases, each providing an increased level of access and sophistication to the website.

The most important part of the system is to be developed in the first phase. This will then be reviewed and the system design revised in the light of what has been learned. The second most important set of requirements will then be developed and implemented and the process repeated twice more.

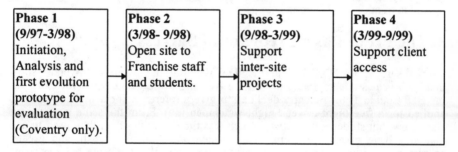

| Phase 1 (9/97-3/98) Initiation, Analysis and first evolution prototype for evaluation (Coventry only). | Phase 2 (3/98- 9/98) Open site to Franchise staff and students. | Phase 3 (9/98-3/99) Support inter-site projects | Phase 4 (3/99-9/99) Support client access |
|---|---|---|---|

Figure 1. Virtual Workspace, phases of development

The first phase (September 1997-March 1998) is concerned with requirements analysis, software evaluation, software selection and prototyping the core website. This will provide (as a minimum) a virtual resource centre (project guides, sample documentation, support facilities), an area for each group where they can advertise themselves and their project, and an area where they can view their marks to date compared graphically against a prediction of their final mark. The HND BIT and HND Computing project students themselves and the tutors running group projects within the Coventry University franchise will evaluate this prototype and their comments will aid the development of the next phase.

The second phase (March 1998-September 1998) will expand the site to include project tutors and project groups at four franchised sites. This will introduce security and administrative difficulties as the site either has to link dynamically to the colleges' own servers, or the franchise tutors must be set up as secondary webmasters of the Coventry site. It has already been established that each franchised college has its own regulations regarding use of the Internet and that there may be difficulties in allowing project groups the necessary access. Franchise students have tended to be more successful in their projects than those at the main site. This is thought to be partly because the cohorts are much smaller (typically a tenth the size) and so students are more aware of what is required of them. It may also be because the franchise project tutor usually also teaches Systems Development Methodology and the inherent link between taught theory and its application in the project is more obvious. It is important therefore that the website enhances the role of the franchise college in their students' eyes rather than detracts from it. Again both students and their tutors will evaluate this evolution of the prototype and their comments will aid the development of the next phase.

The third phase (September 1998-March 1999) will allow virtual project groups to be formed from students studying at different franchise centres. Little additional functionality is anticipated, but administrative difficulties must be overcome. The four colleges each have between one and ten students enrolled on the project module. The requirement for this to be a group project has been resolved in the past by students from one college, travelling to another college for this module. As colleges can be up to fifty miles apart, this is an unsatisfactory solution. Additionally, there is a small number of disabled students within the franchise who have particular problems in travelling daily to college and who are therefore at a disadvantage in group work. The use of the website as a virtual workspace supported by email where necessary and occasional face-to-face meetings, would allow groups to be formed from students at different physical locations.

The final phase (March 1999-September 1999) will allow project clients to access their project group's area to monitor progress and participate in virtual meetings. There may be objections to this from the University or franchised college authorities and careful negotiation may be more time-consuming than the provision of additional function.

# 3  The Project as a Predictor of Success

Internal surveys for HND BIT and HND Computing at Coventry University show that each year students spend more time working in part-time jobs (for example, the BIT Course Tutor recently declined to give a reference for a student who had applied for a five-night-a-week night-watchman job). From the same surveys, we also know that students now spend much less time studying than they used to and that they have greater problems with written and spoken English, and greater problems achieving the expected levels of numeracy. It is therefore not surprising that we see more and more students struggling to complete their project successfully.

## 3.1 Project Failure Compared to Failure in Other Modules

Concern over high HND module failure rates in 1996/7 led us to analyse the relationship between poor project performance and poor course performance.

Out of twenty-four HND Computing students, twelve failed the project and one withdrew from the course. This is by far the worst set of results we have seen.

Of thirty-nine HND BIT students, one withdrew, and the remainder all managed at least to pass the project, but only nine students passed all modules at the first attempt. Additionally, twenty BIT students failed the largely self-directed module Business Policy and Finance (BP&F). The module leader for BP&F feels that similar skills are needed to pass this module as are used in a project, i.e. a high level of self-direction, an early start, good communication work and cooperation with other students.

## 3.2 Late Project Initiation Compared to Failure in Other Modules

The first milestone for the group project is the hand-in and approval of the students Project Specification. This should be signed off by early November; however, some groups did not manage to get their Project Specifications approved until January. When that Project Specification sign off date is set against the students and their eventual results, there is a clear correlation between lateness and eventual module failure.

For BIT students, of twenty-two late students, nineteen failed at least one module (for fifteen of them, this included BP&F). Only two students who belonged in groups handing in their Project Specification late, actually passed all modules.

For Computing students, the findings are even clearer. Of the twelve students who handed in their Project Specification late, ten failed (at least) the project and one withdrew. The only late submitter who passed the project was identified as the only active member in his group.

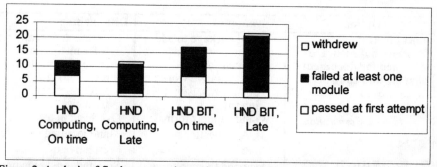

Figure 2. Analysis of final outcomes by student status at first project milestone.

It is therefore suggested that success and activity on the project is associated with success and activity on the course. If the key can be found to start students earlier on their projects, to put in more effort into their projects, this may lead to success in the course as a whole.

# 4 Requirements

Requirements gathering took the form of discussions with students, module staff, franchise staff and several current project clients. The different stakeholders involved in the virtual workspace each have their own requirements, some conflicting. The full set of user requirements are documented in Appendix A.

For module staff, the top priority requirements are
- To increase student awareness of key project milestones
- To make projects visible to first-year students to prepare them for their own projects
- To be able to update any element of the website and give access permissions

For Franchise Staff, the top priority requirements are
- To allow students to share module resources remotely:
- To be able to update any element of the website related to own site and read other elements with permission

For project students' the top priority requirements are
- To be able to contact group members, supervisor and client easily from PC
- To be able to advertise their own skills over the Internet

For project clients, the top priority requirements are expected to be
- To be able to review previous projects
- To be able to monitor progress on their own project.

# 5 Implementation Options

A number of alternative implementation platforms have been considered including Lotus Notes, Microsoft FrontPage 98, Internet MUD (Multi-User Domain/Dungeon) software and in-house development.

| Option | Advantages | Disadvantages |
|---|---|---|
| **Lotus Notes\* [4] Professional software designed for document sharing and control** *\*Lotus Notes is a registered trademark of Lotus Development Corporation* | · Useful package to add to students' CVs <br> · Designed for collaborative work on documents using the Internet <br> · Would support formal QA inspections | · Implemented locally on NT which is not currently available to most staff and students in the franchise <br> · Overhead in teaching and learning skills for effective use |
| **Internet MUD [5] (Multi-User Domain/ Dungeon) software. CoMentor, a MOO (an object oriented MUD) under development at the University of Huddersfield was evaluated. SeeURL :www.hud.ac.uk/ comentor** | · Designed to encourage peer evaluation of essays —good for QA <br> · Sophisticated access and control functions <br> · As the product of a JISC TAP-funded project, will be free to HE when complete (c. September 1998) | · Still under development <br> · Requires customisation to fit requirements of a computing environment <br> · Requires significant administration and software support |
| **Inhouse Developed Software** | · Would allow all required functions to be provided | · Long lead-time <br> · Costly unless funded |

Figure 3. A summary of comparison of some of the software environments considered

MS FrontPage has been selected as the initial implementation platform because it provides the most functionality for the least cost and effort. The only problem encountered so far, is that the discussion group facility is under-used. Investigation suggests that this may be because users feel that the discussion is too public and because they have to access the site specifically to take part in the discussion. This response has been observed on another FrontPage site at Coventry University. Since there is concern within the University about how students might use their website permissions, it may be preferable to use the discussion group function as a virtual noticeboard and find an alternative (such as email plus attachments) to provide the inter-active element. This decision will be an important outcome of the evaluation in March 1998.

| Option | Advantages | Disadvantages |
|---|---|---|
| **MS FrontPage\*, [6] Website authoring and management tool** *Microsoft and FrontPage are registered trademarks of Microsoft Corporation | · Allows fast development of key functions · Provides appealing graphics, themes and icons · Students need no special software other than a web-browser · Only one authoring /administration copy needed for each site · Provides simple access control by logon or IP address | · Discussion facilities require user to log-on to website · Possibility that project groups could misuse their website for their own purposes. · Document sharing is incidental rather than central · Access control is at website-level rather than at document or webpage level |

Figure 4. A summary of the selected software environment

# 6 Development of the Virtual Workspace

The virtual workspace is intended to act as a resource centre, as a common room and as a virtual study for each group. It should ideally provide a means of supporting inter-group quality assurance activities and communication with external clients. The resource centre is the simplest requirement to develop and is compatible with current website provision at Coventry since it consists simply of hot-links to module documentation and useful Internet sites. The common room and virtual study demand that students have limited update access to the site. Additionally, groups may submit their own page, logo or other material which can be made generally accessible once approved by their project tutor.

The initial Intranet site first went live in early November 1997. It was written in raw HTML under Windows 3.1 and ran on the local student file server. The main purpose of this first evolution was to raise awareness amongst both staff and students of the work being carried out and to encourage students to reference the site. It was immediately clear that a simple text-based site had no appeal to the students involved. The access rate rose slightly when a digitised photograph of the student group was added to the site but it still lacked kudos.

More sophisticated graphics for the site were developed voluntarily by one HND Computing student, Abdul Shafaq. He took digitised photographs of student group and module lecturers and created a collage depicting "the class of 1997/8". The colour scheme was changed from pastels to black on bright green in response to his suggestion.

Two project groups asked for their separate photographs to be taken and added to the site. Still the site was pronounced "boring" - partly the format, partly the content. It was clear that web-authoring tools were vital to achieve an adequate level of visual interest and interaction. A sub-project has been commissioned to explore the user interface further, while functionality is expanded.

The website originally conformed to accepted website design principles [7], [8] (simplicity, stability, and standard colours). Interestingly, the very people who could be expected to appreciate this subtlety - students of computing and IT — rejected it and demanded the opposite (complexity in the form of frames, moving objects, sombre or garish colours). The current design tries to adopt a middle path and its achievement of user requirements will be the basis for evaluating success rather than its adherence to HCI principles.

Using MS FrontPage the site has been redeveloped once more using a packaged "theme" called "Zero". This provides a dark grey background covered in ones and zeros; lime green, bright blue, yellow and grey text, and animated icons.

New functionality has also been added, including a hit-counter, Frequently Asked Questions (FAQ) page, feedback form, interactive quality assurance review pages. The site also displays graphs, one showing students their marks to date and the predicted marks for each group, and another showing their success in hitting milestones.

This site was implemented on an Internet server in February 1998 and is now under evaluation by staff and students.

# 7 Benefits to Project Students

The development of the virtual workspace can claim benefits to project students even at this early stage. Firstly, it provides a "home" for project students where their questions can be answered at any time. Secondly, it encourages project students to share good practice and carry out quality appraisals of each other's work. Thirdly it has made students' progress visible long in time for them to remedy their work [2].

An unexpected benefit has been the use by students of the interactive discussion area to raise technical issues and find solutions without involving lecturing staff. In this way it supports collaborative learning, encouraging students to value their peers' technical skills and raising the skills of the whole group [3].

# 8 Findings

The virtual workspace for HND Computing and HND BIT students is still being developed and is expected to have only limited impact on the 1997/8 cohort. However, a prime requirement of the system is that the second year group projects be visible to first year students, in order to prepare them early for the effort required. This will be achieved.

It is certainly true that without this initiative, the rate of failure on HND group projects would increase, results mid-way through 1997/8 confirm this. It will not be until June 1998 that the final impact will be known, however, there are encouraging signs. Many of the students have volunteered to help in the design and construction of this system and in the evaluation of the MOO site at the University of Huddersfield. It is unknown for HND BIT and Computing project students at Coventry to carry out additional (unassessed) work in this way and their enthusiasm gives us hope. One student re-sitting his project from last year has shown great interest in revising the user interface in order to improve the look and feel of the website. Quite unrealistic and uncommitted to his original project, he has already shown levels of skill and professionalism worthy of a BCS and an HND award on this re-sit project.

# 9 Conclusion

The virtual workspace has already encouraged our project students to be more proactive than had been anticipated. Group projects at HND level have there own particular problems, particularly in a franchise, but singleton and degree project students might also respond positively to this type of environment for project development.

By disseminating this material through Project 98, it is hoped that others involved in supporting computing project students can both capitalise on this approach themselves and feedback their findings to the originator.

## References

1. Gilb T. Principles of Software Engineering Management, Addison-Wesley, 1988
2. Youll DP. Making Software Development Visible, Effective Project Control. John Wiley and Sons, 1990
3. Koschmann T. (ed) CSCL: Theory and Practice of an Emerging Paradigm. Lawrence Erlbaum Associates, New Jersey, 1996
4. Lotus Notes 4.5 Technical documentation
5. Internet resource, www.hud.ac.uk/comentor, Multi-user learning environment for social science students
6. Microsoft FrontPage 98 Technical documentation
7. Internet resource, www.useit.com/alertbox/9605.html, Top ten mistakes in web design,
8. Internet resource www.chl.co.uk, Web design guidelines

# Appendix A

## Requirements Catalogue

| User/Code | Shortname | Priority | Description |
|---|---|---|---|
| **Module Staff** | | | |
| • MR1 | Aware | 1 | Increase student awareness of key project milestones |
| • MR2 | Assess | 2 | Increase student awareness of assessment criteria |
| • MR3 | QA | 2 | Encourage inter-group quality assurance activities |
| • MR4 | Progress | 2 | Monitor student progress |
| • MR5 | Prepare | 1 | Make projects visible to first-year students to prepare them for their own projects |
| • MR6 | Pride | 2 | Encourage student pride in projects |
| • MR7 | Professionalism | 3 | Encourage student professionalism |
| • MR8 | StaffSecurity | 1 | Be able to update any element of the website and give access permissions |
| **Franchise Staff** | | | |
| • FR1 | Visibility | 2 | Improve visibility of module development at other sites |
| • FR2 | Share | 1 | Allow students to share module resources remotely |
| • FR3 | Multi-site | 2 | Let project groups to be composed of students from different sites |
| • FR4 | FranchiseSecurity | 1 | Be able to update any element of the website related to own site and read other elements with permission. |
| **Students** | | | |
| • SR1 | Progress | 2 | Be able to assess progress against a standard |
| • SR2 | Skills | 2 | Be able to enhance IT & QA skills through practical use |
| • SR3 | Quality | 2 | Improve the likelihood of producing work of acceptable quality |
| • SR4 | Contact | 1 | Be able to contact group members, supervisor end client easily from networked PC |
| • SR5 | Market | 1 | Be able to advertise own skills over the Internet |
| • SR6 | StudentSecurity | 2 | Be able to read any element of the website related to own group, update own documents and read other elements with permission |
| **Clients** | | | |
| • CR1 | Review | 1 | Be able to review previous projects |
| • CR2 | Monitor | 1 | Be able to monitor progress on their own project |
| • CR3 | Inspect | 2 | Be able to inspect own project documents |
| • CR4 | Comment | 2 | Be able to comment on own project documents |
| • CR5 | ClientSecurity | 2 | Be able to enter own comments and read other elements with permission |

# Group Projects for the Software Engineering of Knowledge Based Systems

M.P.Lee, A. Harrison and A. J. Sammes

Knowledge Engineering Research Centre, Computing & Information Systems Management Group, Department Of Informatics & Simulation, Royal Military College of Science, Cranfield University, Shrivenham, Swindon, Wiltshire, SN6 8LA, UK.

## Abstract

This paper describes the conduct of a project which forms part of a module in Knowledge Based Systems (KBS) contained in the syllabus of our BEng degrees in Command & Control, Communications & Information Systems (CIS) and Software Engineering (SE) presented at the Royal Military College of Science (RMCS) Shrivenham. The paper discusses the difficulties experienced and results achieved by groups of students over the last ten years.

## 1. Introduction

The Royal Military College of Science (RMCS) forms the Faculty of Military Science, Technology and Management of Cranfield University (CU). Courses are presented at both undergraduate and postgraduate levels to the Army, Royal Navy, Royal Air Force, civil servants and civilian students. Undergraduates follow a conventional three-year course leading to the award of BSc or BEng. The Department Of Informatics & Simulation, under the direction of Professor A J Sammes, comprises four groups. Computing & Information Systems Management group (CISM) runs our CIS degree while Computing & Information Systems Engineering group (CISE) runs our SE degree, both as part of wider degree schemes. The other two groups in the department do not run any undergraduate degrees.

The first BSc, now BEng, degree course in Command & Control, Communications & Information Systems (CIS) started at RMCS in 1986. In the first year students take a number of modules which include introductions to software systems design and programming. Software design is based on Jackson Structured Programming (JSP) and a program design language (PDL), while Ada is used as the vehicle for implementing design solutions. In the second year the introductory concepts are brought together into a life cycle based module on software engineering. This is reinforced by a module on advanced programming techniques, which continues the use of Ada as the implementation language. Ada was chosen because of the way the language supports software engineering principles, particularly abstraction and information hiding. In the core year, in parallel with the procedural approach to software production, students are introduced to the techniques associated with Lisp and/or Prolog (Lee, 1996 and Lee et alia, 1994). In the final year all these elements converge with a study of Knowledge Based Systems (KBS) where the incremental approach favoured by the Artificial Intelligence (AI) fraternity using languages like Lisp and expert system shells like Flex is contrasted with the life-cycle approach favoured by software engineers using languages like Ada.

The BEng degree in Software Engineering, which is taught by the CISE group, begins with Java in the first year, includes some Prolog in the second and introduces Ada in the third. Students come together from both degrees for our third year module.

The learning objectives of the module are to:

- Understand the basic principles, technologies and methods of KBS sufficiently well to allow students to evaluate, select and customise a medium-sized KBS.
- Specify and design a KBS using a method such as KADS.
- Implement a KBS is either a Fifth Generation Language (5GL), such as Prolog, or a shell, such as Flex.
- Evaluate the capabilities of a variety of KBS.
- Gain an understanding of neural network technology.
- Demonstrate through appropriate practical design work a commitment to the application of sound information systems engineering principles to the development and use of KBS.

The Knowledge Based Systems module includes a group project where students are required to design and implement a rule and/or frame based system incorporating domain knowledge of their own choosing. Consequently a major part of the task involves knowledge engineering. In order to bring together all the elements of the course involved with software production, it was decided that the project structure should include several groups, each with 5 or 6 students, so that the solution could be developed using a variety of techniques covered by the syllabus. Students were briefed to apply software engineering principles wherever possible (Lees, 1996).

# 2. Syllabus

Knowledge Based Systems is a third year module in both the CIS and SE degree syllabi. The aim of the module is to provide the student with an appreciation of the techniques and tools that are available to support the design and implementation of knowledge based systems. The rationale behind this is that in recent years we have seen an increase in the availability of technology which implements the concepts concerned with knowledge based systems. This technology spans an area extending from expensive research tools down to inexpensive, generally applicable microcomputer based packages. The areas covered in the syllabus are:

- Knowledge representation
- Inferencing strategies

- Uncertainty in reasoning
- Knowledge acquisition
- Tools and applications
- Research topics
- Neural networks
- Team-based project

The recommended text for the module is Hopgood (1995).

# 3. Previous research

It was recognised a long time ago in industry (Baker, 1972) that programming in the large required team projects. It is however only recently that academics have moved from teaching programming in the small by individuals to proper software engineering by groups. Since the late eighties two developments have taken place: the expansion of project work in computer science education and the development of teaching via teamwork.

The first category, of teaching via projects, includes software engineering (King, 1989; Peacock et alia, 1987; Bickerstaff, 1985 and Henry, 1983); business computing (Saadat et alia, 1994; Borovits I et alia, 1990; Klepper, 1989; Little & Margetson, 1989; Burke & Olinsky, 1986 and White 1984) and more general issues (Peacock et alia, 1988; Joel, 1987; Carver, 1985 and Sanders, 1984).

The second category, of teaching via teams, also includes software engineering, the question of assessment and some more general issues. The papers on team projects in software engineering claim various amounts of success (Perkins & Beck, 1980; Collofello & Woodfield, 1982; Hayes 1982; Sathi, 1984 and Waguespack & Haas, 1984). Other papers on assessment present various ways of dealing with the problem of allocating marks to individuals in teams (Sigwart & Van Meer, 1985; Collofello, 1985; Tenny, 1987; Pigford, 1987; Chrisman & Beccue 1987; Jordan, 1987 and Jones & Birtle, 1989). There are also various papers on more general issues in team project teaching (Woodfield & Collofello, 1983; Potvin 1984; Roth & White, 1987 and Farkas, 1988).

It is interesting to note that the majority of papers listed below were published in just one journal, the Bulletin of the Special Interest Group in Computer Science Education of the Association for Computing Machinery.

The recent development of expert systems (ES) and knowledge based systems (KBS) has begun to be taught to undergraduates (Bahill & Ferrell, 1986 and Warman & Modesitt, 1988) and one attempt to integrate knowledge based projects into a systems development course has been published (Kanabar, 1988).

The latter author suggested five reasons why KBS projects are very successful. Firstly, that students obtain useful project management skills, such as project control (compare Smith et alia 1996). Secondly, that practical skills are acquired, such as interviewing. Thirdly, that the theoretical software life cycle is put to the practical test. Fourthly, that good communication skills are learnt (compare

Potvin, 1984) and, fifthly, that new technical skills, deriving from new hardware and software, are acquired.

Kanabar used a KBS life cycle very similar to the classical software engineering life cycle, that is:

- Feasibility study
- KBS Requirements analysis
- KBS Design
- Detailed KBS Design
- KBS Implementation
- Testing

He concludes with 6 "additional points to be considered":

1) that sufficient time should be allocated to evaluate the project characteristics. We concur with the necessity to spend adequate time on the requirements analysis and specification stages of any software development project.

2) that a microcomputer based implementation should be preferred. In view of our background (e.g. Lee et alia, 1989 and 1990; Peacock et alia, 1988 and 1987) we also concur.

3) that a general purpose shell is recommended for implementation. On this point we also agree. Kanabar strongly recommends the use of a general purpose shell because of their flexibility over a skeletal shell or a declarative programming language such as Prolog or Lisp. We have used the Flex system which is a general purpose expert system shell and which sits on top of Prolog.

4) that the students should be asked to use rules only for representing knowledge, a view with which we disagree since we prefer both rules and frames where possible.

5) that, if several sections exist, one of the sections should lecture exclusively to students working on KBS projects. We interpret this to mean that KBS lecturers should come from one academic group only. We disagree with this since we feel that Computer Scientists, Software Engineers and Information Systems practitioners have different perspectives on KBS. The former follow the scientific method of hypothesis, model, experiment and analysis; the engineers follow the complementary engineering approach of requirements, specification, design and test and the IS people prefer business rules, data modelling and Rapid Applications Development (RAD) which is closer to KBS type prototyping.

6) that, if there are several students on a team, each of them should play different roles. We agree with this, although we allowed our teams to decide this matter and the actual roles for themselves (Sullivan, 1993; Davies & Fookes, 1987 and Mantei, 1981).

Kanabar presents a convincing argument for the incorporation of KBS projects into a systems development course, and his work represents the foundation on which our own work is built.

# 4. Project requirements

## 4.1 Knowledge base and Inference engine

In view of the short time given for the project (10 weeks), each group was instructed to use simple rules and frames as means of representing a single knowledge domain. Each group used forward and/or backward chaining inferencing depending on domain.

## 4.2 Knowledge domain

Each group decided at the first of their meetings which knowledge domain they would choose. It was felt that to specify the same domain for each group would make the project considerably less interesting and challenging to the students. The challenge was to identify a suitable domain expert and extract from them the relevant knowledge. It was stipulated that printed matter alone could not be used as the source of knowledge. Thus the students gained some experience of knowledge acquisition techniques.

## 4.3 User interface

It was emphasised at the beginning of the project that the user interface should be of a high standard. In other words it should be very user friendly. Accordingly each system was required to provide the following facilities as a minimum:

- Enable the user to enter rules for storage in a file.
- Enable the user to edit rules in a rule file.
- Have the ability to load rules into the knowledge base from a named rule file.
- The user should be able to consult the system!

It would also be useful to ask the system 'how?' it reached a particular conclusion. A simple rule trace would suffice in reply. Also the user should be able to ask 'why?' the system is asking a particular question. Finally a single step inference facility would be helpful to the user and useful for debugging the knowledge base.

# 5. Project management

Membership of the teams was determined by a member of staff. Having established the teams, a requirement was delivered by the tutor and a series of meetings established. The first project meeting for each team was chaired by the academic supervisor who presented an agenda which included items covering the selection of a student chairman and secretary, the requirement, allocation of roles and the tentative selection of a knowledge domain. Subsequent weekly meetings were controlled by the students who provide an appropriate agenda and minutes to the previous meeting. The tutor was present at most meetings and received minutes from all meetings.

# 6. Paradigms used

Although each group was allowed to formulate it's own approach to the project, all groups have had to begin using the knowledge engineering life-cycle (KELC). This involved the selection of a suitable topic and initial knowledge elicitation. Different groups have then used the software engineering life-cycle (SELC), object-oriented design (OOD) and a program design language (PDL). Other groups have been able to continue with the KELC using a prototyping approach.

The common problems encountered by all the teams which led to major difficulties were:

- Selection of knowledge domains not suitable for forward or backward chaining.
- Underestimating the difficulty of knowledge acquisition.
- Failing to identify an agreed rule syntax at an early stage in the project.
- Initial software specification far too ambitious.
- Unavailability of graphical software for the Human Computer Interface (HCI).

## 6.1 The Knowledge Engineering Approach

All groups began by selecting their own knowledge domain, such as:

- Diving illnesses
- African vaccinations
- Motorbike maintenance
- Aircraft recognition
- Army pay and allowances
- Ammunition identification
- Truck loading
- Electrical supply systems
- Radio communications aerial selection
- Manual of military law
- Soviet tracked vehicle recognition

Each group then needed to find a willing human expert or experts in their chosen domain. Different groups used different knowledge acquisition techniques to elicit information from their expert(s). All groups however found interviewing the most successful means of knowledge elicitation.

The main observations raised regarding the use of software engineering in this type of application were:

- Using objects to implement modularity:
    Enhanced system understanding and
    Produced good models of the problem domain.
- Establishing object granularity and interaction was difficult.
- Modularity and information hiding was difficult to implement.
- Flex was used procedurally rather than declaratively.

# 7. Assessment

The projects were assessed in five ways: a group report (worth 55% of the project marks), an individual report (15%), a mark for individual participation in the team (15%), a group presentation (15%) and a formal examination.

All group reports were of a high standard of both content and presentation, whereas individual reports were often either just excerpts from the group report or working notes. Generating marks for individual participation in group meetings has proved tricky for the tutors, while agreement between tutors on the presentations was easy. The latter were of a consistent high quality, both well prepared and well presented. Each consisted of a one period formal presentation, a software demonstration and a question time open to all tutors and students.

Examination question setting and marking has been performed by just one tutor. Examination questions have been both in essay and note form, the former on more general issues the latter on knowledge acquisition. Typical questions were to compare and contrast the knowledge engineering life-cycle with the software engineering life-cycle and to write an essay on the role of teams in software development with particular reference to knowledge based systems.

The students have been asked to describe the techniques of knowledge acquisition which are more applicable for two out of a list of six domains, three of which were the domains for that year's groups and three were the standard textbook examples. They have had to evaluate the importance of eleven given factors in successful knowledge acquisition. The students have also had to describe the strengths and weaknesses of one technique of knowledge acquisition which they had used and then relate it to knowledge engineering as a whole.

# 8. Student Feedback

At the end of the Lent term in 1998 fourteen students out of eighteen completed a feedback questionnaire with answers on a scale of 1 to 5 from poor to excellent. The question "how do you rate the project as a learning exercise?" scored 4.2 out of 5 rather better than the 3.6 for the module as a whole. The most telling student comment was that "the project has really driven home the importance of good software engineering and successful team working!"

# 9. Recommendations and conclusion

The implementation of software engineering principles in the production of a knowledge based systems is a valuable exercise, however, a knowledge engineering life cycle may need to be carried out in parallel.

We recommend that students should be exposed to both the classical top-down paradigm and the bottom-up reuse of objects approach. Although prototyping helps with knowledge acquisition and validation, we recommend use of the SELC for production and maintenance reasons. The software engineering life-cycle can be applied to the management and design of knowledge based systems even if it is not possible to follow it when implementing code in a shell.

We conclude that these knowledge based system group projects are a valuable learning experience. They reinforce the theory of both software and knowledge engineering and they allow practice in team working.

# 10. Acknowledgements

This paper is published with the permission of the Principal of the Royal Military College of Science. We are grateful to three anonymous referees for their helpful comments.

### References

1. Bahill T. & Ferrell W. R. Teaching an introductory course in expert systems. IEEE Expert 1986; 1:4:59-65
2. Baker F. T. Chief programmer team management of production programming. IBM System Journal 1972; 11:1:56-73
3. Bickerstaff D. D. The evolution of a project oriented course in software engineering. ACM SIGCSE Bulletin 1985; 17:1:13
4. Borovits I. et alia Group processes and the development of information systems. Information & Management 1990; 19:65-72
5. Burke T. E. Integration of student projects in micro-based graduate courses - a pilot experiment. Collegiate Microcomputer 1986; IV:2:159-162
6. Carver D. L. Comparison of techniques in project-based courses. ACM SIGCSE Bulletin 1985; 17:1:9-12
7. Chrisman C. & Beccue B. Evaluating students in systems development group projects. ACM SIGCSE Bulletin 1987; 19:1:366-373
8. Collofello J. S. Monitoring and evaluating individual team members in a software engineering course. ACM SIGCSE Bulletin 1985; 17:1:6-8
9. Collofello J. S. & Woodfield S. N. A project-unified software engineering course sequence. ACM SIGCSE Bulletin 1982; 14:1:13-19
10. Davies L. J. & Fookes A. F. An experimental investigation of team roles in software project management. International CIS Journal 1987; 1:1:23-29
11. Farkas D. Choosing group projects for advanced systems courses. ACM SIGCSE Bulletin 1988; 20:1:109-113

12. Hayes H. Using team projects to teach modular design. Interface. 1982; Winter:18-22

13. Henry S. A project oriented course on software engineering. ACM SIGCSE Bulletin 1983; 15:1:57-61

14. Hopgood A. Knowledge Based Systems for engineers and scientists. CRC, 1993

15. Joel W. J. Realistic student projects. ACM SIGCSE Bulletin 1987; 19:1:244-247

16. Jones A. & Birtle M. An individual assessment technique for group projects in software engineering. Software Engineering Journal 1989; 4:4:226-232

17. Jordan D. L. A comparison of programming team performance on software development projects. ACM SIGCSE Bulletin 1987; 19:3:45-47

18. Kanabar V. Introducing knowledge based projects in a systems development course. ACM SIGCSE Bulletin 1988; 20:1:114-118

19. King P. J. B. Experiences with group projects in software engineering. Software Engineering Journal 1989; 4:4:221-225

20. Klepper R. Self managed teams and MIS productivity: literature, model and field study. Data Base 1989; 20:1:36-38

21. Lee M. P. A novel course in structured systems analysis through Prolog. In: Uso J. L. (ed) Software Engineering in Higher Education II. Computational Mechanics Publications, 1996, pp 153-160, 1-85312-385-4

22. Lee M. P., Pryce J. D. & Harrison A. Prolog as a first programming language. In: King G A (ed) Software Engineering in Higher Education. Computational Mechanics Publications, 1994, pp 275-281, 1-85312-289-0

23. Lee M. P., Peacock D. & Jeffreys S. J. dBASE as a first programming language. Collegiate Microcomputer 1989; VII:2:111-116

24. Lee M. P., Darling M. W. M., Peacock D. & Jeffreys S. Simulating user interfaces with dBASE III+. In: M. A. Life, C. S. Narborough-Hall & W. I. Hamilton (eds) Simulation and the User Interface. Taylor & Francis London, 1990, pp 116-128

25. Lees B Artificial intelligence education for software engineers. In: Uso J. L. (ed) Software Engineering in Higher Education II. Computational Mechanics Publications, 1996, pp 353-360, 1-85312-385-4

26. Little S. E. & Margetson D. B. A project-based approach to information systems design for undergraduates. Australian Computer Journal 1989; 21:2:130-138.

27. Mantei M. The effect of programming team structures on programming tasks. Communications ACM 1981; 24:3:106-113

28. Peacock D., Jeffreys S. & Lee M. P. The use of a structured project to teach program development. ACM SIGCSE Bulletin 1987; 19:4:10-18

29. Peacock D., Ralhan V. K., Lee M. P. & Jeffreys S. A first year course in software design and use. ACM SIGCSE Bulletin 1988; 20:4:2-8

30. Perkins T. E. & Beck L. L. A project-oriented undergraduate course sequence in software engineering. ACM SIGCSE Bulletin 1980; 12:1:32-39

31. Pigford D. V. A management system for monitoring and assessing the group-oriented database project. ACM SIGCSE Bulletin 1987; 19:1:9-18

32. Potvin J. H. Using team reporting projects to teach concepts of audience and written, oral, and interpersonal communication skills. IEEE Transactions on Education 1984; 27:3:129-136

33. Roth R. W. & White A. Dealing with disparate audiences in computer science courses using a project group within a traditional class. ACM SIGCSE Bulletin 1987; 19:1:148-151

34. Saadat S., Rickman R. & Lawrence J. Student group projects – a case study. In: King G A (ed) Software Engineering in Higher Education. Computational Mechanics Publications, 1994, pp 109-118, 1-85312-289-0

35. Sanders D. Managing and evaluating students in a directed project course. ACM SIGCSE Bulletin 1984; 16:1:15-25

36. Sathi H. L. A project-oriented course for software systems development. ACM SIGCSE Bulletin 1984; 16:3:2-4

37. Sigwart D. C. & van Meer G. L. Evaluation of group projects in a software engineering course. ACM SIGCSE Bulletin 1985; 17:2:32-35

38. Smith S., Mannion M. & Hastie C. Encouraging the development of transferable skills through effective group project work. In: Uso J. L. (ed) Software Engineering in Higher Education II. Computational Mechanics Publications, 1996, pp 19-26, 1-85312-385-4

39. Sullivan S. L. A software project management course role-play team-project approach emphasising written and oral communication skills. ACM SIGCSE Bulletin 1993; 283-287

40. Tenny T. Leadership style vs. success in student chief programmer teams. ACM SIGCSE Bulletin 1987; 19:1:103-113

41. Waguespack L. J. A workbench for project oriented software engineering courses. ACM SIGCSE Bulletin 1984; 16:1:137-143

42. Warman D. & Modesitt K. L. A student's view: learning in an introductory expert system course. Expert Systems 1988; 5:1:30-50

43. White K. B. MIS Project teams: an investigation of cognitive style implications. MIS Quarterly 1984; June:95-101

44. Woodfield S. N. & Collofello J. S. Some insights and experiences in teaching team project courses. ACM SIGCSE Bulletin 1983; 5:1:62-65

# The Prof@T Project

Gary Griffiths and Mike Lockyer
School of Computing and Mathematics
University of Teesside
Borough Road, Middlesbrough
TS1 3BA
e-mail : g.griffiths or m.a.lockyer@tees.ac.uk

## 1 Introduction

Prof@T (Professional Skills at Teesside) is a three year project to disseminate excellent practice in teaching personal and professional skills in Computer Science at the University of Teesside. It is one of four computing projects supported by the Higher Education Funding Council for England's (HEFCE) Fund for the Development of Teaching and Learning (FDTL).

## 2 The Prof@T Project

### 2.1 Deliverables

The project is working in five subject areas :

- Group Projects

- Live Projects (i.e. industrially based projects)

- Professional Skills

- Supervised Work Experience (SWE) (i.e. industrial placements)

- Student Support and Monitoring.

The main deliverables of the project are a video and CD-ROM in each of these subject areas. Currently there are draft videos for Live Projects and SWE. Most of the 'live events' for the other three videos have now been shot and they will be scripted, linked and edited during summer 1998.

There are presently 3 CD-ROMs at various stages of development. The Group Projects and Live Projects CDs are drafts without video clips. The SWE CD has the content assembled in hyperlinked word-processed form. The CDs are being developed in HTML so that users can view the material in their own browser. As well as providing a familiar user interface, this approach facilitates the adoption and embedding of the material by making it configurable and editable.

It also allows congruence between the CDs and areas of the Prof@T web site [1]. On the home page of the web site (see Figure 1), the top row of buttons corresponds to the five subject areas of the project. Pressing one of these will take the user to the same content as appears on the CD-ROM for that subject area. This also permits the CD-ROMs to be downloaded.

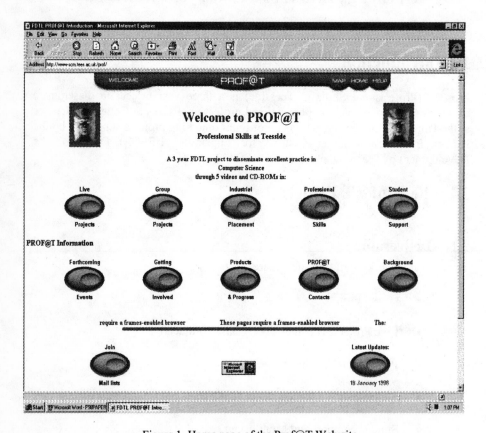

Figure 1. Home page of the Prof@T Web site.

## 2.2 Dissemination

The web site provides one means of dissemination, but a more important mechanism is the pilot centres network. The pilot sites are the universities of

- Derby

- Liverpool John Moores

- Teesside

- Thames Valley

- Ulster

- West of England.

Between November 1997 and February 1998 regional workshops took place at the pilot sites to disseminate and obtain feedback on the draft videos on Live Projects and SWE, and the draft CD on Group Projects. About 70-80 people in total attended these workshops.

The project was also advertised on several e-mail lists (mostly concerning teaching and learning) and about 100 people responded asking for draft materials. About 80% of the respondents were from the UK, and about 80% were in computing (but not the same 80%). The draft materials have now been despatched and a short e-mail questionnaire sent.

The other dissemination mechanism for the project is two national workshops, of which Project98 is the first. To address the themes of Project98 the remainder of this paper will concentrate on the Group Projects and Live Projects subject areas of Prof@T, and the emerging deliverables.

# 3 Group Projects

There are several different types of group projects running at various stages of various courses at Teesside, but perhaps the most innovative is the work on negotiated learning contracts by Malcolm Birtle and Alan Jones over the last 10 years [2]. This approach is used within two group project modules that run throughout the second year of the Software Engineering degree.

While no attempt will be made to describe the work in detail here, its essence is a contract that sets out the deliverables that each member of the group must produce in order to get a certain grade (see Figure 2).

| Student | 1 | 2 | 3 | 4 |
|---|---|---|---|---|
| Grade | | | | |
| A | Acceptance test report and results | | Examination of techniques and management | |
| B | Further functionality | | Functional testing | |
| C | Client pres. | Add. Functions | Functional prog. | Windows prog. |
| D | Object Oriented Design including test specification | | | |
| E | Arch. Design | Acc. Testing | Updated plan | Win. Prog. research |

Figure 2. Sample negotiated learning contract.

These contracts have grades A-E that could be awarded to team members. Each member has five deliverables, corresponding to grades A-E, set out in the contract. A team member must first work on their grade E deliverable. For example, in Figure 2, student 1 will first of all work on architectural design. This will have a checklist associated with it for assessment purposes, and, when this has been satisfied, grade E will be awarded. The team member will then move on to work on their grade D deliverable (in this case object oriented design), and so on.

Unlike other assessment strategies, where a single deliverable is assessed qualitatively to arrive at a grade, within these learning contracts a team member may move from grade E to grade A by successfully working on a series of deliverables. When assessing a deliverable it is checked against a checklist where the outcome can only be pass (award the grade) or fail (re-do the deliverable). Deliverables could be individual or joint (sometimes with the whole team).

Contracts, including the checklists, are negotiated between the team and the supervisor. If there are problems in the team, perhaps one member is not delivering, the contract may be re-negotiated to make the work of that person non-essential, so that the rest of the team are not adversely affected. The onus is then on the non-performing member to re-integrate with the team or, perhaps, fail the assessment.

The current Group projects CD concentrates exclusively on this negotiated learning contracts approach. Figure 3 shows the home page for this subject area on the Prof@T web site and indicates the range of topics covered.

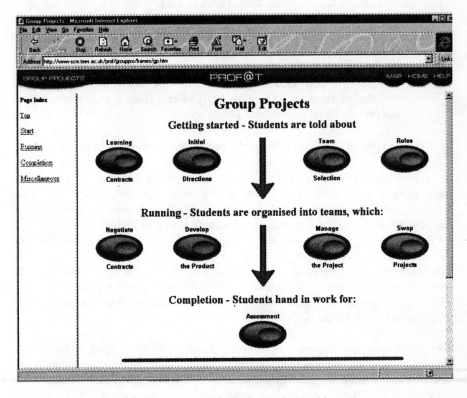

Figure 3. Home page for the Group Projects subject area.

One of the problems with developing this material was that the approach presently adopted is fairly sophisticated, having developed over a number of years. Different contracts are used at different stages of the project and for different levels of achievement. So, we decided to backtrack a few years to a point where this approach was applied more simply and might be used more readily by someone new to the technique.

The draft CD has been through two major iterations during the course of the regional workshops. While being generally well received, some of these yielded as many as 30 points for our consideration. It is intended to extend the Group Projects material in a number of ways to include :

- other group projects at Teesside

- group projects at other institutions

- video clips

- a generic approach to group projects.

Other group projects to be featured from Teesside are :

- an M Sc one week full time case study that uses personal learning goals and audits

- a B Sc first year requirements analysis case study that runs between modules in Structured Systems Analysis and (Human) Communications and includes interviewing and presentations

- an HND BIT one semester group project that is based in industry

It became apparent very early in the project that it would be better if we could not only capture good practice at Teesside, but also distil and disseminate good practice at other institutions (if this was possible). Group projects proved to be a particularly rich area for this and we are now planning to include material from 3 of the pilot sites : Ulster, UWE and Derby. We already have video footage from Ulster of their group projects, which have industrial involvement. We are currently filming a second semester group project at Derby that includes audits, a poster session and presentations. We are planning to feature the group projects at UWE that operate through all taught years of one of the degrees and include community projects and professional skills.

The shooting of the 'live events' for group projects will be finished by May 1998. This will allow the material to be scripted, linked and edited over the summer, and a draft video will be produced by the autumn. It will also give us an opportunity to re-visit the CD-ROM and introduce some video clips as an alternative to some of the text.

All of this activity means that we will have to re-think the front end of the CD. Currently the home page shows the life cycle for one group project at Teesside (see Figure 3). When we have material on a number of group projects from a number of institutions there will need to be a level above this. We are also keen to provide a generic doorway to this material. That is, the way in to the material could be organised by different activities in group projects e.g. team selection, audits, presentations, peer assessment. Selection of one of these activities will then lead the user to a variety of approaches to that activity.

# 4   Live Projects

The Live Projects material on the draft video concentrates on the projects undertaken by direct entrants to the second year of one of the computing degrees at Teesside. These students are sometimes UK students with an HND who want to top up their qualification to an honours degree in two years. More often they are foreign students with an HND level qualification, particularly from France or the Far East. In their first year of study they take a taught semester followed by a live project in the second semester. They then join the other final year degree students for their second year of study.

The live project can be seen as a smaller, but equivalent, experience to the SWE year followed by the sandwich students. It is organised in a similar manner to the one year industrial placements. Figure 4 shows the home page for Live Projects on the Prof@T web site.

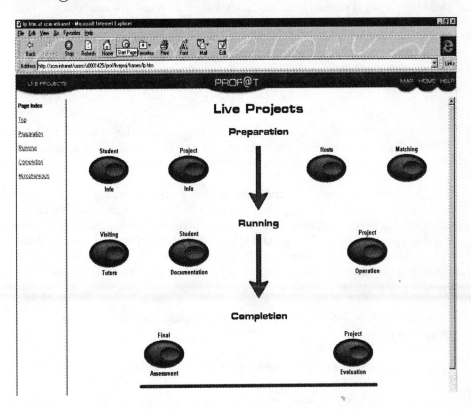

Figure 4. Live Projects home page on the Prof@T web site.

The preparation phase takes place during the taught semester before the live project begins. There are usually 20-30 students and these are all interviewed by the Live Projects tutor. They prepare a formal CV for transmission to potential hosts, and an informal 'pen picture' about their likes and dislikes to help the Live Project tutor in placing them in an appropriate project.

At the same time, details of potential projects are accumulated. These come from a variety of sources. As the services of the live project students are free, many of the projects are community projects with voluntary organisations and charities. Advertisements are placed in the newsletters of these organisations and local newspapers. There is also a flow of projects from other sources : previous live project hosts, staff contacts and the industrial placements section. Most of the projects involve the students in developing software of some sort.

Project hosts fill in a form describing their project and the Live Project tutor selects the appropriate CVs and sends them out. The host then interviews the students and one is selected.

Once the project is running, each student is assigned a Visiting Tutor who will visit twice during the project period, sort out any problems and carry out the assessment. Students are required to complete various pieces of documentation during the project period. In the first two weeks an Action Plan is prepared and agreed with the host and the Visiting Tutor. A diary is kept, with fortnightly entries, and the hosts assess the students on an ongoing basis in the same timeframe.

At the end of the project the student writes a final report. This is assessed by the Visiting Tutor, together with the other student and host documentation generated throughout the project, to arrive at a final assessment for the student.

The draft video currently tells the story of this process featuring two particular projects. One involves an Australian student who helps to install and develop a network at a Special Needs school. The other involves two French students who develop some real-time software at a Go Karting centre. The final version of the video will respond to the comments of evaluators at the regional workshops and on the e-mail list, but it has not yet been decided if it will be extended to cover other types of live projects.

There is currently a draft CD-ROM on Live Projects, but there are a number of things still to do :

- complete the pages under some of the headings

- introduce video clips

- extend the material to cover alternatives.

There are a few areas of the CD that are incomplete. For example, it is intended that all CDs will contain blank copies of forms used, and samples, but these are not all collated and scanned yet.

There are no video clips included yet, although there are placeholders for these. We have now evolved a process for producing the CDs starting from a word-processed transcript of the video material (although this could be any word-processed document).

- **Produce video transcript**
  The video material is produced as a text transcript.

- **Produce outline structure**
  An outline graphical structure is developed that is based on the content of the video transcript and the project style.

- **Integrate transcript and structure**
  The structure and transcript are integrated so that there is a placeholder for all of the transcript material.

- **Produce material in MS-Word**
  The material is produced as a hyperlinked text-based word processor document.

- **Produce pre-draft CD-ROM / WWW material**
  The first HTML draft is produced based on the word-processed version and the project graphics.

- **Review the material with the development team**
  This pre-draft material is reviewed by the development team individually and as a group.

- **Material released within Teesside using the Intranet**
  The material is reviewed internally, in particular the subject expert will provide a detailed review of the material.

- **Material released on the WWW and at regional workshops**
  The material is now live and evaluated extensively, particularly at the regional workshops and by respondents on the e-mail list.

- **Second draft produced**
  A second draft may be produced and evaluated in a similar way, probably including video clips.

- **Final version produced**
  A final version is produced, probably with the addition of new material, particularly from other institutions.

The Live Projects CD will be extended to cover other live projects. This will include other live projects within the School of Computing at Teesside i.e. some

HND level group projects and some B Sc and M Sc individual projects take place in industry. It will also include live projects in other disciplines e.g. the School of Science and Technology at Teesside have a history of offering 'project clinics' to local industry where a student, or group of students, work on an industrial project that the company pays for. Also, there is live project activity at other institutions that we would want to include e.g. the community projects at UWE mentioned above, the Industrial Software Project Support Network FDTL project at Sheffield.

# 5 Conclusions

There are a number of conclusions that can be drawn from the first half of the project.

- The video/CD/Web-based package of materials is a good, though expensive, way of disseminating information.

- The CD/Web development process that we have developed works well and could be used in other contexts.

- It is very important for material to be editable and configurable if it is to be adopted and embedded.

- HTML is a good development technology because it allows the material to be viewed with a familiar software tool/user interface, it is widespread, giving a significant development/configuration population, and it allows a congruence between CD based and Web based material.

- We have developed a good dissemination network based on the web site, e-mail lists and the pilot sites, and it could be used as a mechanism for disseminating other material.

- Collaboration is important when developing materials, but you can't collaborate with everybody. A good approach is to work closely with a small group and cascade the dissemination out from there.

- There is much good practice in project work (and many other things) right across the sector.

- There is much interest and enthusiasm for investigating and adopting good practice.

In the next year, the remainder of the Prof@T deliverables will be produced. These will be disseminated to all Higher Education Institutions covered by HEFCE and DENI before the end of the project in November 1999. After this time, it is intended that the project will carry on, at least as a Web site.

# References

1       http://www-scm.tees.ac.uk/prof/

2       Jones A., Birtle M., An Individual Assessment Technique for Group
        Projects in Software Engineering' Software Engineering Journal, July
        1989, 4, (4), p.226-232.

# PART 3

# New Directions

# VICI: Experiences in Introducing Student run Software Companies into the Curriculum

Mike Holcombe and Andrew Stratton

Department of Computer Science,
University of Sheffield.
Regent Court,
Sheffield, S1 4DP.
U.K.

Abstract.

This paper discusses a novel course run at the University of Sheffield entitled: "Setting up and Running your own I.T. Company." The course is taken by all 4th year students on the M.Eng. in Software Engineering and M.Comp. in Computer Science degrees. The course involves the students organising themselves into companies and trading with a variety of clients. It introduces some of the issues in identifying market opportunities, formulating proposals, negotiating contracts with clients, capturing the requirements, managing the satisfactory construction and delivery of the product, quality assurance, keeping accounts and many issues that relate to the way a real company needs to operate. The paper reports on the current status of the project and on some of the experiences of the staff and the students involved in it. Some conclusions are drawn and recommendations made for those wishing to develop a similar course.

## 1 Introduction

Many comments have been made about the inadequate preparation that many of our graduates appear to have for life in the modern business and industrial world. Engineering employers, particularly, are very vociferous on this point. The recent Dearing Report [1] and much of what underlies the Engineering Council's SARTOR Report [2] focuses on this issue.

It is not just about developing communication and teamwork skills or about having attended modules in business studies or accountancy, it is much more fundamental than that. The belief is that *graduates do not understand the context, the processes and the constraints that apply to business these days*. As such they are poorly prepared for the challenges that the dynamic world of work will pose.

One way in which this can be approached is through the use of industrial placements and sandwich degrees whereby students spend from 3 to 12 months working in a company, either as part of their course or during vacations. This can be very valuable if the placements and vacation experience is of a suitable nature. There are, however, a number of problems with placements of this type. Firstly, the student's experience on a placement is quite hard to monitor in order to assure ourselves and other interested parties that it is *valuable, challenging* and *relevant*. Secondly, a negative experience on a placement could be very damaging to the student's self-esteem, to their understanding of the world of work or to their continuing studies. Furthermore, there is no reason, *per se*, that a placement will help a student to develop the entrepreneurial skills and understandings that are being demanded by the business community.

In [3] a number of comments are made such as: "Universities *seem to be teaching the inappropriate technical and business skills for our industry."* Ian Taylor, CMG.; *"Some older Universities, in particular, do not even see their role as preparing people for work."* Gordon Ewan IT-NTO. These comments reflect widespread attitudes amongst many business people, not always based on reliable information and in many cases anecdotal. It is clear, however, that, even if we think that our graduates are fit for a career in business, some of their prospective employers don't. It may just be a myth, of course, and certainly the demand for our graduates is far in excess of supply (last summer nearly all of the graduates from this department were offered several jobs at salaries significantly higher than a young University lecturer could hope for!). However it is time that we tried to address this perception and to see if we can provide a more realistic type of educational provision that was *real, enterprise-oriented* and *enjoyable*.

## 2 "Setting up and running your own IT company."

This year (1997/8) we have introduced a new module with this title specifically for our 4th year MEng and MComp students. These are our prestige degrees, with high entry requirements and a hurdle at the end of the 2nd year that must be satisfied, of an average mark of at least a good 2-2 standard and no failed component. It is also the main route that we perceive to CEng accreditation following the requirements of SARTOR [2]. So the class is fairly small, talented and enthusiastic. When we first started exploring the idea of setting up such a course we talked to the students - then in their 3rd year. Their response was very enthusiastic and throughout the planning period we worked with them and obtained their support for the basic structure and curriculum details. This was important because the assessment was going to difficult to define precisely in advance and a spirit of trust was needed between staff and students if it was going to work.

The module is of 20 credits (one sixth of the total load), which runs over the full academic year. The basic description is as follows (taken, primarily, from the University's Module Directory):

### COM401/2 Setting up and running your own IT company. (20 Credits)

Pre-requisites: COM301, 302, 303, 304, 306.

[Remarks. The module runs over two semesters. The pre-requisites are the core third year modules and are intended to ensure that the participants have a good grounding in most aspects of a modern computing curriculum (and to restrict entry to an appropriate student cohort).]

**Aims/Description.** This half module involves students forming and running companies that offer IT consultancy and software development services to outside organisations. The emphasis of the work will be on learning how small IT companies are created and managed, the legal and financial frameworks with which such companies operate, the practical management of the companies and their successful trading. Students will involve themselves in the following activities:

- researching market opportunities for software products;
- carrying out IT audits on behalf of local organisations and preparing appropriate IT strategies;
- acting as software/computing consultants to local organisations;
- developing software for clients;
- maintaining software for clients;

During the course of the module students will keep company records, prepare company reports as well as developing analysis and design reports and other consultancy reports for clients.

*Teaching Methods*: Lectures, seminars, practical design work, client presentations.

*Assessment*: Coursework.

The basic background to the module is that in the 2nd year the students have taken part in the Software Hut project [4] which exposed them to the experience of working in teams with a real client trying to construct a suitable solution to the client's business problem. This was used as a vehicle to consider business process modelling, requirements capture and all of the processes involved in the engineering of a piece of high quality software for their client. These skills were then extended with more technical knowledge from their 3rd year programme and their experiences with their 3rd year major individual project and dissertation. Also as part of their third year work they attended a seminar course on software engineering. In the course of this they studied, in some depth, 50 papers from the current software engineering journals (see [5]) and this provided a considerable insight into the *state of the art* in areas as diverse as requirements capture, project management, quality control, testing, design methods and tools etc..

The intention was that the students set up a number of companies and trade with real clients. The companies are to be run as professionally as possible and standard accounting, planning, management and quality control methods used throughout.

As part of the initial training for the exercise the students took part in a series of seminars organised by the Sheffield Training and Enterprise Centre in conjunction with the National Westminster Bank. These were evening sessions aimed at the general public wishing to set up their own companies. They were given by experienced consultants and covered areas such as: financial and business planning, marketing, company law and other related topics. The students reacted enthusiastically to most of these sessions which took place in the first few weeks of term.

To provide a focus and a basic infrastructure for the student companies the Department arranged for a small room to be allocated for their exclusive use which was furnished with 4 PCs and other basic equipment such as phone, kettle etc.

We had identified a number of potential clients prior to the course starting and arranged for these clients to visit the group to discuss possible projects. The students had to negotiate with clients - find out what the client's problem was, whether they thought that they could provide a quality solution, discuss the costs of doing this and trying to agree a contract.

This was the starting point. One client was obtained from some research contacts we had, the other initial client was a company who had previously been involved in a 4 month summer MSc project and wanted the system built by the MSc student extended. It was a fairly small task and thus unsuitable for another MSc project. (In other words the student companies could carry out maintenance for former student projects, something that was not always possible in the past.)

# 3 The basic structure of the module

This course is assessed by coursework, and we had to negotiate what form this will take. The module is highly experimental and everyone involved had to be consulted and involved in order to make it succeed. In the first year there are 6 students on the course. Next year there will be 16 and so some thought has to be given to ways of making it manageable for larger class sizes. For this current year we envisaged 3 companies or divisions which would operate concurrently:

> A. Software development.
> B. Software consultancy.
> C. Software training.

The proposed company structure:

The students decided on a name for the company - VICI or rather 3 names: VICI Development, VICI Consultants, VICI Training.

Each company will have two "officers" a chairman and a finance director. This year, then, each class member is an officer for one company. Everyone will be an "ordinary" member of the other two companies, so each company has 6 personnel. We change roles round in Semester 2 to give everyone experience as chairman and as finance director once. Someone (the finance director) of each company will install and use the Sage package for keeping the accounts. A number of management planning systems had to be set up by the students so that there were methods of identifying the work involved, the way it is to be shared out and some form of monitoring system. The students also had to think about quality control methods, should they use inspections, some formal mechanism (Fagan e.g. or use some of Gilb's ideas.) or what? They must also think about some way of costing activities, some of this will be with real money, other clients will not be charging so there is a need to estimate the cost and account for it in a "virtual" way in the company accounts

Deliverables for assessment purposes.

It was agreed that there should be monthly documentation to be submitted, along with other agreed output, for assessment and planning purposes.

3.1. Monthly real accounts.

3.2. Monthly virtual accounts (which will include notional labour costs based on the number of hours work carried out on the projects and management activities and costed at an appropriate level, for the sake of argument we could cost an hour at something like £10 per hour per person). In some projects include a notional charge to the client based on an estimate of the time required to complete the project.

3.3. Monthly report identifying what was done in the previous month, targets/milestones reached, problems/delays experienced, together with an updated plan for the next month.

3.4. Any deliverables completed in the previous month, requirements documents, design documents, implementations, quality control material, user manuals etc.

Later on a business plan will be prepared in conjunction with the evening course, this will be assessed by the Bank who can provide a professional perspective on the viability of a business plan if some students wished to continue with their company.

A possible structure for assessment.

(i). Customer satisfaction - on the basis of questionnaires given to clients on delivery of the product/course.

(ii). Administrative procedures - based on monthly reports, planning documents, business plans etc.

(iii). Quality control - evidence of a review process, use of software engineering methods in specification, design and validation (testing).

(iv). Profitability - based on the annual virtual accounts - would we have survived financially if the money had been "for real", also the business plans would be assessed under this heading.

We need to apportion the assessment between these (and possibly other) headings. Within these headings we will need to come to some more detailed division. These decisions are still to be agreed. It may seem unsatisfactory that the detailed assessment has not yet been defined. We still do not know the precise nature of the activities during the year. However, the four headings above will form the basis of the assessment.

# 4 The programme of work

The first two jobs were:

4.1. To construct a web based database for a major London hospital that would enable consultants in a medical specialty to consult and submit details of medical cases and the associated treatments on an on-going basis. The task also involved setting up a suitable web database server to be located in London and the emphasis had to be on security, reliability and usability. The client was a Professor from London who visited the Department on a number of occasions to discuss requirements and examine prototypes. E-mail was also used to communicate with this client. There was a fee agreed beforehand by the client.

4.2. To develop an existing sales/stock control system for a philately company in North Wales. This system had been developed by an MSc student as their summer project a year earlier. This client wanted to extend the functionality of the system. A full (formal) specification of the existing system was available and this was very useful. The client visited a couple of times to discuss requirements.

The students were able to make a good start on 4.1 and produced a feasibility study and a rapid prototype for the client. The client then took some time to respond.

The second job has been allocated a lower priority.

4.3. A client from a local teaching hospital proposed 3 database/web projects similar in style to 4.1 and visited the company to discuss the proposals. These are now also under development.

4.4. A consultancy was negotiated with a local technology transfer organisation and is currently on going.

4.5. The students are also keen to provide training courses and have negotiated with two clients. One client is a local organisation which is introducing e-mail and WWW facilities. They want a simple training package to be developed so that their workforce will be able to use e-mail effectively, attaching and retrieving files, undertake simple internet browsing etc.. Initially, there will be 17 people to train but ultimately there are several hundreds who would use the training materials over the internet in the organisation. Another client wishes to have a training course developed to teach the use of Access database packages within their organisation. In these types of contract the hard part is identifying accurately what the client wants and then developing a training package targeted at the right level and using the right medium and educational approach.

4.6. The company is to install a video conferencing system to enable remote communication with future clients to take place using this technology, where appropriate.

4.7. Other consultancy and training opportunities are under discussion.

4.8. As part of their market analysis strategy the group prepared a company brochure and a questionnaire to send out to local organisations and companies. This will provide a valuable resource for the future.

The department also runs an MSc in Advanced Software Engineering and, as is usual in these courses, requires students to undertake a project in the summer. As part of that students also prepare for the project by taking a thesis preparation module in Semester 2. One of the projects offered was participation in the student company scheme and this was chosen by 2 students. So they have been brought into the company and will be carrying out projects of their own within the company. These are outlined below:

4.8. Another medical web based database for an European medical society.

4.9 The development of an oracle database for a major UK charity. This is, as yet, still in the initial stages of negotiation.

# 5 Student expectations

Before the start of the course a questionnaire was designed and circulated to the MEng class to establish what the classes aspirations and expectations were about the fourth year of the MEng degree was like and how they regarded the prospect of this particular module.

The first part of the questionnaire was concerned with the reasons for choosing to stay on to do the fourth year. The results are displayed in Table 1.

## Table 1: Reasons for staying on.

| Reason | Number/% |
|---|---|
| To gain a pg. degree. | 4/67% |
| To have more time to decide on a career. | 3/50% |
| To make themselves more attractive to an employer. | 6/100% |
| To learn more about the subject. | 5/83% |
| Other reasons. | 2/33% |

The next question was directed at possible career sectors, see Table 2.

## Table 2: Career sector interests

| Sector | Number/% |
|--------|----------|
| Commercial | 6/100% |
| Industrial | 5/85% |
| Academic | 5/85% |
| Public | 6/100% |
| Other | 0/0% |

The specific career identified included: Software consultancy, software training, marketing, teaching, management, software engineering, systems analysis and more specifically web development and databases.

A number of specific skills relating to technical issues, communications and business were listed and the class was asked to indicate those that they hoped to develop further during the year on a scale:

1(very important) ......5 (Not important).

See Tables 3, 4 and 5.

## Table 3: Technical skills.

| Skill type | Average rating |
|------------|----------------|
| HTML & WWW | 2.33 |
| Java | 2.75 |
| C$^{++}$ | 1.66 |
| Visual basic & 4GLs | 2.1 |
| Network management | 2.1 |

Some of the procedures that were adopted to ensure that the project management and the quality control were suitable are worthy of further comment. Our attitude was to talk to the group regularly about these issues but not to prescribe in detail what they should do. It was interesting how they changed their attitudes as they progressed and saw that they needed to formalise procedures if they were going to achieve all that they wanted to do.

The weekly business meetings that the companies held (at which no staff attended) were vital and it became apparent that detailed minutes and actions had to be recorded. The monthly reports to us were also of great value and will be part of the assessed material. These reports were structured as follows (a structure that the students refined themselves in consultation with us):

1. Quality checklist (see appendix A);

2. Preface;

3. Development projects - current status (Introduction, schedule from previous month, achievements of current month, problems and processes, schedule for further work, deliverables for this month);

4. Consultancy projects (same structure);

5. Training projects (same structure);

6. Administration (same structure);

7. Appendices (correspondence with clients,

8. Accounts (real and virtual);

9. Minute of business meetings.

Another interesting aspect of the course was that the companies had full responsibility for setting up and administering their Windows 95/NT network which included organising the backup procedures using a Jaz drive and discs. Also the installation of a video conferencing and networking system was part of the company infrastructure that needed planning and implementing. All of these activities gave the students a challenge and were very successfully done. The fact that they were responsible for their own facilities helped to engender a much more mature and professional approach than one might have expected.

Another interesting benefit from the activities, particularly the training contracts, is in developing perspectives on aspects of work that are in marked contrast to the normal student view of life. For example, the training courses they will be providing for an industrial client have to be delivered to a high standard. The client satisfaction will be partly measured by asking the participants of the course to evaluate the quality of the teaching. They are now on the other side of the fence from when they evaluated the teaching of the university lecturers!

**Table 4: Communication skills**

| Skill type | Average rating |
|---|---|
| Customer liaison | 1.5 |
| Presentation skills | 1.5 |
| Report writing | 1.66 |
| Team working | 1.2 |
| Video-conferencing | 3.2 |

**Table 5: Business skills**

| Skill type | Average rating |
|---|---|
| Time management | 1.66 |
| Accounting | 2.5 |
| Work allocation | 2 |
| Business administration | 1.88 |

The results of this, admittedly small sample of 6, are fairly consistent and provide considerable reassurance that the aims of the module are appropriate to the desires of the students.

It is interesting to note that there was still a need to improve both teamwork skills, time management and work allocation (project management). This is despite the fact that the students had been involved in many projects that required them to work in teams from 2 to 6 in almost every year of the course. For example teams of 4-5 take part in the Crossover Project in year 1 where they experience the whole software lifecycle as they build a simple system (requirements capture, formal specification, design, implementation and testing). In the first year each student would have carried out a CADIZ project (building a sizeable formal specification in Z) in partnership with another student. In year two they would have taken part in the Software Hut project, developing a real application for a real client (see [4]). In year

3 they would have carried out a project using the Concurrency Workbench with a colleague (proving properties of a CCS specification) and so on. It really emphasises how *social* software engineering has become.

Another issue identified by the survey is that of presentation skills, report writing and related activities. Again this is after three years of substantial activities of this type in all sorts of courses, including giving seminars based on research papers, [5], as well as presentations relating to their various design exercises.

# 6 Some experiences and reflections

The initial worry was whether we could find enough work of an appropriate type for the students to do. That has not been a problem. In fact, there is, if anything more than enough and was one of the reasons for introducing it into the MSc project system.

In future years there will be more MEng and MComp students taking these modules and this could cause us some management problems. However, if one analyses the amount of effort required to run this module compared with that of an advanced undergraduate module of similar weighting it is probably significantly smaller. There is no lecture preparation required, no laboratory practical preparation. What we have to do is to help the students to make contact with clients, and as the word spreads about the course external clients are beginning to contact us. The lecturers have to monitor the progress through weekly meetings with the company, helping with the planning of the work, ensuring that all the students are contributing suitably, reading the monthly reports and meeting the occasional client.

What have the students learnt?

The experiences gained are many and varied. It has given the students an insight into the responsibilities of business in a way that working for a company could never do. They now realise that satisfying the client is down to them. There is no-one else to blame if it goes wrong, the buck stops with the company management. This simple realisation has dramatically changed their attitudes to the way they organise themselves, to the need to attend to what might seem to be trivial (but necessary) detail.

The mechanisms for managing projects, reviewing the quality of their output and delivering on time have been given a new dimension now since it is they who are seeking client satisfaction now. The clients are *their* clients.

The assessment of the student performance on the course has not yet been completed. It is too soon to say what the outcome of this will be like. There are no established academic markers that we can use in this assessment and so we will have to experiment. Because the students have approached the activities with a great deal of enthusiasm and effort it is to be expected that this will be reflected in their overall grade for the module. This seems to be a common phenomenon with a self selected group of students doing project work.

Each month the company provides a monthly report on activities. This includes the current status of each contract, including a commentary on milestones reached, problems encountered and potential solutions. The monthly accounts are also presented in two forms - virtual accounts where their labour costs are included and real accounts which reflect real expenditure and income. For several months both of these accounts were somewhat negative since no income had come in as no contracts hade been completed. This can be a little dispiriting at first but has now been accepted by the students.

Another assessment source is the documentation associated with each contract. We expect *best practice* in software development to be used, wherever possible.

A further conclusion is that 20 credits is not enough to reflect the work done and next year it will be doubled to 40. There is space in the curriculum to allow for this as the students have 80 credits to cover this activity and any optional modules they wish to take.

# 7 Student feedback

It is still too early to make too many conclusions about the success of the course. We will try to follow up the students after they leave to obtain an evaluation of the usefulness of the course after a year of two. In the interim we have asked for a paragraph or two after they had experienced it over one complete semester.

*"The course funded by the FDTL grant (fondly known as VICI) has been of great interest to myself. The fantastic dreams we had for it at the beginning of the year may not all have been fulfilled, but this is only because the course has taught us many of the problems encountered when setting up a software company, and we now have a much more realistic approach. When I look back to the beginning, it is hard to believe that we were the same people who now have correctly structured meetings, produce monthly reports, and use a strict quality control checklist to assess all the work that we produce. It seems to me that the course is positioned quite nicely in the gap between attending lecture courses, and having time out in industry."*

Grant Bardsley, Feb. 98

## References

1. Report of the National Committee on Higher Education. (The "Dearing Report"), HM Government, H.M.Stationary Office, 1997.

2. Engineering Council, Standards and Routes to Registration. (SARTOR), 1997.

3. Nice degree, shame it's irrelevant. Interface, The Times, October 15, 1997.

4. Andrew Stratton, Mike Holcombe, Peter Croll. Improving the quality of Software Engineering courses through University based Industrial projects. in M. Holcombe, A.Stratton, S. Fincher, G, Griffiths (ed.) Projects in the Computing Curriculum, Proceedings of the Project'98 Workshop, University of Sheffield, Springer-Verlag, 1998.

5. M. Holcombe. A seminar-based course that attempts to provide a more "academic" approach to Software Engineering. To appear in IEEE Trans. Eng. Education.

# Non-technical issues in Undergraduate CS project work

## or

## What are we (all) here for?

Roger D Boyle, Martyn A C Clark

School of Computer Studies

University of Leeds

Leeds, LS2 9JT,

### Abstract

Project work in Computer Science is ubiquitous, but it is not always clear why it has been established or for whom. We note the interest groups involved, and the constraints under which such work is done. We observe that in many circumstances the non-technical aspects of the work are as important as the technical, and discuss what some of them might be. An identification of specific learning objectives is made, and shortage of attempts to meet all of them is noted.

## 1 Projects in Computer Science

Nearly every undergraduate will perform a project. Establishing a definition of project is hard, but usually we can assume that students are exposed to work that is advanced, prolonged and has an identifiable supervisor - a recent survey at the university of Nottingham [1] found over 90% of degree programmes requiring something that could be termed a 'research project', in nearly all cases conducted individually. It is regarded as an essential part of a degree programme; the EPCOS project survey [2, 3] of current practice in Computer Science (CS) reveals that often staff genuinely cannot recall or do not know how long a project has been integral to the degree, in most cases having been there from the very beginning.

CS seems to lie at an extreme of this observation; it is widely accepted that IT professionals in the unfortunately termed 'real world' deal in projects, and that therefore students must be exposed to this sort of thing in order to complete their education. While the project is a major activity in many programmes, the stress placed on it in CS is particularly high. Because, though, it has always been there, it is uncommon to find examples of explicit design of project activity and hence a precise rationale for its existence.

In many disciplines, particularly bench science [4], project work is expected to be a fragment of the supervisor's research; a small part of a project is identified that an undergraduate may be expected to do. The nature of academic computing makes this less common; while it may be possible to conduct a fragment of a project in bench science without a full comprehension of the whole, it is hard to find examples of any except the strongest students generating work of publishable standard in CS. This both deprives the students of the opportunity of participating in 'real' work, and requires us to be quite clear about why we ask them to do what we do. We can also observe that the vocational nature of, for example, systems analysis represents activity quite different to traditional experimental practice.

## 2 Participants

Luck [5] has identified four stakeholders in project work

- students (before the work)

- students (after the work)

- academic staff

- employers

The second category of students has useful and often strong opinions, but for most, their direct interest is limited to negotiating employment interviews. Other obvious players (accrediting organisations, DfEE etc.) may be argued to be acting on behalf of one or more of those given.

The distinction between the student before and after the work is important: Students often have misconceptions about what project work involves, and sometimes negligible preparation. Even with the best of briefings, their opinions afterward often contrast starkly with those before. There is an expectation of predominantly technical learning, but when questioned about their projects, particularly if asked how it could have been improved, graduates will usually draw attention to the organisational, and other 'softer', aspects of the work. Since projects are usually weighted highly [3], they are seen anecdotally both as an opportunity to provide a good grade, and a threat, in the event of failure.

Staff views [6] are usually that the project has a 'finishing' effect, permitting students to demonstrate their full ability on the basis of what they have been taught. When fortunate, it may also contribute economically to research and their own learning but this is not a normal expectation. Thus it is primarily for the student's benefit, and provides an index into their 'true worth'. Potentially, project work can much more easily engage student interest than lecture courses, and represent a value independent form of assessment. The project can also provide an opportunity to reconcile the academic/vocational dilemma in which many computing degrees find themselves, allowing theoretical material to be deployed on a problem (ideally 'live', but often contrived) of some stature. It is common to find [3] that explicit supervisor guidelines do not exist, and that staff adopt a hybrid role of manager, motivator and facilitator, with the balance being a matter of personal inclination, often prompted by student expectation or demand.

Employer views of graduates are well known, and employers of CS graduates are not really different, citing the need for inter-personal and organisational skills [7]. It may be misleading to assume these views are universal, however – SMEs, which are common in the IT industry, often do not get their voices fully heard, but will often report very specific and technical needs. Their requirements are often dictated by a shortage of resources for training, while larger organisations think little of immersing their recruits in a string of formal training courses; for example, 12-month placement students with such organisations report receiving training valued in thousands of pounds, despite their very limited tenure with the company providing it. More prestigious organisations are in a position to cherry-pick their recruits, and will take technical skills for granted by selecting graduates with high grades – they can thus focus selection on other, less tangibly measurable skills. Explicitly, these have been cited as talents of consultation, partnership, project management, commercial understanding and marketing [8, 7]. There is a need for individuals who can 'understand the client', and a move toward measurable competencies such as project management certification. Qualifications such as C.Eng., so prized in the engineering sector, may be seen only as a technical guarantee, the rationale being that such things are only worth what the client interprets, and that Chartered status (as yet) has made little impact on the business areas that the major players occupy.

## 3   Constraints

The project operates within a number of constraints; many of these are historical - 'we do it because we've always done it' - but these are coming under pressure from the rethinking of Higher Education that has developed through the 1990s. The concept of 'graduateness' [9] in particular looks to project work to develop skills of enquiry and investigation that might only have been in place informally hitherto.

The primary constraint within universities on project work is the staff investment. A common format [3] is for one supervisor to handle up to half a dozen independent projects simultaneously, with perhaps an hour per student per week over the project lifetime. This estimate is very approximate, but to it would need to be added preparatory work, assessment and other 'specialist' activity during the project lifetime to keep things on the rails. Given that project tutorials are all different, and frequently driven by student questions rather than staff instructions, these interactions can be exacting and tiring (albeit premium value experiences for students). Staff time is under great pressure, and it is therefore increasingly important to be able to demonstrate that the personal contact provided by project supervision is answering a need.

Careers surveys reveal that the great majority of CS graduates go into employment, and a good proportion of these via a standard recruiting procedure. It has been noted [8] that the purpose of the interview is to determine whether the candidate can put theory into practice, and can articulate evidence. This is very frequently explored via questions about project work, and employers can accordingly be fond of project topics that take theory into relevant practice. If universities make explicit provision for this, it would represent a constraint at variance with the demands of more research oriented projects.

For the overwhelming majority of CS degree programmes, a constraint is accreditation (usually via the BCS). This has always required projects to demonstrate an engineering flavour via a design-implement-evaluate cycle [10]. The precise definition of these terms may be loose (so 'implementation ' does not have to mean coding), but it is expected that the work be significant (thus, not survey based), and should include a literature review and critical appraisal. Group work is not excluded (although individual effort needs to be identifiable). Interestingly, these constraints are in a state of flux with changes in SARTOR [11]. Since these will require (the equivalent of) four years study, and an entry undergraduate level of 24 A level points, it is possible that accreditation will become much less of an issue since so few institutions will be able to achieve it – regardless of the entry barrier, the norm is the three year programme and the climate of HE does not encourage wholesale extension. The new regulations also require an individual project that is much more research based in nature, in addition to group work that resembles the existing BCS project definition.

# 4    A Problem of Definition

We can thus see that the project is not well, or at least not unanimously, defined;

- Students enter it with prior expectations based on often ill-defined preparation; this often causes them to highlight product at the expense of progress, and to preoccupy themselves with technical issues [12]. It is often interpreted as 'a large piece of course-work'.

- Staff will see it as a significant load, and hope it will represent an example of the student's true worth, although there may not be agreement on how. There may be an accent on the supervisor's own study area, and hence a research theme. It is also likely that prospective research students (a small proportion of the cohort) would be exercised in the topics and skills they might later pursue [13].

- Some employers may hope the project will introduce the student to the commercial and industrial interpretation of the word; major tasks, management structures, clients, milestones etc. The view has been expressed [8] that the project permits the student to explore their favoured area of employment – this diverges sharply from the staff view of research projects in which students pursue specialised, perhaps highly theoretical, academic study.

- Other employers seek graduates highly skilled in very specific areas, and would see the project as an opportunity to acquire very specialised knowledge.

- The accrediting body of the profession requires projects to demonstrate a very specific engineering approach; this is probably familiar in theory to students from formally taught material, but may well not coincide with staff experience of their own work. Meanwhile, many employers may be indifferent to accreditation issues.

These different perceptions and expectations provoke tensions meaning that there is rarely unanimity on what the explicit aims of conducting project work might be, still less on what any implicit aims or hidden agenda may be. We can observe, however, that there is a view that the project in CS is not solely an exercise in acquiring or exhibiting technical skills, and that there is a need to identify what else should be going on. Especially in the post-Dearing climate, the *laissez faire* approach of assigning students to supervisors and leaving them to get on with matters (where it is still in use) is not sustainable.

Discussions on projects involving employers and curriculum designers frequently mention the reflective phase; in informal conversation with graduates, this is often the most informative aspect. Some project designs encourage this throughout [14], but interestingly it is omitted from the criteria for accreditation – but then, accreditation is an issue that provokes tensions of its own: It is important for departments to retain it, but the evidence for demand for it from the profession is thin.

The nature of the discipline means that the 'research' project is often inappropriate, or not available. The demands of employers and the views of graduates in regular employment (who make up the majority of our product) are clear that non-technical issues are very important, and require us to think about for whom the project is being done and why, and how.

# 5  Non-technical Issues

We can attempt to enumerate the aspects of project work that fall outside the strictly technical that are seen as desirable to at least one of the players;

- The putting of theory into practice [12]

- A process of enquiry: Students should be engaged in locating information, devising criteria and applying them.

- There should be a process of knowledge integration; while furthering and deepening acquired knowledge, its applicability and inter-relationship should be established. This is particularly important in the wake of widespread modularisation which encourages a compartmentalisation of education.

- 'Soft skills': this is an expression much loved of employers, but is coming to mean the full range of features that employers seek, and is a superset of the 'personal transferable skills' that have become ubiquitous since the early 1990s.

- A reflective phase is most important: It is of great value for the education of the student to be required to stand back at the end of the process and ask what went well and what did not, and thereby be able to measure the change that the project has generated.

Since we are setting criteria, assessment automatically becomes an issue; are these imprecise issues assessable (and should they be)? All projects will generate a report and to some extent this can be used to gauge how far these aims may have been met [3]. It is possible to augment the deliverables list with poster presentations and vivas (which are already used in many places), but there is often a reluctance to introduce these since they are perceived as heavy on staff time. Two economic ways of causing the process rather than the outputs to come under scrutiny are

- A negotiation phase at commencement; this may be on the whole topic, or on aspects of its conduct, or on the nature of its assessment. Anything which causes the student to engage with what is being done and how, or what the 'best' targets may be, will lift the perspective from the purely technical.

- The setting of milestones that permit progress to be obvious. These need not be technical – the preparation of an interim report or literature review, or the submission of a draft report chapter, represent positively useful project activity that can elicit feedback long before completion.

Should these issues be assessed in the same phase and manner as more obviously technical material? Arguably they are largely qualitative in nature, while industry, the BCS (and students) are fonder of quantitative approaches. It seems increasingly likely, post-Dearing, that something along the lines of a 'Learning Log' (or whatever the HE version of the Record of Achievement comes to be called) will become widespread, and perhaps the culminating entries should be devoted to project work. Experiments may already be found around the country [5] of students receiving 'Skills certificates' in addition to degree transcripts.

A deeper issue is the preparation, of both staff and students, for whatever a project comes to represent. Student pre- and post-conceptions can be wildly different, illustrating that they often do not appreciate what is going to happen. There is much anecdotal evidence that students with some employment experience (in particular industrial placement) extract more value from the project experience, but it would be hard to mimic this in preparatory modules. There is some mileage in small scale project work that lays some foundations of good practice, but this is likely to be expensive in staff resource. A positive suggestion is to involve students themselves in preparatory work, perhaps by having exiting finalists give presentations to second years. Certainly, as a checkpoint on experience, the involvement of senior students with juniors has been seen to be of great value [15].

Considering staff preparation, experience suggests it can be very difficult to get all staff to 'buy in' to any changes in delivery or focus, although the more exposure academics have to, for example, the views of industrialists, the more opinions change. It remains very hard though to alter long standing preconceptions. Many projects are double marked, which at least provides some chance of a breadth of opinion in assessment, and in some institutions a moderator for the whole cohort is implicit in the project management [14]. One suggestion is the active involvement of postgraduate research students, who have the benefits of being close to the experience themselves and very manageable by their academic supervisors. The side effect of instilling some professional experience in the postgraduates should not be overlooked.

# 6   A Remedy

We are able to identify four desirable features of project conduct and assessment that are not part of some other aspect or objective;

- The process of enquiry: Projects should develop students' abilities to see a problem in context; to hypothesise solutions; to design and conduct experiments to demonstrate them; to observe, record and draw conclusions. In traditional science, this may be regarded as 'experimental technique'.

- The perception of a whole: This is related to the process of enquiry, and encourages students to see their subject as just that – a whole, rather than a collection of modules which is the characteristic of many CVs, especially weaker ones.

- Reflection: It is well established [16] that learning experiences depend on some reflective phase. Students should always be required to look back and enquire what they have learned, and what may have been done better, or improved.

- Personal transferable skills: The well identified skills of prioritising, scheduling, reporting etc.

The EPCOS consortium [2] is conducting a 36 month study of project practice in a number of areas. A database of existing activity [3] reveals little explicit attention being devoted to these issues, certainly when compared to safer CS territory such as exhibition of software lifecycles. Conceivably this is because neither questions nor answers were phrased with these issues uppermost, and all we might wish to see is happening informally or accidentally. Equally possibly, there may be a lot of lip service being paid to what is widely agreed is important (but difficult).

Specifically, we note that when study is restricted to those that claim to be successful in their learning objectives, project specifications are particularly weak in the second two of these issues, while we can identify attempts to meet the first two. The shortage of explicit attention paid to reflection is especially noteworthy, since this is a skill whose necessity pervades professional life [17, 18]. Work in progress will be attempting to verify that best, or at least good, practice can be packaged for transfer into different programmes in different institutions. Experience will reveal how achievable this is, and how specific to the discipline of CS.

Projects exhibit sharply many of the tensions within current HE; the major employers speak with a loud voice and demand our best graduates, together with a range of soft skills that we have not been accustomed to providing. Meanwhile SMEs, who cannot fund elaborate training departments, are seeking technically competent workers who can hit the ground running with the versatility to fit into a rapidly changing work environment. Staff, many of whom are still audibly yearning for the Old Days, are often not fully persuaded (or sure) of the purpose of the activity, but are usually keen to accentuate the research aspects of project work. Students, meanwhile, enter the whole process in an advanced state of apprehension, unsure whether they are engaged in course-work, the acquisition of a passport to employment, or a life-forming experience. They certainly have some views afterwards, and it would be nice to think we could reduce the apprehension and enhance the benefits to all.

# References

[1] M R Luck. Undergraduate research projects as a route to skills development. *Capability*, 3rd(2), 1997.

[2] S Fincher and M Petre. Using other people's experience of project work: Realising fitness for purpose, 1998. Submitted to the Project 98 workshop, 8th/9th april, Sheffield, UK.

[3] EPCOS Consortium. Project EPCOS. *WWW*, 1996. *http://www.cs.ukc.ac.uk/national/CSDN/html/EPCOS/EPCOS.html.*

[4] J T Leach, J Ryder, and R Driver. ULISP Working papers. Technical Report 1 to 8, University of Leeds, Leeds, LS2 9JT, 1996.

[5] M R Luck. Undergraduate research projects - why bother?, 1998. Given at the EPCOS workshop, 9th January, Leeds, UK.

[6] Graduateness - Towards Honours Projects. *WWW*, 1996. *http://www.lgu.ac.uk/deliberations/graduates/honours/index.html.*

[7] D Tiplady. What the software sector seeks, 1998. Given at the EPCOS workshop, 9th January, Leeds, UK.

[8] P Horn. Skills for the workplace, 1998. Given at the EPCOS workshop, 9th January, Leeds, UK.

[9] HEQC. *The Graduate Standards Programme: Interim Report.* Higher Education Quality Council, London, 1995.

[10] BCS. Course accreditation information for universities and colleges. *WWW*, 1995. *http://www.bcs.org.uk/educat/accinf.htm.*

[11] *Standards and Routes to Registration.* The Engineering Council, 10 Maltravers Street, London, WC2R 3ER, 3rd edition, 1997.

[12] J Ryder and J Leach. Research projects in the UG science course: Students learning about science through enculturation. In G Gibbs, editor, *Improving Student Learning Through Course Design.* Oxford Centre for Staff Learning and Development, 1997.

[13] S Rowett. Experience of a student-led final year degree project. In M Boyle, editor, *Student led Projects at the University of Leeds.* University of Leeds, Leeds, UK, 1995.

[14] B Morris. The role of 'learning conversations' in computing projects, 1998. Given at the EPCOS workshop, 9th January, Leeds, UK.

[15] R D Boyle. Exercising Management among IT Graduates. Technical Report SCS 95.21, School of Computer Studies, University of Leeds, 1995.

[16] D Laurillard. *Rethinking University Teaching.* Routledge, 1993.

[17] D A Schön. *The Reflective Practitioner.* Basic Books, 1983.

[18] D Cannon. New Career, old Problem: Learning from 'things going wrong'. *British Journal of Guidance and Counselling*, 25(4):491–505, 1997.

# PART 4

## Negotiation

# HEFCE EPCOS Project

# Towards a Framework for Transferable Negotiated Learning Practices in Team Projects

**Dr. Malcolm Birtle (m.birtle@tees.ac.uk)**
**School of Computing and Mathematics, University of Teesside,**
**Middlesbrough, TS1 3BA, UK**

## Abstract

Work in progress on a model for evaluating and transferring practice with regard to negotiated learning in team projects is presented. It is for application primarily in the computing discipline. The model is independent of specific teaching and learning practices. Specific teaching and learning methods can be related to the model by a mapping process which matches model elements to the methods. Outline processes for transfer, evaluation of transferred practice, and evaluation of transfer are described. This paper is a contribution to the Higher Education Funding Council for England Fund for the Development of Teaching and Learning project Effective Project Work in Computer Science (EPCOS).

## 1. Negotiated Learning

Project EPCOS (Effective Project work in Computer Science) is a consortium of university computing departments collaborating to capture and disseminate effective and innovative practice in aspects of project work. The partners are the computing departments of Exeter, Imperial, Kent, Leeds, Manchester, Southampton, Teesside, York, and the Open Universities [1]. The objectives of the EPCOS project are

> 1. To identify, make explicit and systematise existing best practices in Computer Science student project methods and techniques in order to make existing knowledge and experience readily accessible for the achievement of threshold standards in Computer Science graduates.

2. For each EPCOS partner to document and evaluate its work with student projects and to realise and improve the contribution of project work to threshold standards in its own area of particular interest.

3. To realise techniques for transferring project work practices between institutions.

4. To execute and evaluate such transfers.

5. To contribute Computer Science-specific material to the literature on project work.

The deliverables from the project will include the results of a questionnaire based on a template produced by consortium members co-ordinated by Centre for Informatics Education Research (Open University). This is intended to capture practice at a number of institutions. The results will be placed on the EPCOS web site to enable examination, cross-referencing and analysis. A summary of the available data has been produced as a poster.

Each project partners has concentrated on an aspect of project work over the life of EPCOS and will produce documents pertinent to their area which may be compiled into a single publication. The particular aspect of project work of interest to Teesside is the element of negotiation in projects. Negotiation in projects takes many forms but the form most commonly described in the literature is the 'learning contract'. However, this is not the only method of including negotiation in projects and Teesside's contribution to EPCOS will attempt to capture the variety of ways that negotiation is practised in undergraduate projects.

Negotiated learning is the concept of enabling students to actively participate in the establishment of learning objectives, organisation of learning resources, the pursuit of objectives, and assessment of achievement. Boud and Jacques [2,3] have described how prescription can compromise the development of autonomy in students by denying them the opportunity to reflect on learning needs and to autonomously set learning objectives. Paul and Shaw [4] have made the point that a negotiated learning process forces participants to define the evidence of learning in detail, and the means of assessment, at an early stage. The student can take a more active role in the whole process of education- *"through choosing methods, to evaluating process and assessing outcomes "*.

An early reference to negotiated learning contracts in the literature was by Frymier [5] and Glasgow [6]. Frymier pointed out that students could clearly understand why penalties were applied or rewards withheld. *"Either learning occurs or it does not. If it does the grade is granted. If it does not all parties involved understand exactly how and why the conditions were not fulfilled"*. Amsden [7] also described an early use of learning contracts. The contractual approach to learning is closely related to approaches developed in corporate training courses such as those described by Biedebach and Burgwadt [8,9,10].

This type of approach is fairly common in work-based learning programmes such as the scheme in place at Leeds University [11]. An early application to projects in a computer science course was described by Joel [12]. Joel provided to the students a means of relating grades to negotiated outcomes of the project. This work does not mention any negotiation with regard to the attributes of deliverables i.e. the characteristics of the deliverable which would merit the grade agreed.

Excellent summaries and practical advice on negotiated learning have been provided in the *"Staff and Educational Development Association (ex Standing Conference on Educational Development) Papers 71 and 72"* [13] and by Tompkins and McGraw [14]. Boud, Anderson and Sampson [15] have provided guidelines and reference manuals [16].

Some further guidance has been published by deLeon [17] and Knowles [18]

The range of uses of learning contracts have been surveyed in Stephenson and Laycock's book *"Using Learning Contracts in Higher Education"*[19]. The major issue identified by them was the move from a pedagogical approach where the teacher is in complete control to an androgogical approach which emphasises co-operation, autonomy and experiential learning.

Flexibility and degree of choice may not be necessarily desirable or possible depending on the situation but the flexible and adaptable nature of the approach means that students can be gradually introduced to autonomous learning. The process can start with a small element of negotiation which increases as the student's approach to learning matures. Negotiation can range from small scale informal discussions between a student and tutor to fully negotiated learning contracts.

Team projects exist in many forms with the common characteristic that they involve groups of students learning in a co-operative manner whilst executing discrete tasks. The purpose of the framework described in this paper is to identify the elements of the negotiated approach to learning which are needed to satisfy the demands and constraints of team projects in the computing discipline. It is anticipated that some practices employed in individual projects will be transferable to the team situation and vice-versa. There are some learning objectives implied or assumed by the model. These are
- to encourage and develop active participation in learning through negotiated learning.
- to develop skills in co-operative working in a computing discipline

The framework exists to provide some structure for the practices identified during the EPCOS project. It will provide a basis for classification and understanding of the purposes of specific teaching practices. It therefore acts as a benchmark and is a basis for evaluation and comparison of practice. It could be used to identify areas of practice that currently lack effective mechanisms in the existing context.

In detail, there are many different mechanisms which can be employed in team projects to enable negotiated learning to take place. This framework is intended to be independent of any specific mechanism or combination of mechanisms. So, for instance, teams may keep log-books, take minutes at meetings, keep project diaries or use some other mechanism to record progress and demonstrate contribution. The framework captures this type of activity and characterises it as a mechanism to provide the framework element of 'visibility'.

The framework will be offered with the team project techniques employed in the School of Computing and Mathematics, University of Teesside together with practices identified at other institutions in the EPCOS questionnaire data. It is anticipated that practices in more institutions will be described in the final deliverable in order to demonstrate the variety of practices available. These techniques address the components of the framework and can be adopted in part for integration into existing practice or as a whole. This allows for interested parties to pick the most appropriate or apparently useful aspects of  practice as appropriate. It is not necessary or  desirable to adopt all the mechanisms offered.

Negotiation in team projects can cover learning objectives, development methods, management methods, and assessment methods and criteria. The amount and scope of negotiation is dependent on the context of the project. 'Context' refers to the environment, culture and overall learning objectives under which the project operates.  Negotiated learning can
- make teams more pro-active in learning
- motivate through increasing autonomy and sense of project ownership
- give students the freedom to develop the synergy of the team and discover the most effective 'modus operandi' for the team.

There are constraints on negotiation. The process needs to be controlled
- to ensure fair assessment
- to ensure comparability between projects
- to define minimum standards
- to relate marks to achievement by an authorised assessor i.e. the validation and verification of learning

# 2. A Framework for Transfer and Learning Mechanisms

The framework consists of a series of elements. These elements address various aspects of student team project work. They can be viewed as partial solutions to problems that can be encountered with team projects. For instance, the problem of individual assessment can be addressed by the elements of visibility, traceability, assessment processes, statement of commitment, and statement of outcomes and responsibilities. Teaching and learning mechanisms are related to framework elements. For each element there may be a number of effective mechanisms capable of satisfying the purpose of the element. For instance, visibility might be provided by minutes of meetings, attendance at supervisor meetings, by producing individual reports or some other mechanism. The most effective mechanism will depend on the context of the project, the capabilities of the participants and the resources available. All elements may not be necessary for every context. The learning objectives of a team project may not require that every element is addressed i.e. that a mechanism exists for the purpose of every element.

| Framework Element | Justification |
|---|---|
| Scope of negotiation | It is the tutor's responsibility to define the knowledge domain and the flexibility of study within the domain. This defines the possibilities for negotiation. |
| Guidelines | The degree of rigour depends on the maturity, commitment, and experience of the participants. Guidelines are required for three types of participant. |
| for supervisors | To provide consistency of approach between supervisors. |
| for individual students | To provide tutoring in negotiation skills and for consistency. |
| for teams | To co-ordinate negotiation activities and for consistency. |
| Statement of commitment | To conclude negotiations and place the statement of outcomes and responsibilities under change control. |
| Relationship of outcomes to grades | To equate effort and reward, and so students can see the relative value of work and achievement. |

134

| Assessment criteria | To define product and process attributes which, when achieved, provides evidence of learning. |
| Statement of outcomes and responsibilities | Provides the basis for visibility of contribution, and the relationships between co-operative activities and outcomes. |
| Visibility mechanisms | So individuals can demonstrate contribution and commitment, and the team can demonstrate co-operative behaviour. |
| Traceability mechanisms | So the team can demonstrate relationships between contributions and co-operative activities. |
| Re-negotiation process | To avoid drift in objectives by exercising change control, and to provide an opportunity to rectify estimation inaccuracies by the team. |
| Mechanism for process definition and improvement | To provide baselines for process assessment and reflection on process improvements. |
| Formative assessment process | To provide a means for feedback and improvement and to provide an opportunity for student involvement in assessment. |
| Summative assessment process | To validate and verify learning. |
| Pre-requisites | To determine the range of applicability of negotiation. |
| Moderation process | To ensure comparability of learning objectives and assessment between teams. |

## 3. Mechanisms and Dependencies

A major concern of the EPCOS project is the means of transfer of effective practice. This framework is an attempt to capture and structure examples of negotiation practice in a form that allows selective uptake and transfer. Examples of practice will be drawn from the EPCOS data gathering exercise and from practice at Teesside. Examples of teaching and learning mechanisms for negotiated learning in team projects are currently available in Jones [20], and Birtle [21, 22, 23]. These and others drawn from other institutions will be included in the final EPCOS deliverables and in the PROF@T FDTL project.

There are two dependencies which the EPCOS partners have identified as crucial to analysis and transfer of practice.
**Critical Dependency-** a given teaching and learning mechanism cannot be transferred without also transferring a mechanism it depends on.

**Critical Adjacency**-A given teaching and learning mechanism can be transferred by itself, but in its originating context it is closely attached to another mechanism, and they should be considered together.

For instance, standardised minutes may be used to capture the outcomes of team meetings in order to provide visibility. The form of these minutes may be critically dependent on the existence of a formal standard. The effective transfer of this practice of minute taking may be dependent on the transfer of the standard. Therefore, the transfer involves two aspects of practice rather than one. Alternatively, the view may be taken that a specific standard is not required and it is possible to transfer the practice without necessarily adopting the specific standard. This could be seen as a critical adjacency between the practices.

## 4. The EPCOS Transfer and Evaluation Process

The aims of transfer are
- to determine if the framework can be employed to characterise effective practice in general
- to assess the independence of the framework from specific learning mechanisms i.e. that the framework can be effective without prescribing specific learning methods.
- to assess the process of matching learning mechanisms to framework elements i.e that a learning mechanism delivers a framework element
- to provide mechanisms for each framework element where needed by the adopting partner

It is expected that **some** of the learning mechanisms described from Teesside will be transferred and integrated into existing practice of at least one of the EPCOS partners. (It is unlikely, and not expected that any participant would want to adopt all aspects of team project work at Teesside). The framework can be tested by benchmarking the practice as a whole by matching learning mechanisms used by the adopting partner with elements of the framework. The ease of integration, and effectiveness, of any learning mechanism will need to be assessed (if any mechanism from Teesside is adopted). Effectiveness will be assessed by determining if the mechanism satisfies the appropriate element(s) in the framework within the context of the adopting environment. The adopting partner will need to benchmark existing costs and keep a record of any additional costs incurred through integrating the framework approach with existing reflective activities on teaching. The notion of 'field records' can be useful for this type of activity. This involves participants maintaining structured logs of observations and measurements (if desirable and easy to obtain). The adopting partner will be asked to record their experiences using 'field observations'. A template for these observations will be provided. Practitioners will be asked to record changes in learning outcomes as part of their field observations. Advice and techniques for capturing student experience for evaluation purposes will be provided with the framework through published material. Ideally, existing evaluation mechanisms at the adopting institution will be exploited to assess student's experience to keep costs manageable. The impact of inertia due to departmental change procedures will also be included in field notes and then analysed and reported by the originator. This should provide some information on institutional barriers to change. The resources required for support from the originator will be recorded and reported by the originator. 'Field notes', the EPCOS template, evaluation feedback from participants, and empirical data should provide enough information for the identification and analysis of problems associated with transferability.

Evaluation of the transfer will be in two parts. The first evaluation prepares the practice for transfer, and the second evaluation covers the transfer experience.

## 4.1 Preparation for transfer

Each element in the framework has a stated purpose or objective. The framework will cover any dependencies and adjacencies within the practices offered. Dependencies and adjacencies need to be considered at the receiver to ensure that transferred practice can be adopted without conflict with existing practices. Transfer of practice could be considered by
- assessing current practice against the elements in the framework,
- using the elements to identify current need ,
- considering the adoption of an associated mechanism for the element pertinent to the need

The framework consists of elements with some potential teaching and learning mechanisms which address the purposes of the elements. A problem with team work can be mapped to one or more elements. Then mechanisms to address the problem can be identified. Associated with each example of practice will be
- information on evaluation of that practice
- any known problems encountered in the process of production
- any problems anticipated during transfer
- a statement of known benefits of the practice

Elements can be taken as a whole or in parts depending on the context of the receiver. It may be that many of the elements are already addressed and the receiver wishes to address problems/issues/objectives related to a sub-set of the elements. A map of the elements, mechanisms, dependencies and adjacencies of existing practice at the receiver should be made. This should be compared with the framework to assess comparability between the context of the importer and exporter of practice. Examination of the relative dependencies and adjacencies should illuminate the possibilities for transfer.

One aim of producing the framework is to provide a benchmark against which practitioners can test their practice and identify practices that could lead to improvements or problem resolution. The following aspects of existing practice need to be addressed for applicability within a context before an attempt at transfer

- Are all the elements in the framework necessary in this context?
- Are there any elements of effective practice missing from current practice?
- Can any current problems be addressed by any of the framework elements?

An attempt was made to identify instances of negotiation during the EPCOS data gathering exercise. Table 1:Relationship between Framework Elements and EPCOS Template indicates the way that reported practice might relate to framework elements. The 'question refers' column following refers to the EPCOS data gathering template available at the EPCOS web site [1].

| Framework Element | Criteria (question to ask) | Question refers (x-ref to EPCOS data gathering template) |
|---|---|---|
| Scope of negotiation | Objectives and degree of flexibility should be explicit | 3.5 partic. ii,4.1 |
| Guidelines | Transferable advice to teams and supervisors should be explicit | |
| for supervisors | | |
| for individual students | | |
| for teams | | |
| Statement of commitment | There should be a point in the negotiation process where participants commit to outcomes. | |
| Relationship of outcomes to grades | There should be a clear mapping of deliverables and compliant processes to grades | 5.8 |
| Assessment criteria | Criteria, even if negotiated, should be explicit and defined in advance of relevant process | 5.1 |

| Statement of outcomes and responsibilities | There should be clear statement relating individual responsibilities to outcomes. | 1.4,3.5 partic. i, 4.1, 7.4 |
|---|---|---|
| Visibility mechanisms | Each individual should be able to demonstrate individual contribution | 5.5,7.6 |
| Traceability mechanisms | each individual should be able to demonstrate how their contribution adds value to the co-operative activity | 7.6 |
| Re-negotiation process | Changes to team objectives should only take place in a controlled and moderated manner | |
| Mechanism for process definition and improvement | Teams should be able to articulate their development and management processes, and have the means to improve on them | 4.2, 4.3 |
| Formative assessment process | There should be a feedback mechanism which enables teams and individuals to improve | 4.8 5.4, 5.6, 5.13, 5.14 |
| Summative assessment process | The process of producing marks should be explicit and defined for assessors | 5.2, 5.4, 5.8, 5.9, 5.11, |
| Pre-requisites | The skills and knowledge required to qualify for a negotiated approach should be defined | 2.3, 2.5 |
| Moderation process | The equivalence of the negotiated outcomes between teams should be monitored and controlled | 4.4 |

Table 1:Relationship between Framework Elements and EPCOS Template

## 4.2  Evaluation of Transferred Practice

The following  evaluation criteria are transferable i.e.common, across elements
- Has the identified problem been resolved?

- Is there any consistent negative feedback from practitioners regarding the transferred practice?

Table 2:Evaluation Criteria for Framework Elements lists the evaluation criteria for each of the elements. This indicates the type of test that could be applied to a teaching and learning mechanism for each element in order to assess effectiveness. It is likely that these evaluation criteria will be more detailed in the final deliverable. The table also indicates the typical means of acquiring evaluation data for each element. It is unlikely that mechanisms for every element have been transferred so the evaluation process may not be so onerous as this table might suggest. Evaluation will only cover a sub-set of the elements of the framework for any particular transfer.

| Framework Element | Criteria (the practice will be successful if) | Data collection mechanism |
|---|---|---|
| Scope of negotiation | Descriptives document exists and student feedback positive | Document inspection and student feedback |
| Guidelines | Seen to be explicit and timely provision. Little duplicated guidance from supervisors. | Supervisor feedback |
| for supervisors | | |
| for individual students | | |
| for teams | | |
| Statement of commitment | Visible signatures, dates and line of responsibility. | Document inspection |
| Relationship to grades | Supervisors clear about mechanism | Supervisor feedback |
| Assessment criteria | Visible to supervisors and students before application | Document inspection |
| Statement of outcomes and responsibilities | Students clear about responsibilities | Student feedback |
| Visibility mechanisms | Ease of discovering individual contribution | Document inspection |
| Traceability mechanisms | Ease of discovering adequacy of document information | Document inspection |

| Re-negotiation process | Any changes controlled and documented | Document inspection |
|---|---|---|
| Mechanism for process definition and improvement | Teams have standardised means of defining process. A consistency of approach. | Document inspection |
| Formative assessment process | Teams receiving feedback and acting on it. Involvement of teams in process | Student and supervisor feedback. Document inspection. |
| Summative assessment process | Relationships of product and process attributes to marks and grades explicit. | Document inspection |
| Pre-requisites | No complaints about processes beyond student capabilities. | Student feedback |
| Moderation process | Project outcomes and processes of equivalent standard | Project co-ordinator feedback |

**Table 2:Evaluation Criteria for Framework Elements**

# 5. Evaluating the Transfer

The second part of EPCOS evaluation considers the transfer of practice itself. The evaluation criteria are transferable between mechanisms and will be transferable across all EPCOS sub-projects in detail. These criteria will cover

- Adoption and continuity of practice
- Commitment to further development of practice
- Modified adoption of practice
- Breadth of adoption of practice
- Evidence of improvement (positive feedback) of practice
- Identified problem(s) resolved

This information will be collected by a third party not connected with either the importer or exporter of practice.

# 6. Acknowledgments

Thanks to EPCOS consortium partners for valuable discussion and feedback and to all contributors involved in the data gathering exercise.

# 7. References

[1] http://www.cs.ukc.ac.uk/national/CSDN/html/EPCOS/EPCOS.html
[2] Boud D. Ed. (1981), *Developing Student Autonomy in Learning*, Kogan Page Ltd., London, UK
[3] Jacques D. (1985), *"Learning in Groups"*, Croom Helm Ltd., London, UK, 1985
[4] Paul V., Shaw M. (1992), "A Practical Guide to Introducing Contract Learning" , *In Standing Conference on Educational Development Paper no. 71*, Brown S, and Baume D. Ed., Standing Conference on Educational Development, Birmingham, UK, pp.7-21
[5] Frymier J.R. (1966), *The Nature of the Educational Method*, Columbus, Ohio, Charles E. Merrill Publishing Co.
[6] Glasgow J., *'Performance of High School Students on Grade Contracts'*, Unpublished Thesis, Ohio State University, 1967
[7] Amsden S. (1970), "Have you Tried Contracting for Grades", *English Journal*, 59, 3, 1279-1282
[8] Biedenbach J.M., Ed. (1972), "Special Issue on Continuing Education", *IEEE Trans. on Education*, E-15, 2
[9] Burgwardt F.C. Ed. (1976), "Special Issue on Continuing Education", *IEEE Transactions on Education*, E-19, pp.1
[10] Ed. Burgwardt F.C., Biedenbach J.M, Ed.(1976) "Education in Industry-Some Approaches to Life-long Learning", *IEEE Trans. on Education*, E-19, pp.119-123
[11] http://education.leeds.ac.uk/~edu/wblp/a7.htm
[12] Joel W.J. (1987), "Realistic Student Projects", *Bulletin of the Special Interest Group in Computer Science Education*, 19, 1, 244-247
[13] Brown S, and Baume D. Ed.,(1992) , *Learning Contracts:Volume One A Theoretical Perspective* , Standing Conference on Educational Development Paper no. 71 and no.72, Standing Conference on Educational Development, Birmingham, UK
[14] Tompkins C., McGraw M., 'The Negotiated Learning Contract', in Boud D., *Developing Student Autonomy in Learning* , (Kogan Page Ltd 1981 and 1988), 2nd Ed., ed. Boud D. pp.172.

[15] Boud D., Anderson G., Sampson J. (1994), "Improving the Use of Learning Contracts", In *Proceedings of the National Teaching Workshop*, Australian National University, Canberra, Australia, pp.120-127

[16] http://uniserve.edu.au/caut/NTW1994/TitlePage.html

[17]http://carbon.cudenver.edu/~ldeleo/pad5220/learning_contracts/about_contrac ts/menu.html

[18] Knowles M.S. (1986), *Using Learning Contracts*, Jossey-Bass, San Francisco

[19] Stephenson J., Laycock M. Ed. (1993), *Using Learning Contracts in Higher Education*, Kogan-Page, London and Philadelphia.

[20] Jones A., Birtle M.,'An Individual Assessment Technique for Group Projects in Software Engineering', *Software Engineering Journal*, 4, (4), July 1989, pp.226-232

[21] Birtle M., 'Developing Student Autonomy and Process Improvement in Software Engineering Team Projects', Ph.D. Thesis, University of Lancaster, 1996

[22] Birtle M., 'Negotiated Learning in Team Projects, *Annals of Software Engineering*, 1998, *submitted to*

[23] http://www-scm.tees.ac.uk/research/epcos/epcos.htm

# The role of learning conversations (and the learning coach) in Computing Projects in Higher Education in the UK

Brian Morris

Division of Business, Brunel University,

Middlesex, United Kingdom

There are opportunities to enhance the learning that takes place within computing projects in Higher Education in England and Wales. The application of Self Organised Learning (SOL) ideas in conjunction with teaching on Project Management for student negotiated self-selected computing projects for small to medium size enterprises has proved encouraging. The anatomy of learning conversations, found with SOL, has proved very useful in coaching students carrying out final year HND computing projects.

Key words:      SOL, learning, learnong coach, project, project management

---

# 1    Has Teaching Prevented Learning?

For some time I have felt there is something wrong with learning on student computing projects. I have come to believe that teaching can get in the way of real learning. This might seem an unusual view, but others agree with it. Dr Stephanie Pace Marshall (Executive Director, Illinois Mathematics and Science Academy, USA) is one. A year ago she gave a lecture to the Royal Society of Arts entitled: "Does education and training get in the way of learning?" [1] which is discussed below.  An associated question is "Why has distance learning NOT proved to be a flop?"  Surely learners must have a lecturer or teacher? People cannot learn very well on their own, can they?

In Higher Education great importance is attached to the **final year Project.** Our degree at Brunel requires 40 credits out of 120 credits for the Project in the final year. This is standard across the University and represents 33% of final year effort. It is a major factor in contributing to the degree classification.  Our HND Computing requires the completion of a substantial 30 credit project out of 120 credits in the second year. This is combined with the study of Project Management which, if assessed, moves the credit total to 45 out of 120 in the second year. This is between 25% to 37% of final year effort. These figures are replicated in most United Kingdom Universities.

Yet the *organisation* of the final year project is a variable matter. Firstly, there is a tension between lecturers teaching students on modules throughot the couse of study and, secondly, lecturers expecting students to **"get on with"** their own learning, largely by themselves, in the final year project. Current practice may be sketched as follows. Students may have a one-on-one tutorial with a Project Supervisor once a month - say eight times from October, November, December, January, February, March, April, May.

Typically these sessions last forty minutes. Eight such meetings of forty minutes imply just over 5 student-staffhours per student for the academic year. For thirty students this will be 30x5 = 150 staffhours. By contrast the cost of taking all students all year in the new Learning Coach mode (together with teaching elements of Project Management) is 3.5 hrs x 30 weeks = 105 staff-hours. On efficiencygrounds since 105 staffhours is less than 150 staffhours the move to this approach is justified. But the purpose of this paper is to explore learning, not efficiency.

What do we make of the traditional supervisor role? What is the implication of "supervision" if it does not suggest some features of 'project management'? Many would agree that teaching project management helps students gain an insight into their concurrent project processes.

Following traditional practice, the final year Project report is scrutinised academically. The student may not be present. Therefore, as a learning experience, it is, in my view, separated, isolated and over-rated. Some may say this lonely isolated experience breeds the tenacity needed for researchers, others - and I include myself here - are very uneasy about it. Does it promote learning in an effective way?

Industrialists are making similar points about our graduates and diplomates. David Tiplady, Systems Integration Principal with UNISYS, made the following points at a recent conference [2] on Projects at Leeds University:

> We need graduates with the following skills: Consultative, Partnership, Project Management, Commercial, Business, Technology, Marketing.... You can help us by embracing the notion that **soft skills are key.** Team skills - have teams constantly forming and reforming, look at interpersonal and leadership styles, Consultative skills - develop presentation and communication skills by matching the message to client needs, Commercial skills - understand a balance sheet and simple contractual law, Marketing - sensitivity to the marketing concept, anticipating customer's needs and selling the right products and services, Project Management - work planning and delegating.

It was clear that Common Skills / Key Skills / Transferable Skills were highly valued qualities amongst the cream of all graduates interviewed at UNISYS. Does the lonely research path promote these qualities? Indeed, should it? Does the occasional meeting with a Supervisor develop Common Skills? Not necessarily. It seems a culture change in HE is needed to embrace the sort of ideas David Tiplady is advocating over and above the standard computing graduate product.

My unease with the student-supervisor system lead to an imperative for change: something different must happen. Ackoff, in his wonderful paper "The art and science of mess management" [3], captures this need for change:

> We must redesign the educational process. The focus on design of those of us in academia leaves us with need to develop a new kind of education; it leaves us with the need to develop an adequate *methodology of design, a logic of creativity.* This must be very different from the conventional logic of classes because it must be a logic of uniqueness, of individuality. It cannot be an inductive or deductive logic such as is adequate for clinical judgement or scientific inference. It must be a logic of intuition from which creativity springs. (my italics)

In my unease with final year computing projects I withdrew to the HND Projects to try out some ideas based around soft systems, project management and common skills. If these ideas work for HND students before two years are completed then they should work with final year degree students. The advantage of this approach was simply the fact that I controlled the timetabling for HND Information Systems for Business and HND Multimedia Production.

Further, there was the realisation that psychology has moved on and is increasingly relevant to learning. The domain of Psychology has progressed from Behaviourism (man as a machine) through Freudian Psychology (man as a sexual being) to Human Psychology (man as a learning being). The key idea was to use Self Organised Learning ideas, developed by George Kelly, Carl Rogers [4, 5] and Laurie Thomas [6], and employ a Rogerian approach with HND students in 'learning conversations' on a weekly basis throughout their final year computing project. For a discussion of these approaches see Harri-Augstein & Webb [7].

# 2    Models Of Project Organisation

This paper suggests a **classification** of projects in HE may be based on the type of learning (other-organised learning or self-organised learning) contrasted against the project team size (solo or many). A grid for this is given below in Figure 1

| Size<br>Learning type | Solo | Many |
|---|---|---|
| Other-organisedlearning | Cell 1 | Cell 2 |
| Self-organisedlearning | Cell 3 | Cell 4 |

Figure 1

Cell 1 is typified by a supervisor who has a problem he wishes the student to work on. The student is guided by the supervisor. The problem is not owned by the student. This is characteristic of many University departments. The examination paper is a classic exemplar of other-organised learning.

Cell 2 is typified by a department that creates teams of people from different disciplines and requires them to work on a problem the department has set. Southampton University follow such a scheme for their engineering students.

Cell 3 is typified by a department requiring students to identify a range of possible client needs amongst local small to medium size enterprises (SMEs) and working on it alone (or exceptionally in a pair). Given a free choice, based on HND Computing Information Systems projects at Brunel, the relative frequencies of working alone (solo) are as follows:
> 1996: solo 73%, pair 27%;
> 1997: solo 93%, pair 7%;
> 1998: solo 100%, pair 0%.

Cell 4 is typified by a group of people meeting to plan their learning *ab initio*. This unusual aproach is typified by the MBA run at Roffey Park for Sussex University. This is based on Self Managed Learning (SML) lines. Students work part-time in sets of six on a project to plan the content, learning, budgeting and approval mechanisms for their own assessment in the first year of the course. The resulting extended essay has to be approved, by both the other members of the set and the external examiner, before progression can take place.

This paper focuses on a change in approach from cell 1 to cell 3 (with elements of cell 4 being allowed).

However other classifications exist. Following Gray [8] the current organisation of Projects may be categorised in three ways. The first is a "Loose programme model" with little control or observation. Gray then describes a second in which he describes super-projects as a Programme. (Bringing home 45-95 student projects is itself an example of a super-project or programme. Gray's ideas here have particular relevance to all University departments, with regard to theses and projects that must be completed in volume.) These consist of a number of projects which are controlled by a central programme management unit. This may be termed a "Strong programme model". A possible exemplar might be a central University registry unit organising examinations during an examination fortnight. He then refers to learning organisations to identify a third model: the "Open programme model". In this the possibility exists for Project Managers to have easy access to information on the objectives, progress and deliverables in other projects without demanding synchronicity between projects.

It is this Open programme model, in conjunction with a Rogerian aproach to Self-Organised Learning, which may be a future model for student projects in Higher Education. **Constructed meaning** is shared between students, meaning is **rehearsed** and **articulated**, learning is promoted and exposed to appropriate and timely criticism, the whole is orchestrated by a **learning coach** and good practice may be passed around a department.

The current student/supervisor or "Loose programme model" may be sketched, using systems analysis notation, as follows in Figure 2

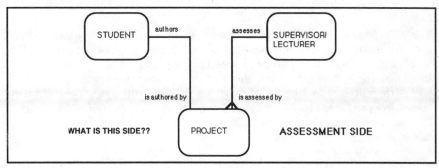

Figure 2

- A Lecturer assesses one or more Projects, each Project must be assessed by one Lecturer.
- Each Student authors one and only one Project, each Project is authored by one Student.

The right hand side is predominantly about assessment. Other relationships might be "the lecturer manages many projects". That would suggest the lecturer has a project management function.

What is happening on the left hand side? Learning? Certainly not teaching. As it stands not very much is learned about student learning under the student/supervisor organisation scheme. During the final year, this paper suggests, we do not really <u>know</u> very much about what happens to students and their **learning** on the left hand side. Perhaps we should know a lot more than we do. If we did know more about student learning possibly that knowledge would validate the quality of the assessment process. A benefit might be that plagiarism would fade away.

## 3      The Implications Of The Knowledge Era

As Don Tapscott [9] suggests there are **six** big new learning themes in our networked Knowledge Era. These are listed below:-:

- Increasingly, work and learning are becoming the same thing.
- Learning is becoming a life long challenge.
- Learning is shifting away from the formal schools and Universities.
- Some educational institutions are working hard to reinvent themselves for relevance. But progress is slow.
- Organisational consciousness is required to create learning organisations
- The new media can transform education, creating a working-learning *infostructure* for the Digital Economy.

Or, more simply, **one big theme - learning to learn.**

The MIT Media Lab, in conjunction with sponsors Lego and Nintendo, has explored the relationship between playing and learning. They are finding the best learning comes from **passion**. Passion may be instilled by teachers, passion should be felt by students. Once the student's passion for his/her project has ignited it will sustain him/her through to a successful conclusion. Passion comes from self-interest and an awareness of its value to oneself and to others. One senses rewards and the possibility of recognition. Dr Marshall touches on this in row 11 of Figure 3 below.

Perhaps we cannot put passion on the curriculum. But what about something like this as a process of building passion in our students? I suggest we ask students, at a series of presentations, to <u>articulate</u> their views on their project work under the following headings:

- **Self organised learning:** models of active generative learning, articulation of purpose, choosing to learn, learning styles; psychology of learning.

- **Aspiration:** the desire to do well, the will to complete, the production of an impressive portfolio of work, the determination to produce a fully authored high-quality multimedia system.; the need to impress others with professional attitudes. Good work habits. Professionalism

- **Motivation:** theories of motivation, awareness of personality types, team roles, the need to lead others v the need to follow others; the nature of management.

We are aware of societal change which includes the abolition of the binary divide, the expansion of University places, the reduction of student grants and the "decline in donnish dominion" (*pace* Halsey). We are aware also of technological change - such as such as cable, Web, compact disc and video - and its impact society and universities. The emergence of the World Wide Web (WWW) however seems to be having a big impact on the lecturer's role. Tapscott suggests the lecturers' role is being **redefined**

- <u>away from</u> being a FACT REPEATER

- <u>towards becoming</u> **both** MOTIVATOR **and** FACILITATOR

There is evidence of this move away from 'fact repeater' to 'motivator and facilitator' happening around us. Colleagues at Brunel, in the Division of Business Studies, are beginning to use the Web to store notes and make slide show tutorials available to students on their Web pages. No doubt that activity is replicated at many Universities in England now.

This FACILITATOR role is emerging strongly at Brunel on the Web - albeit at a distance. It is commonplace for students at Brunel (Business Division) to find lecturer's notes on the Web, to find slide shows that make active and interesting points on the subject of study. Some lecturers have developed whole sites dedicated to various areas of interest such as (i) Business Organisation and (ii) Wine Industries. Brunel central administration publishes examination timetables on the Web too. There is no doubt the Web intranet is being used for the facilitator role.

But what of the MOTIVATOR role? Where is the **passion**? Where is the challenge to students' learning, aspirations and motivation? How do we cultivate student <u>determination</u> - such an important trait amongst researchers? Where is that indefinable something that MOTIVATES students so that they become determined to do well. Do we see ourselves as motivators? Should we? What are we here for: - <u>Fact Repeater</u> **or** <u>Motivator and Facilitator</u>? How do we turn **student work avoidance** into **student work commitment?**

How do we get students to stop thinking of **"This is stuff we have to regurgitate"** and to start saying **"This is meat and drink to me. Let me consume some more."**

How do we get students away from **professing to work** and into **professionalism at their work?**

As Tapscott [10] says:

> The job of classroom teachers (/ lecturers) will become more like that of a <u>coach.</u>

It is as if our Web based students are saying "Give me the motivation, give me the tools and leave the rest to me!". Harri-Augstein & Thomas [11] point out that:

> Whilst the task supervisor is often highly skilled and informed about the learning domain, he or she is usually not in conversation with a Learning Coach and does not see any need for it. The domain is manipulated and arranged for teaching purposes, not for learning purposes.

Evidently Harri-Augstein & Thomas do feel teaching is getting in the way of learning. Yet they offer a way out of the impasse via a model showing how the learning coach should function. The learning coach, via "learning conversations", gives students the confidence to go ahead and <u>learn</u> on their own. Having explored these approaches on the two HNDs in Information Systems Multimedia Production course, I am finding this to be the case. I feel HE needs to adopt a new role in the use of its staff to support learning on computing projects: that role is the <u>learning coach</u>

Coaching is subtle. It has to be flexible. In this instance it attempts to get students to learn how to learn to do projects. To move the student from competence to commitment the coach must examine each student's confidence and motivation. Confidence is derived from self-esteem and assuredness, whereas motivation is derived from interest and enthusiasm for the task in hand. With competence and commitment, generative learning may take place.

As Dr Stephanie Marshall said in her address to the RSA (*op cit*):

> Generative learning and the creation of knowledge are the core competencies underlying the future health and sustainability of all our institutions and social systems; **the quality of our future is inextricably connected to our capacity to learn**; this capacity and the creativity and imagination it evokes, will be the new source and measure of wealth in the knowledge era.

This is important. Dr Marshall is directly assessing the implications of the Knowledge Era. Why does she hold the above view? She holds this view because, she believes, our view of education is fatally flawed.    Marshall has identified what she calls **twelve erroneous assumptions**. These are listed in Fig 3 (with my italicised comments):-

| # | Erroneous Assumption | Should be |
|---|---|---|
| 1 | Learning is passive and incremental | ...dynamic and developmental |
| 2 | Learning is acquired information | ...constructed meaning and pattern formulation |
| 3 | Potential & capability are finite & bounded. Cannot be enhanced | ...can be enhanced |
| 4 | Intelligence is a fixed capacity. It is not learnable. (*analogy - you cannot change your sex.*) | ... not fixed. It is learnable. (*analogy - you can change / improve your fitness*) |

| 5 | Learning is defined by the calendar and not by demonstrations of and performances of understanding (*take Mathematics exam on this day and <u>not</u> on that day.*) | ...learning is defined by demonstrations of and performances of understanding and not by the calendar (*take the Driving test when you are ready.*) |
|---|---|---|
| 6 | More important is content coverage and reproduction (*DELINEATION & IMITATION*) | ... more important is genuine understanding. (*ILLUMINATION & CREATION*) |
| 7 | Best is rote memory (*The reproduced word perfect answer*) | ... best is spatial memory. (*Seeing relationships between things.*) |
| 8 | Prior knowledge is unimportant for future learning (*We will do it to you. See comment about Monty Roberts later.*) | .... prior knowledge is important for future learning (*You have to develop from where you are.*) |
| 9 | Best is context segmentation (*EPISTEMOLOGICAL - how what we know fits together*) | ... best is concept integration (*ONTOLOGICAL - becoming more knowledgeable*) |
| 10 | Reliable evaluation can only be objective and external. It is not connected within real world settings. (*MULTIPLE CHOICE TEST*) | ... reliable evaluation is qualitative and self correcting and is in the real world. (*MEANINGFUL CONVERSATION*) |
| 11 | Competition and external rewards are the most powerful motivators - not collaboration. (*POSITION*) | ...collaboration and internal rewards are the most powerful motivators - not competition. (*PASSION*) |
| 12 | Primary conditions of thoughtfulness are clarity, certainty, agreement, important answers and unambiguousness (these are thought to be tough and have rigour) (*PLATO analogy - he gave what he thought were important answers*) | ...primary conditions of thoughtfulness are mystery, uncertainty, disagreement, important questions and ambiguity. (-but some would say these are soft and are lacking in rigour.) (*SOCRATES analogy -he asked important questions*) |

Figure 3

We seem to be looking at something like McGregor's Theory X and Y . (With the emphasis in the right hand column - the Y.)

The point is these erroneous assumptions justify the notion of the <u>powerful teacher and a powerless learner</u> and a "one size fits all" system that stifles the student's natural desire to learn. It is the perfect description for training - the efficient and prescribed delivery of information and skills **but not for learning.** As Harri-Augstein & Thomas point out [12] "...(institutions) assume that if you teach, then people learn".

The *current* management of projects in higher education seems to me to resemble "the powerful teacher and the powerless learner".

Marshall goes on to say:

> If we want to create powerful self-directed, collaborative and adaptive inquiries, we must ground our educational transformation and our leadership in the science of our times (how the brain works, chaos theory, emergence, integration and not reductionism ...)... we must **create learning communities** that encourage the purposeful and soulful engagement of student in their work.
>
> We must move away from isolated classrooms and unconnected schools to the creation of learning communities.

As learning organisations, Universities and Higher Education would want to create learning communities, surely?

Monty Roberts [13], the world famous horse trainer, reduced the time taken to break-in a wild horse from six weeks to three hours. To do this he eschewed the traditional methods ... and it was the insight into the true nature of learning given him by a teacher at school. This quote is his book:

> The most influential teacher in my educational career was a nun by the name of Sister Agnes Patricia. The thing I will always remember about her is that she taught me about teaching itself. It was her belief that no teacher could ever teach anyone anything. She felt her task as a teacher was to create a learning environment in which the student can learn.
>
> Her opinion was that knowledge needs to be pulled into the brain by the student, not pushed into it by the teacher. Knowledge was not to be forced on a student. The brain has to be receptive, malleable and most importantly desirous of that knowledge.
>
> I apply the same philosophy to training horses. ....**There is no such thing as teaching, only learning**.

Perhaps we need to change our attitudes to teaching and learning to enjoy results akin to Monty Roberts. Self Organised Learning represents such a change in attitude.

# 4 Self Organised Learning

## 4.1 What is SOL?

SOL proponents Harri-Augstein & Thomas [14] define learning as "the conversational construction of personally significant, relevant and viable meaning" and meaning as "purposeful patterns of thoughts and feelings which are the basis of our anticipations and actions". Harri-Augstein & Webb [15] give a fuller discussion of Self Organised Learning in their book "Learning to change".

Motivating students in their project work is a challenge. What is to be done if, as Monty Roberts states, "there is no such thing as teaching, only learning"? This is where both **Self Organised Learning (SOL)** applied to student negotiated project work, together with concurrent teaching on Project Management, has proved to be so useful to me. With its anatomy of seven different learning conversations SOL gives a very powerful approach to coaching Project work. It is based on the idea that 'learning is the construction of meaning'. The long time span (30 weeks) allocated to student projects gives opportunities to apply SOL techniques.

Indeed, SOL's System 7 gives an insight into a *range* of learning conversations with significant people other than the students themselves. SOL's System Seven can be applied effectively to a department to improve its learning support, resources and learning policies.

There are other approaches than SOL. Morris [16] has argued that Self Organised Learning together with a study of Project Management is comparable to the Problem Based Learning techniques used so extensively and successfully in the the field of medical education. Self Managed Learning (SML) has been mentioned earlier as practised at Roffey Park with 'sets' of managers on MBA courses. But, in my view, SOL offers the most comprehensive approach to student centred computing projects in HE.

## 4.2 SOL in Action.

I take all the Project students in HND year two for Project seminars one morning a week all year. This is a timetabled slot. The focus is primarily learning (nevertheless the efficiency gains are a nice by-product.) Essentially, the students tell me what they are thinking of doing on their Project. They are together in a group. Their interest is very "peaky" - with highs and lows - starting with the enormity of what they are about to do. They are shown past projects - all nicely produced. I go into **learning coach** mode. The **trigger question** is asked

> "Do you want to be holding in your hands in a years time your very own project? Do you want to be able to show it to a future employer with pride? Do you realise hundreds of students have been in precisely the position you are in now and have won through to success?" ...

Then I start to manage students' projects. We have a shared interest: the student wants to successfully complete his project, I as learning coach want to bring home thirty successfully completed projects. I have to be responsible for a super-project or Programme to use Gray's phrase.

It seems natural to teach "_project management_" at these sessions. It is the most natural thing for me to talk about whenever students have nothing to say. Perhaps I should call it "Project management for learning".

Once started I require students to (a) identify three projects that are of interest to them, (b) select one from the three identified by generating criteria, building a spread sheet, scoring projects for criteria and weighting the criteria, and (c) developing a feasibility study which scopes the main areas in the project. All of these are via ten minute presentations followed by questions and answers. Each encounter with a student, in front of his colleagues, lasts around 20 - 30 minutes.

This can be seen more clearly in Figure 4 . This is an elaboration of figure 1, but with greater attention paid to the learning side.

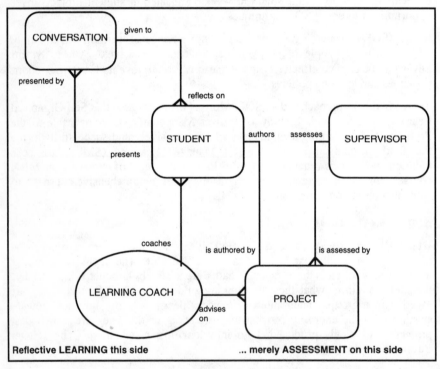

Figure 4

Notice two new entities have been added. The first is the 'conversation' which includes the presentation given by the student and the comments on it by other students and assessors. The second entity is the 'learning coach' who (i) advises on the project - both specifically and generally- and (ii) coaches the student by pointing out ways work may be improved and suggesting there are dangers that might be profitably avoided.

To get through the whole group of say 25 to 30 students takes a semester. Some might wonder "Why waste time?". The simple response is that the initial stage of project selection is the most uncertain and the most hazardous. It is important to ensure the student is choosing the right project for him/her. At this point of project selection "Why this project? What does it consist of?" are relevant questions.

At this stage "How do I progress this project?" is irrelevant. Students are inclined to rush into something they think is acceptable. The learning coach should ensure students remain focused on **why-what** questions at the beginning of the project and keep them off **what-how** questions till their project has been identified, selected and shown to be feasible.

Traditionally, students are not required to demonstrate their project's acceptability over a longish period of time - it is common practice to accept three hundred words at the beginning of the academic year as the Project Outline. This paper suggests this is too little, too early. Requiring students to justify what they hope to do in a more elaborate and student centred way seems to pay dividends. For once students know they are doing the right project they can then concentrate on doing that project 'right'.

In the early stages of project selection students come to see the value of Checkland's [17] Soft Systems Methodology (SSM). It encourages them to respond to their own questions - such as: "Why must I do a project? Why do I want to do something in my best area? Why do I want to impress an employer with a well produced project report?" SSM, in root definitions, invites students to consider a world view! This quite overwhelms some students. They have become so accustomed to other-organised learning that it is difficult for them to articulate their self-organised learning. That is a dire commentary on the learning experience of much of HE. In this early phase SSM helps the student select the project right for him/her..

During this phase the students need to be supported by the learning coach. The learning conversations may leave them downhearted - but, to follow a sporting analogy, better to be down hearted on the training ground than on the pitch during the big match. Having been exhorted to keep their shape, at the end of the first semester of the final year real learning kicks in.

## 4.3 Application Of Self Organised Learning

How is SOL applied to a typical cohort of HND Computing students? What do students do at their Project / Project Management seminars? Students are informed and reminded of the general processes and procedures for carrying out their project.

A set of graded assessment elements for negotiating HND Computing project work, used at Brunel, is as follows:

## HND Computing Project 199*

All elements are assessed directly by two or more assessors.

**Elements**

Element 1 is assessed by three presentations to the group and the learning coach with the occasional assistance of any relevant available staff.

Elements 2, 3, 4 were assessed by two people - learning coach and assessor.

Element 5 is assessed by two assessors (excluding the learning coach) - employers are invited to attend.

**1= Seminar Activities, (drawn out over four months October to January)**

    a.      presentation at which three possible projects were identified (October)

    b.      articulated reasons for project selected with students own criteria (November / December)

    c.      feasibility study presented, with handouts, to class, (January / February)

**2=Demonstration to two lecturers, (a key event in late May** - the second assessor and the learning coach are present as the student demonstrates the system built and field questions on his/her report. This normally takes 45 minutes per student. Four students are dealt with by these two assessors in a single session of a morning or an afternoon.)

    a.      demonstrated content showed student had a good grasp of subject

    b.      demonstration was logical, clear and comprehensive

    c.      demonstration had style and was well prepared

**3= Breadth & Presentation of Report, (a key event in late May - see 2)**

    a.      produced artefact would not embarrass an employer

    b.      showed perception in recording facts and overcoming difficulties in report

    c.      proposed solutions that were adequate and relevant

**4= Depth and technical grasp in the report. (a key event in May - see 2)**

    a.      exhibits strong design features and use of tools

    b.      shows evidence of significant technical learning

    c.      evident the report is complete with concise and realistic conclusion

**5=Presentation to first year. (last week of course, June, establishes a feedback loop with the year below.)**

    a.      explained technical issue in depth to year 1 - an audience of forty students

    b.      presented a range of technical issues in breadth to year 1

    c.      gave a well prepared and interesting slide-show presentation to year 1

It is emphasised the Project is an important piece of work. Then at the first seminars students are reminded of my request that they find three clients with relevant and interesting information system needs. They are required to have something to say: they must tell me and the rest of the group what they are thinking of doing. They will negotiate their way towards a viable project. Not in a casual way, but in rather a formal way via a **presentation with evidence** (evidence brought to the group from outside). The presentations are all standardised to ten minutes and are carefully timed. For the presentations acceptable evidence would be letters, forms, and other details from potential project. Evidence of some kind of negotiation with the outside world is required. After all, an HND is a vocational course.

But they are in my place, standing up at the front of the class, giving a ten minute presentation while I sit with the students - as a listener. The body language is completely different to what they are used to. They feel the scrutiny, and I maintain it focuses their minds wonderfully. The group is invited to ask the student questions about the presenter's reasons for choosing a particular Project idea. A student might ask why the acetates have been hand written. Another might suggest the presenter use a friend to place the acetates on the overhead projector thereby giving the presenter an opportunity to pause, relax and collect his thoughts.

Essentially the focus is on reality. In his rejection of what he terms 'narrative education' Paulo Freire [18] proposes a 'problem-posing' model of education which "... presupposes a dialogical situation in which teachers and students confront reality and help each other to reflect on it critically". He goes on to say:

> Whereas (narrative) education anaesthetizes and inhibits creative power, problem-posing education involves a constant unveling of reality. The former attempts to maintain the submersion of consciousness; the latter strives for the emergence of consciousness and critical intervention in in reality.

This is what Marshall calls **generative real-world activity**. I am really trying to get the students to set themselves small achievable problems. I am trying to get them to organise themselves. I am trying to get them to construct and articulate their meanings as they negotiate through - with all its uncertainty and ambiguity - what Patching [19] terms a 'Human Activity System (HAS)'.

I am trying to get them to do what interests them. I am trying to get them to step back and look at the big picture, to use soft systems, to realise they are in a HAS and, to use Ackoff's memorable phrase, " must become involved **in mess management"** and later become involved in **"a logic of creativity".** I try to follow a Rogerian approach and put myself at the students feet. I want them to know I am attending to what they have to say.

As time goes by the other students stop watching and slowly start participating. They begin to ask questions, to push their colleague, to air their private worries in the guise of a general question, to discuss what was said. Both presence and anonymity are guaranteed. They are present while presentations and questions are taking place, and yet because the subject matter is so important to them they reflect on their thoughts privately and anonymously. The project experience is no longer isolated and fragmented - rather it is communal and thought about.

As Harri-Augstein & Webb suggest [20] the learning coach needs to support the student during the early softer stages of SOL. Student competence varies throughout the thirty weeks of the project. This is represented diagrammatically below in Figure 5.

In phase 1 time is spent ensuring students understand the process of negotiating their way to a project of their choice. In phase 2 time is spent supporting students through a possible loss of confidence. In phase 3 students may define personal criteria for success.

However no specific evidence is cited to justify the supposition that learning coach **support** is needed for Computing project work. The grades for the first three presentations in Element 1 were used to monitor student changes in competence as measured by grades given for presentation performance. On HND courses the top grade is Distinction (D), the second grade is Merit (M) and the last sussesful grade is Pass (P). Work that is not satisfactory is graded Fail (F). Thus in comparative terms D > M > P > F.

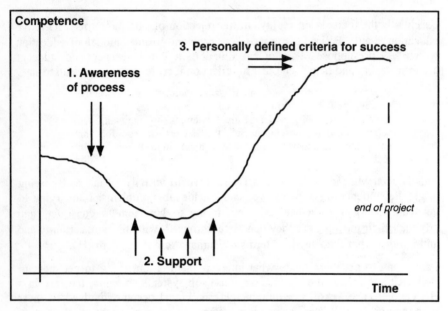

Figure 5

From Figure 5, the change in competence from Sepember to late October suggests a loss in perfomance. The change in competence from late October to December suggests a gain in perfomance. The change in competence from December to late January suggests no change in perfomance. The evidence that students' performance drops in phase 2 is apparent from the evidence in Figure 6. Then, after support during phase 2, competence picks up as students' awareness increases as they realize and internalize what they need to do personally.

There is indicative evidence to show that this support is necessary - particularly during the first half of the project from October to February in each academic year from 1995-96, 1996-97 and 1997-98. In the grids below, for these three successive academic years, the modal categories are highlighted in bold (see Figure 6, Figure 7, Figure 8).

| Performance for AY 95-96 | 1 (Oct) | 2 (Dec) | 3 (Feb) | 4 (Jun) |
|---|---|---|---|---|
|  | 1995 | 1995 | 1996 | 1996 |
| Gain | 09% | **68%** | 05% | 13% |
| As expected | 27% | 27% | **68%** | **50%** |
| Drop | **64%** | 05% | 27% | 37% |
| *22 students* |  |  |  |  |

Figure 6.

In Figure 6 the students enter the second year expecting to do reasonably well. There is an expectation they will do good work worthy of a Merit grade. In the first presentation students identify three possible clients and the project associated with each client. This presentation is given to their peers, with me in the audience as coach and assessor. Their expected performance drops. It is quite a shock to many students: 64% do not do as well as they expected.

Time passes and students watch other students do as badly as they did. This gives a perverse pleasure, but equally a real desire to know what they must do to improve. At the second presentation students generate criteria for choosing a project and score each criteria with points on a scale of their choosing. Some students rate certain criteria more impoortantly than others and so a weighting is introduced. To stop any one view dominating the project selection process, around fifteen criteria are looked for. In Figure 6, column two, there is a performance gain - 68% of students improve compared to their performance in presentation 1.

Students are supported as a group by the learning coach throughout this period. At the third presentation, there is not much change in the level of performance compared to the second presentation.

Finally, in column four, the final overall grade is compared with the performance at presentation three. The 'as expected' category is dominant just as in column three. A specualtion might be that column three is a good predictor of column four the final module grade. Certainly the period between February and June is characterside by students becoming very purposive and focused about their project. They are even ready to identify factors assessors should take into account when assessing the student's project.

| Performance   for AY 96-97 | 1 (Oct) | 2 (Dec) | 3 (Feb) | 4 (Jun) |
|---|---|---|---|---|
| | 1996 | 1996 | 1997 | 1997 |
| Gain | 14% | **56%** | 11% | **58%** |
| As expected | 28% | 24% | 28% | 28% |
| Drop | **58%** | 21% | **62%** | 14% |
| *29 students* | | | | |

Figure 7.

In Figure 7 for academic year 96-97 there is evidence of a drop after presentation 1, followed by a gain after presentation 2. There was a drop in performance at presentation 3 from which students bounced back at the end of the course in column four. The idea of using column three as a predictor for column four is negated.

In the current academic year the final grades for projects will be available in June. The data so far in Figure 8 indicates a similar pattern to figures 4 & 5. There is a drop in expected performance. Students become aware of the project processes. They are supported to December and an improvement in performance results. By February they are performing as expected.

By the time students get the marksheet for the project demonstration they are ready to specify criteria that may be taken into account by assessors. This will happen for the first time in May this year.

| Performance   for AY 97-98 | 1 (Oct) | 2 (Dec) | 3 (Feb) | 4 (Jun) |
|---|---|---|---|---|
| | 1997 | 1997 | 1998 | 1998 |
| Gain | 22% | **52%** | 04% | *NA* |
| As expected | 33% | 33% | **56%** | *NA* |
| Drop | **44%** | 15% | 41% | *NA* |
| *27 students* | | | | |

Figure 8.

This process of negotiation promotes generative learning, and in my view, motivates the students. But to what extent should we be motivators? And to what extent is this connected to Project Management? This is discussed in the next section.

# 5 Project Management, Motivation and Soft Systems Methodology

## 5.1 Project Management Principles

The Association for Project Management (APM) has published a Body of Knowledge [21] - it is what a formal Project Manager should know. There are forty (40) competence statements in it. The Body of Knowledge only once mentions motivation and learning. Interestingly motivation is in its definition of Project Management. It defines Project Management as

> 1.3 - the planning, organisation, monitoring and control of all aspects of a project and the **motivation** of all involved to achieve the project objectives safely and within agreed time, cost and performance criteria.

Learning is mentioned in a rather wide and impersonal sense as in

> 1.12 -Post Project Appraisal
>
> Post Project Appraisal, sometimes called the Post Project Evaluation, completes the project management process once the product is in use. It provides feed-back in order to **learn** for the future. There are two main stages:
>
> 1) immediately, to apply the lessons **learned** to the next project
>
> 2) A longer term review to determine what, if any, adjustments should be made to company policies and procedures.

The methodology PRINCE recommends use of presentations to monitor project progress. There is a case for widening its scope, in the context of student computing projects, away from detector purposes to include both detector and effector purposes. Particularly in relation to student learning.

## 5.2 Motivation to learn

The reference to motivation (1.3 above) does imply people. Compare Tapscott's "Motivator and facilitator" with the APM definition of Project Management "planner... and motivator" and we have a happy overlap in aims. Good learning and good Project Management can go hand in hand.

However this definition seems to *assume* we know precisely what the project is. For other-organised work this is the case. But this is not the situation our students are in. If they are required to exercise their creativity in order to improve their learning they have the problem of identifying which project to do before deciding how to best carry it out. This is where SSM is so useful and so rich.

The reference to learning (1.12 above) represents too little too late - it occurs at the post Project Appraisal. In my appraisal of projects it seems sensible to give appraisal - individually and severally - throughout the life-cycle on a regular basis.

Don Tapscott suggests the lecturer should be both facilitator and motivator? The Web will not motivate students learning even though it may facilitate learning. Many students cannot motivate themselves. This paper maintains there is a new and emerging role in Higher Education for lecturers - namely the learning coach.

There is, in my view, a qualitative sense of purpose and control in adopting the learning coach approach. The coach detects errors as they arise at presentations and in assessing presentations directly gives timely advice that effectimportant changes in each students attitude to their learning and work..

Incorporating the idea of the Learning Coach, Figure 4, and reflection on learning, into the earlier diagram, on the left hand side, it becomes a richer model for managing projects - or, following Gray, an Open programme model.

This learning coach approach is closer to the student, more is found out about each students work directly and from an early stage. The student constructs his/her meaning, then he/she shares meaning with the group. "**Sharing meaning**" has a powerful effect on students' learning. Nothing someone wants to discuss is excluded.

Students become constructively critical. The quality of their questions improves as time goes by. The learning coach gives advice after each ten minute presentation and question-and-answer session. Students critique each others work. They each share a collaborative experience; they feel they can learn from others and others, equally, can learn from them.

Consequently the **quality** of both assessment and learning is better. The students' work becomes known by a wider group - they can enjoy a fellow student's work / presentation / successful project.

## 5.3    Systems Thinking: situating the student.

Yeo [22] in the conclusion to his imaginative paper "Systems thinking and project management - time to reunite" says (with my emphases):

> "The author of this paper considers the work on Soft Systems
> Methodology as a **complement** to traditional systems  thinking
> to be important to the field of project management. The secret of
> success in project management, as in any other field of
> management, is **learning**, especially when dealing with **soft,  ill
> structured and initially ambiguous problem situations**. The
> learning has to be **continual, purposeful** and **focused**. The
> **learning process that is stimulating and purposeful brings
> fulfilment and meaning to those who are involved**, in the
> course of helping to contribute to the overall objectives."

Yeo points to the importance of both learning and particularly making choices in the early stages where projects are soft, ill-structured and unclear. In my experience of using SOL in conjuction with Checkland & Scholes [23] soft systems methods I believe Yeo's conjecture is correct.

# 6    Conclusion And The Way Ahead

Since October 1997 student presentations have been put on to the Web for later consultation,further feedback and a record of what has been said. This will be evaluated in the future. But primarily the following points have been part of my experience over the past few years:

- the student constructs meaning,

- the student shares meaning,

- the learning coach explores the student's meaning,

- the other students learn to evaluate a wide range of relevant shared meanings,

- the "conversations" are indicators of emergent purposive activity,

- the cohort keeps its shape in a joint yet individual learning experience,

- students become reflective about their own learning,

- the learning coach practices motivation and wants to learn about motivation

- the mess of learning and variation in motivation is managed,

- colleagues appreciate what has occurred

This process is collaborative, it is real, it is about learning (rather than emphasising assessment), the effective individual learner becomes part of a high performance group - not isolated with a once-a-month supervisor.    Students develop an *esprit de corps*.    They are motivated to do well.    They enjoy the achievements of other students who do well. A learning community emerges.

With the students negotiating as much as possible of the Computing Project they rapidly acquire a sense of ownership of both their project and their learning. However a key question is "Does this learning coach model transfer to other people who wish to follow the learning coach role within the University or between Universities?".    Some might say this evidence is based on one individual for whom it works: it does not follow it will work for other people. Under what conditions does the learning coach role transfer to others (if at all)?

Further, it may be argued that if doing projects is a good way to learn then students should carry out a Project every year so that the learning community emerging in year 1 becomes a better learning community in year 2 and finally becomes a superb learning community in year 3. It will make an interesting study to see to what extent Universities have a project at each level of their courses.

Negotiated creative work has been included in part within HND assignments at Brunel.    This attempts to keep the creative spirit alive and promote learning autonomy.

The implications for recruiting researchers in a department are profound. Would Ph. D completion rates increase if this approach was adopted and the necessary organisational anatomy created?

These are open questions, but one thing is sure: the situation for me, managing super-projects or an Open Programme, is so different to the *status quo ante* and is so much more fulfilling. As J Burdett [24] suggests coaching is poorly understood. The application of SOL at Brunel University has made more comrehensible the process of coaching students doing computing projects.

## References

[1] Marshall, S. Does education and training get in the way of learning?. Proceedings of the RSA, Vol CXLV No 5477 p 37-38. RSA, London, January 1997.

[2] Tiplady, D. Presentation notes on behalf of UNISYS. EPCOS conference Leeds University in January 1998.

[3] Ackoff,R. The Art & Science of mess management, Interfaces 1981; Vol 11, No 1 pp 20-26. In: Mabey, C & Mayon-White, B (ed): Managing change (2nd edition). Chapman, London, 1993.

[4] Rogers, C. Personal Thoughts on Teaching and Learning. In: Kirschenbaum, H & Henderson, V (ed): The Carl Rogers Reader. Constable, London, 1990.

[5] Rogers, C. The Interpersonal Relationship in the Facilitation of Learning. In: Kirschenbaum, H & Henderson, V (ed): The Carl Rogers Reader. Constable, London, 1990.

[6] Harri-Augstein S & Thomas, L. Learning conversations. Routledge, London, 1991.

[7] Harri-Augstein, S & Webb, I. Learning to Change. McGraw Hill, London, 1995.

[8] Gray, R. Alternative approaches to programme management. International Journal of Project Management 1997;Vol 15, No1 pp 5-9.

[9] Tapscott, D. The Digital Economy. McGraw Hill, New York, 1995.

[10 ibid, page 207

[11] ibid, ref 6

[12] ibid, page 224

[13] Roberts, M. The man who listens to horses. Arrow, London, 1997, p 133.

[14] ibid, pp 6-7

[15] ibid, reference 7

[16] Morris, B. Project Management *is* problem based learning. Problem Based Learning Conference, Brunel University, Uxbridge, 1997.

[17] Checkland, P. Systems Thinking, Systems Practice, John Wiley, Chichester, 1981.

[18] Freire, P. The Pedagogy of the Oppressed. Penguin, London, 1972.

[19] Patching, D. Practical Soft Systems Analysis. Pitman, London, 1990.

[20] ibid, p 56

[21]     Association of Project Management (http://www.apm.org.uk/ as at 6 April 1998) The APM address is 85 Oxford Road, High Wycombe, UK

[22]     Yeo, T Y.   Systems thimking and project management - time to reunite. International Journal of Project Management Vol 11, No 2 pp 111 - 117, 1993

[23]     Checkland, P, and Scholes, J.  Soft systems methodology in action. Wiley, Chichester, 1990.

[24]     Burdett, J. To coach, or not to coach - that is the question! In: Mabey, C & Iles, P (ed): Managing Learning, Routledge, London, 1994, pp 133 -145.

# PART 5

# Managing Projects

# Computing Science Projects at the University of Glasgow

## Richard Cooper and Ray Welland

Dept. of Computing Science, University of Glasgow, Glasgow G12 8QQ, Scotland

**Abstract**

The Computing Science department makes heavy use of projects for teaching the essential techniques of software development. This paper discusses how we gather, allocate, manage and assess these projects. Clearly, when a large number of projects are involved there needs to be central control of the process and the mechanisms (including IT mechanisms) for simplifying the management are discussed. The paper also shows how the projects provide benefits in terms of administration, teaching and research quite separate from the educative benefit to the students.

## 1    Introduction

Although the teaching of Computing Science must involve a considerable amount of theoretical material, the discipline essentially remains intensely practical. It is impossible to learn to program a computer without writing and testing programs. Creating a database application properly can only be learned by using a database system. Understanding the merits of good user interface design requires both that the student experiences the use of software of all kinds and that he or she can build and evaluate fresh interfaces.

Furthermore, learning how to create large scale, robust applications can only be achieved by having the student participate in the creation of such applications. In doing so, he or she will encounter two kinds of practical difficulty. Firstly, there will be a variety of engineering issues regarding the fitting together of software components. Secondly, there must be issues in relating to others collaborating on the creation of the software – including colleagues in the software implementation, managers of the software design process and customers to whose needs the software is supposed to cater.

It is therefore vital that a Computing Science course provides students with the ability to encounter such difficulties in a structured and supportive environment. Accordingly, we place great emphasis on providing students with significant projects as learning experiences. Moreover, the examination of these projects constitutes a major aspect of the assessment of the student, since only then can we be sure that we are graduating students with the confidence that they are going to be able to apply their learning in practice.

This paper describes the role that project work plays in our courses and discusses management issues regarding the projects, including finding appropriate projects, the allocation process, managing running projects and assessing the resulting dissertation. For a large number of projects, the use of automatic techniques are important in keeping the project co-ordinator's job tractable. It ends with a discussion of the value of projects in teaching computing.

## 2. Computing Science Courses at Glasgow

At the undergraduate level, the Computing Science department at the University of Glasgow provides Honours degree courses in Computing Science and in Software Engineering and contributes to a joint degree in Electronics and Software Engineering as well as to joint Honours degrees with other disciplines. At the postgraduate level, the department offers a taught M.Sc. course in Advanced Information Systems and is the major contributor to the conversion M.Sc. in Information Technology. All of these degrees require that the student submit at least one dissertation based on a significant piece of project work.

Glasgow follows the Scottish undergraduate system in requiring students normally to attend courses for four years. In the first year, a student will typically take modules in three separate subject areas. In the second year, this reduces to modules in two subject areas. Only in the third and fourth year do students focus on the courses of a single discipline – the third year taking them to ordinary degree level and the fourth year to honours degree level. A small number of students take a combined honours course in two subjects. In recent years, we have had students combining computing with mathematics, geography, psychology and history, for instance.

The first and second year students are not given a separate project, although they will certainly be provided with a significant amount of course-based practical work. Third year single Honours students are required to carry out a team project and all fourth year students carry out a solo project (whose scope is somewhat reduced for combined Honours students). Students of both M.Sc. courses complete their year of study with a prolonged project.

Third year team projects run throughout the year concurrently with a Software Engineering course and are intended to reinforce the teaching of techniques for the reliable design of large scale software. At the beginning of the third year, the students carry out a small warm-up project as part of the Software Engineering module. For this project, teams of five or six students are allocated at random, since we feel that this is closer to the reality of working in industry.. Although this is a small scale project, it is intended to illustrate the whole software life cycle from identifying requirements (starting from a deliberately vague specification) through to the production of a working prototype and involving the creation of proper documentation throughout the process.

For their main project, the students work in teams of between four and six people and are made responsible for the whole process of designing and producing a piece of software. Thus, guided by the principles taught in Software Engineering and by the project supervisor, the students must create a working group structure and also appropriate styles of documentation. They must also partition the problem appropriately and create software interfaces that ensure the smooth integration of their individual work.

The fourth year project is tackled alone and requires that the student be able to plan and design software which can be implemented and documented in the time available – a nominal 240 person hours are scheduled for the work on the project, although combined Honours students only have 160 hours.

Students taking their degree in Software Engineering, rather than Computing Science, will have had an industrial placement in the vacation between third and fourth years. The procurement, management and assessment of industrial placements is a significant problem which we are not going to discuss in this paper. However, it is intended that the fourth year project for these students will build upon their summer work in some way. At one extreme, this could mean that students continue software development in conjunction with their summer employer. On the other hand, it may mean that some aspect of the student's summer work generates an interest in a software engineering topic which is pursued in a final year project.

Whereas undergraduate students carry out their project work simultaneously with the rest of their studies, M.Sc. students work on the project only after completing the taught component of the course. Students on the Advanced Information Systems have six months in which to complete a project which relates to the topics of the course – persistent systems, information retrieval, multimedia design, and creative media systems. Information Technology students have three months after their exams to carry out a project which demonstrates the IT skills that they have been taught. Unlike the other projects discussed here, most IT projects are supervised outside of the Computing Science Department (CS), although the management of the projects is managed from CS and all projects are assessed by either a CS academic or by an academic from another department with proven IT skills.

All in all, this means finding and supervising a large number of projects. There are typically around 15 third year projects, 50 fourth year projects and 100 M.Sc. IT projects, plus a small but growing number of M.Sc. AIS projects. This places a considerable workload on the department in terms of finding enough projects, finding supervisors, hardware and software and assessing the resulting dissertation. These problems will be discussed in the succeeding sections.

## 3. Attracting Suitable Projects

Characterising the nature of an appropriate project has recently become much less straightforward. Previously, we could comfortably assert that, at the very least, the student had to demonstrate considerable skill in using a high level programming language. There has now been an explosion of tools that facilitate the software creation process. Integrated packages, database connectivity tools, web site constructors, 4GLs and so on have transformed the process of software manufacture. Although, at base, we still believe that programming ability is fundamental to the competent software engineer, there must now be much more emphasis on the use of tools and the re-use of code.

Consequently, we increasingly see the proposal of projects which, in reality, require a fairly modest amount of coding. However, they do demand that the student master one or, more usually, several software components and learn how to integrate their use. This may vary from the tightly coupled world of Microsoft Access and

Visual Basic to the more loose confederation of a Java program, JDBC and a database system such as FoxPro. At present, we can be fairly comfortable with this kind of project, since there is a lack of suitable documentation – i.e. texts which discuss the fitting together of a particular constellation of components in sufficient generality. The student therefore is engaged in an exploratory task in finding the appropriate implementation route. However, as techniques become standardised, such projects could easily become quite trivial to accomplish. Clearly we need to monitor this situation quite closely.

We therefore typically contrast three kinds of project:

- *Software Engineering Projects.* These require the design and implementation of a significant piece of software. Ideally, the student will produce a succession of design documents – requirements, external design and internal design; implement the software; carry out an evaluation; and then write a dissertation about their work, together with additional documentation such as a user manual and data dictionary.

- *Application Based Projects.* Such projects, of increasing importance, require the student to create a piece of software in the context of pre-existing software tools, such as database systems, office packages or 4GLs. Clearly such projects place much less emphasis on programming skills, rather focussing on the student's design skills and the ability to master one or more complex pieces of software and to integrate their use, by creating an application which uses them. There is usually an expectation that such projects should produce a more polished final application, since the implementation problems should be less acute. It is also expected that the evaluation phase will be carried out more thoroughly. Such projects usually arise from the needs of external customers and, as they have a genuine need for the product, they can be expected to test the product more extensively and a more focussed critical eye, than, for instance can a pool of the student's class mates.

- *Research Projects.* These projects are not mainly concerned with producing a piece of software. Instead they focus on an attempt to understand and improve an exploratory technique. Work on these projects will entail reading the research literature, coming to terms with advanced concepts, suggesting a new development of these concepts and, usually, implementing a piece of software which demonstrates the use of these concepts.

Each class requires a different mix of these three kinds of project. The team projects are usually of the first kind. The fourth year projects can be of any of the three kinds. For instance, students strongly interested in a research career will probably opt for the last. The M.Sc. AIS projects should overwhelmingly have a research flavour. The M.Sc. IT projects, on the other hand, will only rarely have much research content. Graduates on that course need to have demonstrated practical skills and so their projects tend either to be software engineering or application based projects.

We seek project proposals from a variety of sources:

- Academic and research staff in the CS department are asked at regular intervals to propose projects and they respond with proposals which reflect their teaching, research or personal interests. The department has a comprehensive points allocation system for various teaching tasks and project supervision counts towards an academic's target teaching load.

- The students themselves may propose projects that they would like to work on. If a supervisor can be found to manage the supervision then this can be a highly appropriate source of proposals.
- The CS department has strong industrial contacts, including an industrial association, and so proposals from local firms are also frequently available. This can be a very good route with which a student can make contact with a potential employer.
- Finally, (and particularly in the case of the M.Sc. IT) we have projects proposed from elsewhere in the university.

The third and fourth sources are particularly important to us. Our students have benefited greatly from dealing with real customers. Attending lectures about the elicitation of requirements and the problems of interacting with customers is no substitute for actually doing it! However, it is necessary to compromise between the customers' product requirements and the academic objectives of project work.

In order to make proposing a project much simpler, we have created an HTML form for submission. At present, this is only in place for the M.Sc. IT with its more distributed proposer base, but it is envisaged that this will be used by the other courses in time. Figure 1 shows the form for the M.Sc. IT.

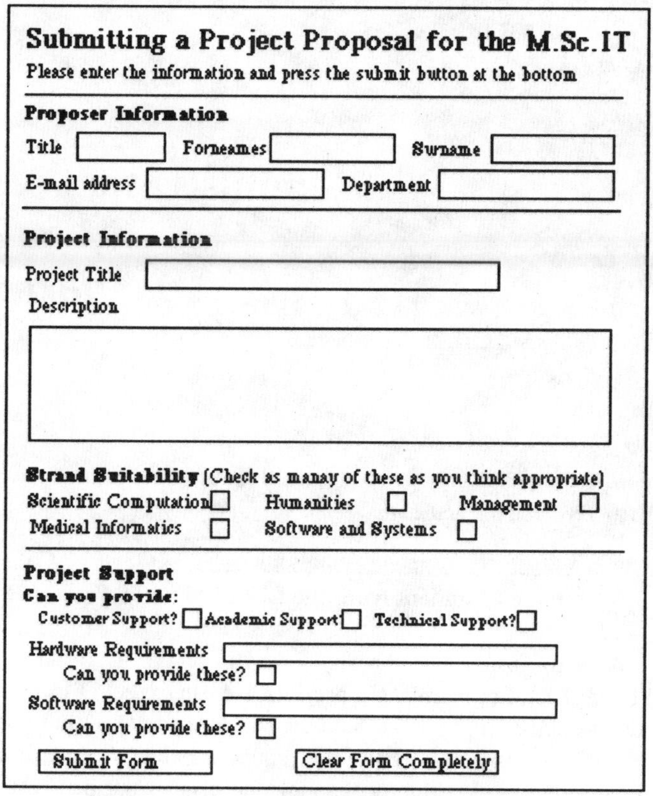
**Submitting a Project Proposal for the M.Sc.IT**

Please enter the information and press the submit button at the bottom

**Proposer Information**

Title ☐ Forneames ☐ Surname ☐

E-mail address ☐ Department ☐

**Project Information**

Project Title ☐

Description

**Strand Suitability** (Check as manay of these as you think appropriate)

Scientific Computation ☐ Humanities ☐ Management ☐

Medical Informatics ☐ Software and Systems ☐

**Project Support**

**Can you provide:**

Customer Support? ☐ Academic Support ☐ Technical Support? ☐

Hardware Requirements ☐

Can you provide these? ☐

Software Requirements ☐

Can you provide these? ☐

Submit Form | Clear Form Completely

**Figure 1. Submission Form for the M.Sc. IT**

The form firstly asked basic details about the proposer and then the project and its description which is entered in a text area, preferably as HTML source. The rest of the form requires a little more explanation. Firstly, the M.Sc. is divided into a number of strands, with the qualification reading, for instance, M.Sc. in Information Technology (Health Informatics). If the student wishes to gain that qualification, then firstly, he or she must take the appropriate modules, but secondly, the project taken must be deemed suitable. The form allows proposers to indicate the strands for which the project is suitable. Each strand has a designated co-ordinator and he or she vets the proposals that are indicated as being suitable. This constitutes a preliminary acceptance test, a further check being made once the project is underway.

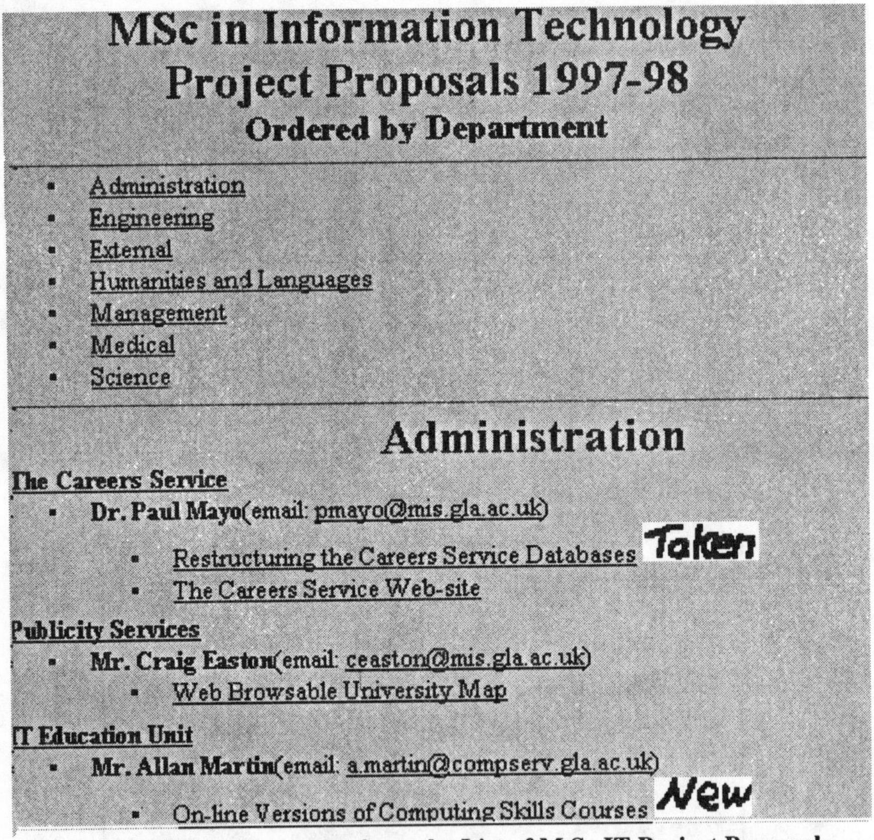

# MSc in Information Technology
# Project Proposals 1997-98
### Ordered by Department

* Administration
* Engineering
* External
* Humanities and Languages
* Management
* Medical
* Science

# Administration

**The Careers Service**
* Dr. Paul Mayo(email: pmayo@mis.gla.ac.uk)
    * Restructuring the Careers Service Databases *Taken*
    * The Careers Service Web-site

**Publicity Services**
* Mr. Craig Easton(email: ceaston@mis.gla.ac.uk)
    * Web Browsable University Map

**IT Education Unit**
* Mr. Allan Martin(email: a.martin@compserv.gla.ac.uk)
    * On-line Versions of Computing Skills Courses *New*

**Figure 2  Web Page Fragment from the List of M.Sc.IT Project Proposals**

Next we need to ensure that the student will receive adequate support while working on the project. For internal CS projects, we can expect of the supervisor that he or she have the ability (a) to understand the problem domain; (b) to be a qualified academic supervisor; and (c) to have the required technical expertise. If any of these are lacking then will certainly be someone else in the department who can fulfill the missing role. External projects are much more likely to be proposed by members of the university staff who either do not have IT expertise or are not academics – administrators frequently propose projects. Therefore, it is important that the project co-ordinator ensures the creation of a supervisory team to fulfill all of the roles. The form highlights potential problems and shortfalls. Similarly, it is not unusual for external proposers not to have either the appropriate hardware or software for the project. If the project is to run, the co-ordinator must again arrange to make up for the shortfall if possible or to veto the project if not.

The submitted information is then fed into a database, with the various fields of the form being stored in three tables representing proposals; supervisors; and departments or other sources of the proposal. This database is then used to generate automatically a set of web pages that the students can explore when they are asked to choose a project. The pages include an index of projects by supervisor and another by department. Figure 2 shows the latter – departments being divided into categories (Administration, Engineering, etc.) to help the students focus their interest. Note also that newly proposed projects are flagged as are already allocated projects. Figure 3 shows the web page generated for a single project description, which includes hyperlinks to e-mail the proposer and to the web site of the department..

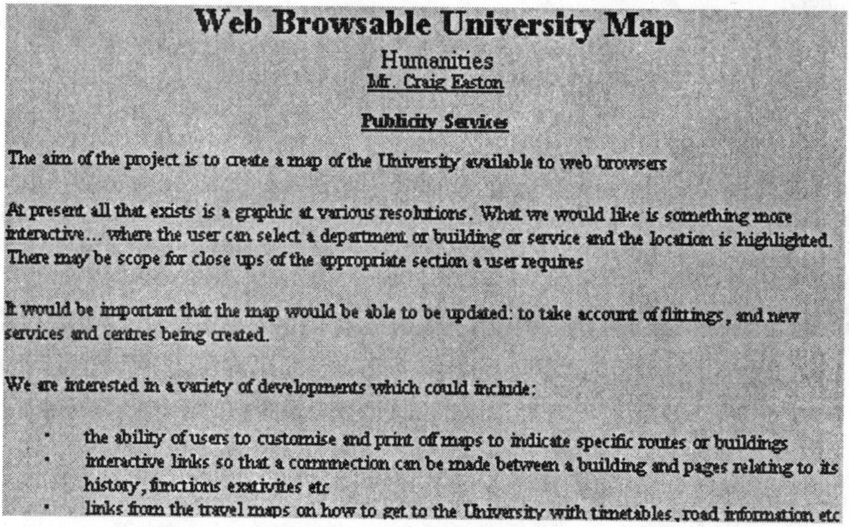

# Web Browsable University Map

### Humanities
#### Mr. Craig Easton

#### Publicity Services

The aim of the project is to create a map of the University available to web browsers

At present all that exists is a graphic at various resolutions. What we would like is something more interactive... where the user can select a department or building or service and the location is highlighted. There may be scope for close ups of the appropriate section a user requires

It would be important that the map would be able to be updated: to take account of flittings, and new services and centres being created.

We are interested in a variety of developments which could include:

* the ability of users to customise and print off maps to indicate specific routes or buildings
* interactive links so that a communication can be made between a building and pages relating to its history, functions exativites etc
* links from the travel maps on how to get to the University with timetables, road information etc

**Figure 3. Example Web Page Advertising a Project**

# 4. Allocating Projects

The students are asked to view the web pages containing project proposals and to contact the proposers for more information. They are then asked to indicate their choice to the project co-ordinator. This is achieved in different ways for the different classes.

The M.Sc. AIS being a class in which the number of students is small compared both to the proposals and to the number of potential supervisors is dealt with in an entirely *ad hoc* fashion. The M.Sc. IT is dealt with also in an *ad hoc* manner, but for a different reason. As the proposers and supervisors are spread so widely and the class is so large (many more than 100 at this stage), it is infeasible to impose a rigid time scale for all staff and students. Consequently, the students are left to agree a project with a potential supervisor and to inform the project co-ordinator as soon as they have done so. For both courses, a publicly visible web page of assignments, similar to Figure 4, is maintained to ensure that the information is correct. This is generated from the same database that held the proposals, but requiring an extra table for student information. Note that the public availability of the web pages also acts as publicity for the course for prospective students considering the courses for next year. Finally, proposals which have been taken up are marked in the proposal pages as being no longer available.

The undergraduate project allocation, being internal to the Computing Science department, is more closely managed. Students are issued with a ballot form on which they indicate up to ten choices in order. For solo projects, the data from these forms is fed into a program – itself the product of an earlier student project – that generates 'good matchings' automatically. The algorithm used is a variation of a classical approach to the Assignment Problem[1]. Different weights can be attached to force the program to generate a matching satisfy one of a number of criteria, namely:

   i)     to maximise the number of first choices and, subject to that criterion, to maximise the number of second choices, etc.;

   ii)    to minimise the value of n, where the $n^{th}$ choice is the worst allocated, and subject to that, to minimise the number of $n^{th}$ choices, then $(n-1)^{th}$ choices, etc.;

   iii)   to minimise the average choice allocated.

In practice, the three strategies usually produce very similar allocations, although the first strategy tends to produce a very poor allocation to a small number of students. We look at all three matchings and usually plump for the second option, because this removes the possibility of a particular student suffering significantly to benefit the rest of the class.

Team project ballots can be filled in by one or more students – thus allowing the students to self-select their teams. There is an issue in allowing this. Students will already have worked in teams and so have a fair idea of how well they work with some of their colleagues. If their previous experience was good, they are likely to opt for the same people they had in the previous group. This means that people who have worked well together will be assigned to a group immediately. Those who did not work well together will be left to be assigned to a group by the project co-ordinator. As they will now be a reduced portion of the class, there will be a high chance that they are re-allocated to the same groups. In general, self-selection tends to re-create previous groupings.

The ballot forms are used to allocate the students to projects. Now the allocation is more difficult because some forms are for one student, while others can have up to six names on them. It is believed that a version of the automatic assignment program could be constructed to provide at least an initial matching. However, the problem does not correspond to the standard assignment problem and it is likely to be a much more computationally complex task to find an optimal solution, so a heuristic approach might be preferred. In any case, we have never built such a program and so the allocation is carried out by hand. This process is like making a jigsaw puzzle and is best done with cut out pieces of paper and a template. Eventually (and usually with the aid of negotiation) the process is completed. The allocation is then publicised on the web, Figure 4 showing a fragment of the team project allocation.

## CS 3

| Supervisor | Title | Name | Reader |
|---|---|---|---|
| Steve Brewster | Web Pages for the partially Sighted | Gillian Taggart<br>Bryan Robertson<br>Steven McCann<br>Mark Anderson<br>Stefan Pacevitch<br>Thomas Kelly | Mark Dunlop |
| Rich Cooper | Book Store Web Pages | Colin Melville<br>David Green<br>Paul Lynch<br>Peter McElroy<br>Tommy McLaughlan<br>Scott Corker | David Watt |
| | | Eric Cheung | |

**Figure 4. Web Page Fragment for the Allocation of Team Projects.**

## 5. Project Management and Assessment

Having allocated the projects, the day-to-day management is left up to the supervisor. The supervisor will usually see the student at least once a week and will ensure that adequate progress is being made by requesting documents and demonstrations at appropriate intervals. For each course, the project co-ordinator also makes a milestone check. This takes the form of a submission by the student of a one page description of the project with the intended goals clearly stated. This is required about a third of the way through the project time and lets the co-ordinator know that the project is underway and is clearly defined – i.e. that both the student and the supervisor are working on the project.

Another milestone is expected of undergraduates – this time in the form of an early version of the introductory chapter of the project dissertation. This is required as coursework for the Communication Skills modules which are taught as very short courses mid-way through the year. The module deals partly with presentation skills and partly with writing skills. One of the lectures deals with writing summary documents and the draft introduction must be written so that the student can implement the recommendations taught in the lecture.

The other use of the Communication Skills module is to prepare the students for presentations of their projects. Undergraduate students are expected to produce presentations of their projects to an audience of their classmates and their teachers. For each year, this is organised as a kind of mini-conference, with sessions of three or four presentations of projects on related subjects, each having an academic chairperson. This gives the students valuable practice in honing their ability to present material in public – a vital requirement in present day industry. It also gives staff the ability to learn about some useful topic by attending sessions – if our busy schedule permits this. Unfortunately, the resource implications of a university-wide course have prevented this from put into practice for the M.Sc. class.

The dissertation submission must include a full project report (varying in length depending upon the course), full documentation (user manuals, requirements documents, external specifications, internal specifications such as ER diagrams, DFDs and so on, listings and a project log). The last of these is particularly important for assessing team projects, since these tend to highlight the different levels of contribution by the different team members. Group projects receive an overall mark, which is then adjusted for the individuals in the group to account for differentials in contribution.

Assessment is carried out independently by two markers, one of whom will normally be the project supervisor. Each of the markers produces a mark out of 100 for the project as a whole. The second marker should be independent of the project, but it has sometimes been the practice that another academic has been involved in the project supervision and is also the second marker – in such cases, we are intending to switch to ensuring an independent marker. For the undergraduate students, the project presentation is taken as part of the material to be assessed and the marker is given a form which essentially requires the mark to be composed of subsidiary marks on aspects such as design, implementation, project report and so on. In fact, marking using such a form sometimes gives the marker some difficulties in that the sum of the component marks does not correspond to the marker's overall assessment. Tailoring the component marks can occasionally be a tricky task.

More importantly, there is a clear problem in ensuring that all markers are using a common standard. This has been found to be a problem even within CS, but is even worse with the M.Sc.IT, since now marking is split between departments. Within CS, a number of techniques have been used to ensure some uniformity:
  i) ensuring that pairs of markers do not mark more than one project;
  ii) having someone (for instance, the project co-ordinator) mark many projects so as to provide a common metric against which to judge the other markers;
  iii) re-assessing (with a third marker) any project in which there is a wide discrepancy between the two marks;
  iv) comparing project marks against exam marks and re-assessing projects which appear too highly or lowly rated;
  v) using statistics programs which calculate an average for each marker and ensure a balance across all markers;

vi) (in the case of the M.Sc.IT) ensuring that at least one marker is from CS or is known to be IT competent.

In fact, each of these can only be a partial solution against different value systems of different assessors. One particular variation has been found to be significant within CS. Whereas, there is usually a high degree of agreement for projects which are poor or are in the mid-range (up to upper second class quality), there can be considerable disagreement when marking very good projects (first class projects are usually assessed at above 70%). Roughly speaking, two attitudes dominate. On one side, some markers assert that "if I give the student a first class mark, then I am already praising it highly and so I need extra value for every mark I give over 71". Others take the view that the project should be judged against perfection – "Starting from 100%, what reasons can I find for deducting marks?" The latter viewpoint will frequently assess a project more than 10 marks higher than the former. We have had to introduce strong guidelines partitioning the 70-100 mark range so that there is some better reason for agreement. An assessment of over 90, for instance, is taken to mean that a paper extracted from the work would very likely be publishable in a major conference – clearly rendering this mark extraordinary.

# 6. Other Befits from Student Projects

All of the projects that have been discussed have education as their central purpose. However, we have found that student projects have helped us in three ways. Firstly, a number of projects have contributed in important ways to the administrative functions of both the department, in particular, and the university in general. Secondly, we have built teaching tools using student projects. Thirdly, departmental research has been greatly helped.

## Administrative Tools

One administrative project has already been mentioned – the one which created the solo project allocation program. Here are a number of other projects which have helped with administrative tasks:

- As part of the drive to remove discrimination against disabled students, all universities have been required to examine building access and to produce a plan to remove potential barriers. Last year, an M.Sc. IT project set up a database to house the findings of this audit and provided an application on top of this. This allowed the user to select any room in the university and a particular disability condition and then to respond to the question "Can a student with this disability get to this room and, if not, why not?"

- Another M.Sc. project created an application for the Faculty of Social Sciences, which enables it to check the progress of students more easily. As students progress through the university system, they are monitored by an application that can check for problems of various kinds and produce summary information on demand.

- In common with all university departments, we at CS have an increasing requirement to seek out new students and to publicise the department. Accordingly, we have designed and built a multimedia document which describes the department and the university and which includes hypertext, sound and video. This was built by a third year team project and completed by them as paid programmers over the summer following their project. It is now available as a CD-ROM which has been distributed to schools.

- A similar project was recently completed by an M.Sc. IT student to capture the CS departmental history to celebrate the department's fortieth anniversary. This resulted in a web site[2] which comprised a variety of textual and aural history of the past forty years.

## Teaching Tools

There is a greater and greater emphasis on the creation of teaching software. For instance, in Glasgow, both this university and Strathclyde University are contributing to the Clyde Virtual University [3]. This aims to provide on-line teaching material for a wide range of disciplines. Many projects, particularly those for the M.Sc. IT, have been involved in creating such courseware. For example, a series of student projects have built a set of computer-based tutorials on anatomy (notably of the nervous system). As another example, the first author is building a suite of database system teaching tools largely from the use of student projects.

As another example, several teams of third year students have undertaken projects for the University's Hunterian Museum, gradually building up a high-quality WWW site with different features [4]. None of these projects has involved the implementation of significant pieces of software. In each case, there have been interesting technical challenges in using existing software and major design issues but these have to be balanced against the Museum's desire to capture large quantities of data. The compromise is to regard the student project as providing a framework for the final product which can be expanded by paying somebody to carry out the data capture required to fill in all the details.

We have completed six projects for the Museum and there are currently another four in progress. The initial projects were concerned with fairly basic Web site construction: designing an attractive overall style for the Museum's web site, providing a consistent framework for future development and evaluating the results using Museum visitors, both locally and remotely. Building on this basic structure, there have been projects involving adding video clips to animate some of the material on Roman armour, using image maps to illustrate Captain Cook's voyages of exploration, adding audio for Latin inscriptions and more recently for aiding blind and partially-sighted visitors to the museum. We have used QTVR (Quick Time Virtual Reality) to provide panoramas of the Mackintosh House and to display small objects from the Museum in 3-D.

In addition to the general educational objectives of exposing the students to team work, each of these projects has shared a number of valuable features:

- *Requirements elicitation.* The students have had to talk to the staff in the Museum, understand their requirements and define a reasonable project which was achievable within the limited time frame of a student project. The major problem was usually over-enthusiastic customers who expected too much from the students, as you explain the possibilities and present prototypes the customers generate more and more ideas! A certain amount of tactful intervention from Computing Science staff supervisors was sometimes required to ensure that students did not get overwhelmed with low-level work.

- *Design skills and software evaluation.* In each projects there has been a significant design component in working out how to present the information and artefacts in an suitable manner. There has also been a requirement to evaluate available software and learn how to use it. In many cases the available software has been poorly documented and rather 'flaky'! For example, when we first used QTVR panoramas there was very little useful documentation on how to stitch the components of the panoramas together and quite a lot of experimental work was required to achieve a satisfactory result which did not leave the user totally disorientated.

- *Evaluation.* We have encouraged each project team to use HCI evaluation techniques to get feedback on their work. In most cases we have managed to get some local feedback from visitors to the Museum, comparing the Web site with the real thing, and also from remote sites using the Web. For example, for the video clip project a subject in San Francisco downloaded the video clips at various times of the day to evaluate the feasibility of using this technology [5,6].

- *Documentation.* Each project has produced a normal project report but they have also been required to provide accurate user documentation for those who are going to continue these projects. For example, the QTVR teams have built up documentation on how to construct panoramas and how to handle the presentation of small objects using the object rig. They have provided tutorials on the use of the technology and trouble-shooting hints to help other users avoid some of the pitfalls they encountered.

These projects are critically dependent on the co-operation of the Museum staff who have proved extremely enthusiastic and supportive. Any project with real customers obviously depends on their willingness to participate but one of the additional problems of this group of Museum projects has been that many of the objects which the students have been working with are extremely valuable and in many cases fragile and irreplaceable! The curatorial staff of the Museum have been extremely helpful in overcoming a wide variety of problems.

## Research Prototypes

Our research has also benefited greatly from the work carried out in student projects. Such projects can be used to demonstrate the feasibility of a research idea. The first author used a series of research type projects to develop an idea which culminated in two funded projects.

We have encouraged students to undertake projects associated with larger research projects. These projects must be small and well-defined and must not be critical to the outcome of the research project. Recently, the second author has had experience of MSc IT students working with research projects. In the first case, two MSc students developed a graphical editor and visualisation tool for a PhD student who was developing a formal specification language. The tools were not critical to the PhD student's research, but provided him with a useful demonstrator and helped him with the presentation of his work as he had to explain it to the two MSc students (several times!).

The second experience was getting another two MSc IT students to develop graphical tools associated with an EPSRC-funded project. Again, the main thrust of the research project is language based and the students' projects provided useful graphical demonstrators for the technology. One of the students subsequently went on to become a Research Assistant on the project, having established his credentials via the MSc project. We have found that good students enjoy the challenge of these research-related projects and this type of project has the advantage of spreading the supervisory load. Much of the technical input is provided by research students and research assistants, who also gain valuable experience in project supervision. However, assessment is still carried out in the normal way by the academic staff.

In summary, student projects can enhance research work in four ways:

i) Early prototypes explore new, untried and yet-to-be-resourced ideas.
ii) Demonstration applications testify to the success of the products of the project. An enhanced range of example applications can often add greatly to the perceived outcome of a research project.
iii) Additional or enhanced user interfaces make the functionality (usually the research component) more easily accessed.
iv) Aspects of the project can be tackled which, although desirable, are neither in the main core of the proposed work, nor can feasibly be attempted within the resources provided.

To exploit student projects more systematically (and particularly the first of these kinds of benefit), the department has recently attracted a large grant as part of the Revelation initiative [7]. Revelation proposes "a foundation for advanced and precise digital communications experiments" and has been used to create the infrastructure (support staff and powerful hardware) to support student projects. Revelation is at once a support environment for student based projects in the future and is itself the result of past student projects, such as the ones for the Hunterian Museum. Student based projects are proposed by staff from anywhere in the University with the explicit goal of turning research ideas in fundable proposals. Often such attempts falter due to a lack of hardware or other support. Revelation is designed to fill this gap.

## 7. Conclusions

The Computing Science Department at the University of Glasgow makes heavy use of projects in its teaching. This is vital in a subject in which practical skills are paramount. Students hone their software development by being involved in the creation of software, which may be quite large or complex. Hopefully, the techniques taught as software engineering can be seen to be beneficial. Managing such a large number of projects could easily become unwieldy and so a number of (semi-)automatic tools have been built to make the co-ordinator's life a little easier.

However, involvement in student projects has been shown to have wider benefit than just the education of the students. Administration, teaching and research can all benefit from the development of software. Moreover, the close involvement of supervisor and student is one of the main mechanisms by which our department breaks down the barrier between teacher and student – thus creating an educative environment which is at once more pleasant and more powerful.

## Acknowledgements

The authors would like to thank Rob Irving and David Watt for their useful comments and Chris Johnson for important contributions in the development of the support system for project management. They would also like to thank the many hundreds of students who have taken part in projects for the department and have helped shape the staff's understanding of Computing Science as part of their work.

## Bibliography

1. C.H. Papdimitrou and K. Sterglitz, "Combinatorial Optimization", Prentice Hall, 1982
2. http://www.dcs.gla.ac.uk/anniversary/
3. http://cvu.strath.ac.uk/admin/index.html
4. http://www.gla.ac.uk/Museum/index.html
5. C.W.Johnson, Ten Golden Rules for Video over the Web, *in* "Human Factors for World Wide Web Development", J.Ratner, E.Grosse and C. Forsythe (eds.), Lawrence Erlbaum, New York, pp. 207-224.
6. http://www.dcs.gla.ac.uk/~johnson/papers/video.html
7. http://www.revelation.gla.ac.uk/

# The Sheffield University Maxi Project
# The Industrial Project Manager's Perspective

Stan Price, BSc[Eng.]; C.Eng.; M.R.Ae.S; M.B.C.S.
Price Project Services Ltd, 23 New Mount St., Manchester M4 4DE

## Abstract

The Sheffield University Computer Science Department Maxi Project for MSc Students is managed by an experienced industrial IT project manager. This paper describes how he does this and the thinking behind it and the way it has evolved.

## 1  Introduction

Sheffield University, Department of Computer Science conceived the idea for the Maxi Project for it's MSc students in 1988. The concept involved the use of an industrially experienced Information Technology [IT] project manager [1] to manage teams of students as if they were his or her staff working in an industrial environment. I have performed the role since it's conception on my own, apart from two years when student numbers were such that a second industrial project manager was required.

I have therefore played a significant role in deciding how the Maxi Project operates. This modus operandi has been continuously developed since it's conception. New ideas have been introduced, evaluated and if found not to be sufficiently beneficial they have been dropped. This paper does not therefore just describe how the Maxi Project is currently operated, but also describes it's development including features that have been tried and rejected and the reasons why.

The Maxi is a mandatory module for most of the Department of Computer Science MScs. Over the years these MScs have addressed topics including software engineering, advanced software engineering, software systems technology, artificial intelligence and expert systems and, in recent years, telematics.

## 2  The Author

The Author has been involved in IT for thirty-two years. After an initial three years as first a programmer and then a systems analyst in an engineering environment I started to manage small to medium sized projects. After a period of some six years

I became one of the first in the United Kingdom [UK] to have the job title Software Engineer. Despite this technical title, I was the project officer instrumental in procuring the UK's en-route air traffic control system software from the United States [US] Federal Aviation Agency [FAA]. This software represented some 3,000 man-years of development activity. My ongoing relevant work included a similar role on the Metropolitan Police Command and Control System Project.

After a period involved in the sales and marketing of a variety of bespoke IT systems I became an independent consultant. In this capacity I have been involved in IT projects in a number of ways viz:-

      -controlling a number of IT projects,
      -monitoring a number of IT research projects,
      -acting as an expert witness in litigation subsequent to the failure of IT
      projects.

I have also conceived and taught IT project management courses for a number of organisations in both higher education and commercial training. Some of my previous ideas are contained in a book [2]. However since it was written in 1984 my ideas have developed and been refined.

# 3 Education Value

Despite the above training experience I would not describe myself as a professional educator. The educational value of the Maxi Project is in the student's learning by doing. However, a project manager has to, at times, act as a coach and in this capacity I illustrate concepts by anecdotes from my experience. I have the conceit to believe that these may have some educational value.

Apart from this, it is for others, especially my employer, Sheffield University Department of Computer Science, and my students, to comment on the educational value of what I do.

# 4 Philosophy

The way I manage the Maxi Project is partly dictated by what the University requires and the constraints specific to the academic environment as well as the normal project constraints. However subject to that, it embodies a number of my beliefs about IT project management. Incidentally, most of these are applicable to project management generally. The principal relevant beliefs are:-

- Project Management is not a mechanistic task which consists simply of a number of administrative activities. It involves activities such as creating a culture, team building and staff motivation [principally by carrots but occasionally and if necessary by sticks].

- An IT project involves a number of creative activities which cannot always be scheduled and put into a strict chronological order. Therefore, although a framework for any particular project is required this must allow a high degree of flexibility so that creativity can flourish. It is interesting that the World's largest software producer, Microsoft, attempts to achieve the same balance [3].

- Any project is a social activity and it is important to take measures against anything that would impact the social cohesion of the project team and so threaten the attainment of the project's objectives. Note however, a little creative tension is not necessarily a bad thing.

- It is impossible to foresee everything that must be done at the start of the project. Even if one did not forget anything unforeseeable threats and opportunities will arise during the course of a project. It is therefore important that the project manager aided by his or her team has formal and informal processes for the timely detection of events that require actions and then their timely enactment.

- The informing of the project team of the actions that they will have to carry out and the subsequent requests to do so should be done in such a way that the project team is challenged and not threatened to a consistent level throughout the project.

- Progress should be measured against both time and resource expenditure. Also work should be constantly checked to see that either or both are not being achieved at the expense of quality.

# 5 Planning the Maxi

The Maxi for the following academic year is planned in August/September. Every year the Maxi has run from the start of the first term or semester to the end of the second term or semester.

The activities that require face-to-face contact between myself and the students are scheduled for one afternoon per week throughout this period. Not all of these afternoons are in fact allocated. There is a gap between semesters and some weeks it is more sensible to let the students get on with their work. This must however be balanced against the importance of regular meetings to ensure a satisfactory rate of progress is achieved.

The first afternoon is primarily occupied by my delivery, for some 2 to 3 hours, of background lectures plus the project's overall briefing which is also given by me. All other afternoons are divided between half hour lectures, termed briefings, and tutorials with each student team. The briefings are intended for and attended by all the students i.e. all the teams and are the forum for my dissemination of information which is common to all students and all student teams. These include briefings on what is required in each stage of the Maxi, arrangements for the semester break and the final afternoon of the Maxi etc.

The tutorials last 15 to 20 minutes and are held with each team. Given that normally 12 teams have to be seen within a single afternoon I ensure that I am completely prepared and the students are "encouraged" to be the same. The tutorials as well as including normal discussions of their progress and identifying problems, also incorporate such activities as Fagin's Inspections, End of Stage Reviews. Towards the end of the project, when there is actually work to be seen, these tutorials are held in the computer science laboratories.

Apart from my face-to-face work with students significant time has to be spent in my own Manchester office planning, administrating and marking. These are taken account of but not included in the Maxi planning.

Despite my reservations about how realistic it is to a real project, the Maxi is based on a waterfall model embodying five stages. These stages are typically Feasibility, Requirements Capture, Design and Test Preparation, Coding and Implementation. The break between semesters presents a real problem. Ideally the coding stage should start before the break. However, the difficulties of a stop-go stage are felt to be too severe and so the start of the Coding stage is deferred to the second semester. This tends to mean more is required of the students during the second semester. It also allows a less arduous synchronisation of the Maxi requirements and the timing of when students are taught relevant material within the academic modules of their MSc.

The planning activity results in a two page briefing document with diary and plan plus an example stage plan which are distributed in document form to the students on the first afternoon of the Maxi. A User Briefing is also produced and distributed to the appropriate users.

Fig. 1 shows a typical MAXI project diary.

SHEFFIELD UNIVERSITY - DEPARTMENT OF COMPUTER SCIENCE
MASTER OF SCIENCE COURSES

MAXI PROJECT 97 DIARY [REVISED 05/12/97]

| Week | Date Wed | Project Stage | Lecture/Briefing | Tutorials | Deliverables |
|---|---|---|---|---|---|
| 1 | 1/10/97 | 1 | Project & Stage 1 | No | |
| 2 | 8/10/97 | 1 | No | Yes | Project Budget, Stage 1 Plan |
| 3 | 15/10/97 | 1 | Stage 2 | Yes | |
| 4 | 22/10/97 | 2 | No | Yes | Stage 1, Stage 2 Plan |
| 5 | 29/10/97 | 2 | No | Yes | |
| 6 | 5/11/97 | 2 | No | No | |
| 7 | 11/11/97* | 2 | - | - | Draft Stage 2 (DS2) |
| | 12/11/97 | | Stage 3 | DS2 Inspection | |
| 8 | 19/11/97 | 3 | No | Yes | Stage 2, Stage 3 Plan |
| 9 | 26/11/97 | 3 | No | Stages 1/2 Review | Stages 1/2 Stats |
| 10 | 3/12/97 | 3 | No | No | |
| 11 | 9/12/97* | 3 | - | - | Draft Stage 3(DS3) |
| | 10/12/97 | | Stage 4 | DS3 Inspection | |
| 12 | 17/12/97 | 4 | Yes | Yes | Stage 3, Stage 4 Plan |
| 20 | 11/2/98 | 4 | Stage 5 | Stage 3 Review | Stage 3 Stats |
| 21 | 18/2/98 | 4 | No | Yes | Stage 4A, Stage 5 Plan |
| 22 | 25/2/98 | 4/5 | No | No | |
| 23 | 4/3//98 | 4/5 | No | Yes | Stage 4B |
| 24 | 11/3/98 | 4/5 | No | No | |
| 25 | 18/3/98 | 4/5 | Yes | Yes | Stage 4 |
| 26 | 25/3/98 | 5 | No | Product Marking | Stage 5 (everything) |

Apart from 1/10/97 all briefings will be at 1.30pm. The timings of individual team tutorials and the lecture rooms for briefings and the seminar rooms for tutorials (1997 only) will be given on the appropriate notice boards.

* Tuesdays

**PLEASE ENTER THESE DATES IN YOUR DIARY**

**Fig. 1**

For the first few years of the Maxi student teams were encouraged to produce their own overall schedule but this made the overall management of the Maxi within the budget impossible. Also, many students found it too difficult.

# 6 Choice of Application and User

An application project and associated user is selected each year for each type of MSc. Typically there are three applications being addressed in one year with several student teams allocated to each one.

Getting real industrial applications is extremely difficult. Although the applications owner may be said to be getting something for nothing in fact they have to devote significant time, particularly for their requirements to be elicited. This is more than the normal industrial situation where they would have to do this only once, whereas with the Maxi they have to do it for each student team. This presents a significant obstacle to industrial co-operation.

My own involvement with the users is limited. It is the job of the student teams to handle the face-to-face contact, as would be the case in the industrial situation assuming I was the project controller i.e. the project manager's superview. What involvement I do have is generally limited to problems with the user which the student teams cannot resolve e.g. the user's typical tardiness in providing test data.

Apart from test data the only items generally required from the user are a "wish list" at the start of the Maxi and a mark for each team at the end. The former is given to the students simultaneously with my briefing documents.

# 7 Formation of Student Teams

A team is generally composed of individuals on the same MSc course. The ideal number for a student team is five. This is based on general industrial experience where the communication overhead starts to become excessive within larger teams. It also fits in with the five Maxi stages in that it allows each student, within a team, to act as a stage manager. Teams of a different number are formed where the numbers on a particular MSc course make it inevitable. Six is the largest number allowed in a team. If this is the case, the third stage of the Maxi is divided into two viz Design and Test Preparation with a student managing each so that each student in the team still has an opportunity of stage management. Teams of three and four are common. Here some students have the misfortune to have to manage two stages, however they are compensated by having the higher of their two stage manager marks used in the overall marking. As an inducement they are told of this in advance.

A team of two has proved to be too risky apart from anything else it only requires one to drop out and the team is unviable. In these circumstances, and in others e.g. a breakdown of relations in a team, team transfers are contemplated although the later these occur in the life of the Maxi the greater the difficulty.

Apart from seeing that teams are largely composed of students on the same course and that teams are equally endowed with English speaking competence no other criteria is used in deciding the constituents of teams. Early in the Maxi a much more complex team selection process was attempted. This categorised students as leaders, doers, communicators etc. but it was abandoned as it did not offer any apparent benefits.

# 8 Stage Managers

Subject to issues related to team size, as described above, and the requirement that each student will be stage manager, once the students agree amongst themselves which stages they will manage each stage manager has to produce a stage plan by the date shown in the overall plan produced by me. This will be based on the stage briefing which I will have normally given them a week before. At the end of the stage the stage manager has to produce statistics showing how predicted effort in the stage plan compared with actual effort. Each student in the team is required to sign this to indicate they agree on the hours worked. Based on a notional hourly charge rate the cost of the stage is thus determined.

# 9 Fagin's Inspections and End-of-Stage Reviews

The critical requirements and design and test documents are subject to a simulation of a Fagin's Inspection which I conduct in the relevant tutorials. In order for me to achieve this the overall plan requires drafts of these documents to be submitted a week in advance with sufficient lead time for me to examine them before the Inspection [see fig. 1]. The students have the opportunity to improve the documents before their final submission a week later. In accordance with the spirit of Fagin's Inspections they are not allowed to influence the Maxi Marking. The students, in addition to these inspections, are encouraged to perform their own within the teams on other documents and code.

Typically two end of stage reviews are held. A combined Feasibility and Requirements i.e. Stage 1 & 2 Review and a Design and Test Document i.e. Stage 3 Review. The Agenda followed is a cut down and modified version of that advocated by the PRINCE project management methodology. It is:-

- Actual against Planned Progress in terms of time and resources [money]
- Quality
- Outstanding concerns
- Updated Risk Analysis
- Go/No Go Decision
- Future Plans & Concerns.

# 10 Financial Control

As part of the Feasibility Stage the student teams are encouraged to produce a guestimate of the cost of their Maxi Project. The Key element is of course the number of man-hours required. This is converted to money by an arbitrary fee rate per hour which I give the students. The cost of the project is broken down into stage costs and it is these that are compared with actual costs, both stage and accumulative, at the end-of-stage reviews. Whilst the dubious nature of the figures is acknowledged to the students, the importance of financial control in real life industrial projects is constantly emphasised.

# 11 The Project Stages

Brief details follow of what is required in each stage given the Feasibility, Requirements, Design & Test Preparation, Coding and Implementation life cycle alluded to earlier.

## 11.1 Feasibility

A Feasibility Report has to be produced by each team approximately three weeks into the project. This should address the feasibility of and the justification of and for the project and include an overall estimate of the cost of the project and a simplified risk analysis.
Apart from my briefing the teams are ill-prepared for this. The advantages of it being a normal industrial requirement and acting as an immediate spur to get the teams working together are felt to outweigh any disadvantages stemming from this ill-preparation.

## 11.2 Requirements

A Report agreed and signed by the user is produced approximately seven weeks into the project. This should address both the functional and non-functional requirements and also any constraints on the design of how these requirements are to be met. The students are expected to negotiate with the user what these requirements will consist of. Unless there are significant problems I do not get involved. I do however advise the student teams how to go about the negotiations.

## 11.3 Design and Test Preparation

A Report showing how the system will be designed to meet the requirements allowing for the constraints is produced approximately eleven weeks into the project. Amongst the issues it will address will be:-

-Choice of Hardware.
-Programming Language Chosen.
-Design of User Manual.
-Choice of System Operatives and their training requirements.

Simultaneously a short document describing how acceptance testing is to be carried out will be produced. Attached to it will be a number of Acceptance Test Specifications and a blank proforma to be used for the reporting on the outcome of these tests each time they are attempted.

## 11.4  Coding

The document deliverables from this stage are the program listings [possibly on a floppy] and a road map overview of them for software maintenance purposes. The stage should proceed with the evolutionary development of the software. Normally I inspect this at three discrete times [shown in the overall plan] and the User should do likewise. The student teams are encouraged to perform modular testing but this is not examined.

## 11.5  Implementation

This involves the carrying out, including completing test report proformas, of the Acceptance Tests specified earlier until they are successful. It also involves the production of a User Manual. It culminates in the delivery of the finished system and all it's attendant documents etc. on the final afternoon of the Maxi. The total list is:-

Feasibility Report
Requirements Document
Design Document
Test Document.
User Manual
Software Listings
Software Documentation [Roadmap]
Test Reports
Change Notes
Acceptance form
Outstanding Statistics
Demonstration

The first 4 will be the documents I have already marked and returned to the user.

The stage plans and stage 1, 2, 3 statistics I will have retained.

# 12 Marking

Each team is given an overall mark for the Maxi comprising individual marks for most of the main items referred to above, apart from Stage Plans and Statistics. The individual items are given weightings dependant on their importance to the whole project [e.g. Requirements carries a high weighting] and each item's mark is multiplied by it's weighting before it is accumulated into the overall team score.

The final product, as demonstrated to me and the user, is marked by myself and the user. These marks, which comprise two separate items, carry a high weighting such that:-

> a team may score highly on documents but poorly on the product in which case it will tend to fail, or score poorly on documents but highly on the product in which case it will tend to pass.

An important point is that the product is marked in relation to it's requirements including any amendments documented in change notes. Thus when comparing product marks between teams, without reference to the requirements, it may seem that a "better" product has a lower mark to an "inferior" product, to some students chagrin.

The teams are marked out of 80%. The remaining 20% is for individual students. The team mark plus the individual student mark out of the remaining 20% represents the total individual student's mark for the Maxi Module.

Half [i.e. 10%] of this 20% is award on the basis of the student's performance as stage manager. If he or she has managed two or more stages the highest mark is used. This is derived from the quality of the stage plans and the presentation of statistics.

The other half [i.e. 10%] is awarded on the basis of the individual student's contribution to the team. I determine this from the individual's contribution:-

> -as shown by the stage statistics,
> -by the number of test documents, lines of codes [authorship is requested in the form of comment lines], and
> -their performance in tutorials.

The imperfections and hence dangers of this marking schema are recognised. All I can say is that I believe I have never failed a student who deserved to pass but students have passed who may have deserved to fail.

# 13 Problems

Some of the problems in trying to simulate an industrial software product in an academic teaching environment have been alluded to previously. There are others. Overall the significant ones are:-

- The impact on the user and the teams of several teams addressing the same requirement simultaneously.

- The constraints imposed by the equipment/software choices available in the University.

- The normal employer's power of termination of employment or the threat of it is absent.

- The stop-go nature of the project as imposed by it being spread over two terms and the introduction of the semester system which has exacerbated this.

- Budgetary limitations which preclude the full gambit of stage reviews, inspections etc.

- The need to schedule the project mindful of an academic teaching schedule.

However, any industrial environment would impose similar problems and restrictions and therefore I believe the Maxi is a relevant exercise for the students in learning to produce something whilst attempting to overcome obstacles.

# 14 General Observations

When I first managed the Maxi I was surprised to find the students were not as self-motivated and confident as I would expect from those attempting to gain a Master degree. This was one of the factors why the overall plan became prescriptive in terms of deadlines.

The second major observation is the difficulty many students have in seeing what the purpose of an IT project is. Many see the introduction of any form of IT as an object in itself. Maybe this is just symptomatic of an underlying problem within the IT sector generally.

However, despite the difficulties and problems most student teams produce a credible working product at the end of the Maxi. Only in a few cases does this reach a marketable standard but this in itself is, I believe, a valuable lesson for the students

## Acknowledgements

My thanks to my colleagues and friends and indeed students in the Department of Computer Science at Sheffield University for giving me the opportunity to pass on some of my experience.

## References

1.      Mike Holcombe and Hugh Lafferty. Using Computer Professionals for Managing Student Software Projects. Conference Proceedings Developments in Teaching computer Science. University of Kent Canterbury 1992.

2.      Stan Price. Managing Computer Projects. John Wiley and Sons

3.      Michael Cusumana and Richard Selby. How Microsoft Builds Software. Communications of the ACM vol. 40 no. 6 June 1997.

# Perceptions of Final Year Project Outcomes

Dr Peter Capon

Department of Computer Science, University of Manchester

Manchester M13 9PL, U.K.

pcc@cs.man.ac.uk

## Abstract

Students highly value the experience of a good final year design and implementation project. The definition of a good project is by no means trivial but can be crucial to success. A student learns both by managing the process and delivering a product. An ideal project will succeed in both but there can be many obstacles to complete success.

A survey of students shows a variety of well defined expectations. Often these expectations concern the learning process and are independent of the final technical outcome. Supervisors often have a stronger expectation of technical success as a proof of competence but make greater allowance when failure to deliver is for legitimate reasons.

Clear definition of expected project outcome both in terms of learning objectives and project deliverables will maximise the likelihood of a satisfactory outcome.

In his wide ranging article, Denning [1] argues that the Graduate Engineer must be able to demonstrate practical competence in action. Students must learn "good practical engineering, how to complete their work rigorously and how to be self-learners". Good practical engineering concerns both process and product. The outcome of a project concerns both these aspects. We should neither be entirely satisfied with an excellent process which in the end fails to deliver nor with a functional end product produced in an entirely ad-hoc and arbitrary manner. In assessing a project, measurement of the quality of the outcome should reflect a balance between these two aspects.

This paper reports the results of a survey of the outcomes of final year Computer Science projects at Manchester University. The aim was to investigate students' perceptions of project outcome and compare them with the supervisors' views. To what extent do student and supervisor share a common view? To what extent does a good outcome depend on the technical success of a project?

Some of the factors influencing the project outcome include the initial definition of the project, the ability of the student, the motivation of the student, the quality of tools used and support provided and the quality of the supervision.

Kantipudi [3] identifies many reasons for 'failure' of group software projects. He splits these reasons into technical issues, personal issues and management issues. The management and personal issues identified mainly relate to group dynamics so are less relevant to an individual project. The technical reasons are directly relevant here. These included lack of experience with the language or environment used, underestimating the size of the task and underestimating the time needed for a manageable task therefore leaving it too late. Kantipudi identifies the major causes of technical failures as direct consequences of student inexperience.

The projects considered here are individual final year projects of nominal 240 hours duration completed over 20 weeks. They are 'engineering' projects intended to satisfy the present (Sartor 90)[2] accreditation requirements of the BCS and IEE. Design and implementation are essential to the project. In 1997 81% of projects were defined by academic staff and bid for by students while 19% were student defined. The bidding process favours better students so a weaker student is less likely to be allocated a popular first choice.

Project deliverables include a seminar presentation, a demonstration of the finished product and a written report of 5000-9000 words. The marking scheme provides that half the marks are awarded on technical merit alone. The other half of the marks, for the seminar, demonstration and report, depend much less on the technical outcome of the project.

# 1   Project Definition

In this section we discuss issues related to the questions 'What sort of project is likely to lead to a satisfactory outcome?' and 'What are the obvious pitfalls?'. To what extent does a good outcome depend on a good project definition?

It is clear that our expectations change as a result of changing technology. Some previously good projects have become trivial regeneration of existing software. Despite the existence of many more tools it is often harder to create an end product that will impress.

Conversely, producing an impressive end product is increasingly dependent on the mastery of such tools. A considerable amount of background and software may have to be understood even to get off the ground. Very few projects now are just a straightforward program in a simple language. At the very least interfacing to some potentially complex library package is required. In an industrial situation several weeks, or possibly months, will be spent learning a particular development environment but there is seldom sufficient time in a crowded curriculum. The continuation of the trend towards use of such tools has ongoing implications for future project definition. To what extent is successfully learning the environment a satisfactory outcome? How much care should be taken to identify environments in which the student is likely to be productive and ensure that students have some pre-awareness of what is available?

To what extent are we flexible on the deliverables we expect? When does a project with no technical deliverables cease to be an engineering project? Insistence on a significant implementation component may be to the detriment of good design. With limited time available and an emphasis on design, a well executed design should be an equally acceptable deliverable for a project. However it is difficult to measure the quality of a design if there is no implementation based on it. There is a suspicion that students who hate implementation will seize upon design projects as a supposed 'soft' option. It is possible to define perfectly good investigative or comparative studies which are not engineering projects in the sense defined here and which do not meet the Engineering Council requirements. Can such studies replace an implementation oriented project as part of a Computer Science degree? We do not consider this question further here.

A project should be sufficiently challenging to ensure that the student learns something significant through undertaking it. Indeed the best projects may generate a research paper. To what extent should we try to match the expected difficulty of a project to the student's past performance? Giving a student a project that is too difficult does nobody any good. Some students have acquired such limited skills in previous course-work that a demanding project merely causes the student to flounder around and waste the supervisor's time. However apparently weak students sometimes complete quite challenging projects exceptionally well. We do not know how to discriminate the two types of student and how to treat them if we could. It seems particularly difficult to set projects appropriate for weaker students. As an external examiner commented, there must be no glass ceiling, all students must have the opportunity to surprise their supervisor in what they achieve. Some would happily settle for something that will teach them no more than their A-level project. Such a 'lazy' project is typically scoped by the student, requires no new tools to be learned, has a straightforward implementation and can be done at home. We need learning objectives that avoid this danger.

## 2   Towards a student view

It is clear that most students are strongly motivated in their final year project. Some of the positive aspects for student motivation are:

- The project is primarily a student centred learning activity

- Students are enthusiastic about the project content. At the project definition stage they either choose projects that interest them or create their own project in their preferred area of interest.

- Learning is self-paced. Our formal labs in previous years of the course proceed on a rather rigid timetable of fixed deliverables. The flexibility for the student to define their own work-plan is welcome.

- The student scopes the project. Even if there is a fixed objective the student has considerable control over the scale of what is delivered.

Here are some suggestions of what might be regarded as a good outcome from the student viewpoint which will be compared with the survey results in the next section.

- Relevance to proposed career

- A salable technical skill

- Meeting the defined project objectives

- A good mark

- Completion to timetable

On the other hand various outcomes might be regarded as bad from the student viewpoint, regardless of whether shortcomings outside the student's control are compensated in the assessment:

- Failure to learn any lessons from the process

- Technical failure through external circumstances

- Technical failure through student's fault

- A poor mark

- Poor presentation or report

- Disagreements with supervisor

# 3 A Student survey

It is clear from the literature that the outcome of student surveys on the benefits of project work is generally positive. For example Melody Moore reports in [5] and [6] that "students got a lot out of the labs. Even when progress was frustratingly slow they felt the intangible lessons they had learned were valuable".

A survey of students in Manchester reaching the end of their projects was held in April 1997, using the following survey questions:

1. What did you most hope to get out of the project?

2. Do you think you got this? If not why not?

3. How successful overall was the project? Give reasons.

4. What do you think you learned?

5. Were you required to learn new tools or techniques? If so what?

6. What was the hardest thing you had to do in the project?

The survey received 23 responses out of 132 students. Although this is a small sample, responses were entirely voluntary and the responses all gave good quality detailed answers.

Consider first the representativeness of the sample. The distribution of responses by degree class was:

|  | Degree class | | | | |
| --- | --- | --- | --- | --- | --- |
|  | 1st | 2.1 | 2.2 | 3rd | Pass |
| No of Responses | 6 | 7 | 8 | 2 | 0 |
| % of Responses | 26 | 30 | 35 | 9 | 0 |
| % in Degree class | 18 | 32 | 28 | 19 | 3 |

Comparing the final two rows of the table the sample under-represented weak students in the 3rd/Pass classes but 1st and 2nd class are reasonably represented.

The comparison of degree class with project class given in the table below shows that 15 students received the same degree class and project class. Of the 8 who did not 5 had a project mark one degree class higher than the degree awarded, one received a 2.2 with 1st class project and one a 1st with a 2.1 project and one a 2.1 with a 2.2 project. In no case, in this sample, did a student receive a project mark which changed the degree class he would have been awarded on exam performance alone.

|  |  | Degree class | | | |
| --- | --- | --- | --- | --- | --- |
|  |  | 1st | 2.1 | 2.2 | 3 |
|  | 1st | 5 | 1 | 1 |  |
| Project | 2.1 | 1 | 5 | 3 |  |
| Class | 2.2 |  | 1 | 4 | 1 |
|  | 3 |  |  |  | 1 |

9 students received the same project mark and overall mark (within 2%), 10 performed better in the project and 4 worse in the project. Those who performed better were on average 9% better with the best 20% better; none of those who performed worse were more than 5% worse. This correlates with an overall project average for the year 4% better (at 60.8%) than the overall average.

## 3.1  Survey responses

Consider now the responses to the individual questions:

1. What did you most hope to get out of the project?

   - 15 described this in terms of a personal skill that would be useful in the future, either technical or managerial
   - 5 described it as a successful technical outcome
   - 3 in terms of a desired degree classification.

The clear majority (15) therefore saw the main benefit of the project as a personal skill, either technical or managerial, acquired. 10 students described the skill acquired as technical, often citing specific skills such as C++ programming or graphics and user interface design. The remaining 5 cited organisation or experience of a large project as the main benefit. Only a minority (5) saw technical success as the main benefit.

This question was designed to elicit actual student definitions of a good outcome. Most responses could be described as concerning a desired learning outcome only loosely dependent on the technical success of the project. Acquiring a technical skill and experience of a large project are two such outcomes.

2. Do you think you got this? If not why not?

   For those who answered question 1 as personal skill, 11 said yes, 3 in part and 1 no. For those who answered technical outcome, none said yes, 2 in part and 3 no. For those who answered degree class all 3 said yes.

   Those who categorised the benefit in terms of personal skills acquired were far more likely to have believed they achieved their objective than those who stated their main objective as the technical outcome alone. For example, the objective of learning a technical skill could be satisfactorily achieved even if not all the technical aims of the project were met.

3. How successful overall was the project? Give reasons.

   5 said very successful, 10 successful, 5 moderately, and 3 not at all successful.

   The table below shows some correlation with the previous answer. However, one student who failed to achieve his objectives nevertheless rated the project a success and one who achieved his objectives rated it a failure.

|  |  | Q3 View of success | | | |
|---|---|---|---|---|---|
|  |  | Very Succ | Successful | Moderate | Failure |
| Q2 | Yes | 5 | 6 | 2 | 1 |
| Achieved | Partly |  | 3 | 2 |  |
| Objectives | No |  | 1 | 1 | 2 |

4. What do you think you learned?

   - 10 students described what they had learned primarily in terms of a technical skill
   - 7 in terms of a personal or managerial skill or a lesson
   - 6 in terms of both.

   In this sample every student claimed to have learned something. Possible this alone is sufficient to declare all these projects successful.

5. Were you required to learn new tools or techniques? If so what?

   19 students learned between them a wide variety of tools and techniques. These included new languages such as Java, C++, Perl and Tck/Tk and libraries or packages such as AVS, XView or OpenGL.

   4 students said they did not need to learn new tools but in fact cited learning to cope with the scale or complexity of what was required as something they learned from the project.

6. What was the hardest thing you had to do in the project?

- 10 understand something concerned with the project itself or with the tools to be used
- 6 some aspect of the design
- 6 some aspect of the implementation
- 1 accept the limitations of what he could achieve

7. What one change, if any, would have made the project better and why? This question, by its very nature, produced the greatest diversity of answer:

- 6 said better hardware resources or software tools
- 5 better design or project planning
- 3 more time
- 2 start learning earlier
- 2 choose different software
- 2 none
- 1 more supervisor hand-holding
- 1 choose an easier project
- 1 no answer given

# 4   Supervisor Evaluation

In Manchester the supervisor writes a report at the time of marking, to which comments by the marking moderator (the lab organiser) are added. Comparison between this report and the student survey may identify differences between the student's and the supervisor's perceptions.

The student survey and the supervisors' reports and marking were completely independent. The survey was conducted after the projects were completed but before the projects were marked or the supervisors' reports written. In this section we attempt to correlate the supervisor's opinion with the student's opinion. We then relate this to the marks actually obtained in the project and for the degree overall.

For this purpose we classified the supervisor's statement of degree of success of a project and compared it with the student assessment recorded in question 3 of the survey.

5 students stated their projects were very successful and in all 5 cases the supervisor agreed. Of these 5 projects, 3 obtained 1st class project marks and 2 2.1 marks. In terms of degree result 2 were 1st class, 1 was 2.1 and 2 were 2.2. No project marks were worse that the overall result and 3 students performed 5, 10 and 20% respectively better than their overall mark. The latter student obtained a 1st class project mark but only a 2.2 degree result.

| | | Supervisor view of success | | | |
| --- | --- | --- | --- | --- | --- |
| | | Very Succ | Successful | Moderate | Failure |
| Student View | Very Succ. | 5 | | | |
| | Successful | | | 6 | 4 |
| | Moderate | | | 2 | 3 |
| | Failure | | | | 3 |

In 6 cases the student and supervisor agreed that the project had been successful. These comprised three marginally 1st class and three 2.1 projects, resulting in degree results: one 1st class, two 2.1 and three 2.2. 4 of the 6 had better projects than overall results.

In 3 cases the student and supervisor agreed the project was moderately successful but in 2 of these cases a 1st class degree result was obtained. One project was 1st but the other top 2.1. The third was a 2.2 project with a 2.1 degree.

In all 3 cases where the student judged the project a failure the supervisor considered it a moderate or partial success. These students obtained project marks the same as overall degree with one 2.1 and two 2.2s.

In 2 cases the student considered the project moderately successful but the supervisor judged it successful. Both these projects obtained 1st class marks.

In 4 cases the student considered the project successful but the supervisor judged it only moderately so. Degree results were 2.1, 2.2 and two 3rd class.

It appears that there is a high degree of correlation between the student's and the supervisor's assessment of success. However the student's estimate is moderated to a greater extent by his expectation. So some good students with good projects tended to qualify the degree of perceived success by their own expectations while supervisors gave a possibly more objective and positive evaluation. Similarly where students of average ability considered their projects a failure the supervisor generally found redeeming features. However, some weaker students were satisfied that they were successful in their own terms but the supervisor's view was more qualified.

# 5 Case studies

## 5.1 Case study A: A possibly unsuccessful project

In project A the student stated that what he hoped to get out of the project was the delivery of the technical goals. He failed to achieve this and judged the project a failure. The supervisor considered the project a partial success. The overall degree and project mark awarded were both 2.2 class.

There were difficulties with the selection of this project. The student was unsuccessful in his initial choices as he chose projects which were very popular and allocated to other students. The choice of this project was something of a last resort at a very late stage in the allocation process.

The project required practical experimentation to test a hypothesis based on some difficult theory. It was to be programmed straightforwardly in C and did not require the learning of new tools. The supervisor stated that the student did not need to understand the theory and that the practical experiments were straightforward. Nevertheless he reported that the student had difficulties understanding the project throughout and that technical understanding was the weakest aspect of the student's performance.

The student appeared, to the supervisor, happy with the project as it proceeded and maintained regular contact with the supervisor. However he reported in the survey afterwards that the project was intrinsically not suitable for an average undergraduate.

Possibly as a result of difficulties in understanding, the student found it difficult to be enthusiastic about the project and progress was slow throughout most of the project. However towards the end of the project the student was reported as working hard and was able to conduct some of the experiments required.

In retrospect the student feels he would have achieved more and perhaps learned more with an easier project. To him problems of theoretical understanding of statistical methods and neural networks were a major obstacle. It does appear that to him the choice of project was a major negative factor and that the project would have been better suited to an abler student.

Nevertheless a satisfactory mark, relative to the student's exam performance, was achieved. A different project might have resulted in a more satisfactory learning outcome but not necessarily a better mark.

## 5.2   Case study B: A very successful project

This project was judged very successful by the student, the supervisor and the lab organiser acting as a second marker. It was awarded a good 1st class mark but the degree class the student obtained was 2.2.

The project definition was created by the student himself and was related to his desire the write games programs for a living. The project was a 3-D interactive model designer for constructing 3D polygonal surface models of considerable complexity. A complete working program of some 7000 lines was designed, implemented and evaluated by 3 separate users. The lab organiser, himself a 3D modelling expert, judged the project one of the most technically impressive he had seen.

The student was highly motivated. His stated aim was to get experience of a large project and he was pleased he got that. He also claimed that he 'learned how to write good software' through this project.

This student arrived at University with good A levels (24 points) and considerable programming experience. He has tended to under-achieve in examinations and also in the formal set laboratory exercises in the first two years. His exam performance was particularly weak in formal and mathematical subjects. An open question is what would have motivated him to achieve a better all round performance.

One of the successes of this project is that it has not been allowed to degenerate into a 'code hacking' exercise. The project definition has been abstracted sufficiently away from 'games programming' to be soundly based. A good project life-cycle methodology of requirements, design, implementation and evaluation has been followed. Although it might be expected that a practically oriented Computer Scientist does well in a practically oriented project, the project has achieved more than it. Significant learning objectives have been met.

# 6   Conclusion

In a rapidly changing subject, such as Computer Science, there is a constant need to reevaluate learning outcomes. Changing technology results in rapid changes in the technical definition of a good project. The success of such projects depends on a student undertaking a project sufficiently challenging that project completion is a significant achievement. However a project which fails to achieve its technical objectives may still be a valuable and positive learning experience even if that value is difficult to measure. If the student knows how the technical objectives would be met if the project were started over again then something significant has indeed been learned by undertaking the project. If due attention is paid to both the process and the product, in project definition, execution and assessment, then our projects will be successful.

Student surveys inform our understanding of learning outcome and should influence the definition and execution of the next cycle of projects. Good practice will identify expected learning outcomes early in the project lifecycle. Agreement between supervisor and student will ensure that an acceptable list of outcomes is defined and will maximise the likelihood of these being achieved.

# 7   Acknowledgements

The work was conducted under the H.E.F.C.E. Fund for Development of Teaching and Learning Project EPCOS (Effective project work in Computer Science)

# References

[1] Peter J. Denning, Educating a New Engineer, Communications of the A.C.M. Vol 35 No 12, December 1992, pp 82-97.

[2] The Engineering Council: Standards and Routes to Registration (SARTOR), 2nd Edition 1990 and 3rd Edition 1997.

[3] Manmahesh Kantipudi et al, Software Engineering Course Projects: Failures and recommendations, in C Sledge (Ed.), Software Engineering Education, LNCS vol 640, Springer-Verlag 1992, pp324-338.

[4] University of Manchester Department of Computer Science: Third Year Single Honours Project Laboratory (CS3900) 1997/8.

[5] Melody Moore and Colin Potts, Learning by Doing: Goals and Experiences of Two Software Engineering Courses, in Jorge L. Díaz-Herrera (Ed.), Software Engineering Education, LNCS vol 750, Springer-Verlag 1994, pp151-164.

[6] Melody Moore and Terence Brennan, Process Improvement in the Classroom, in Rosalind L. Ibrahim(Ed.), Software Engineering Education, LNCS vol 895, Springer-Verlag 1995, pp123-130.

# POSTER

# Group Projects

Lesley F. Wright
Liverpool John Moores University,
Liverpool, United Kingdom

#### Abstract

This is a description of the first run of a course using a new method of assessment. Although group work had previously formed a major part of the assessment, this was the first use of a real-world example.

## Introduction

I teach a first year course in reasoning and communication. The course has been designed to teach the students various skills including group skills and working in teams. This leads to such concepts as delegation, what makes a good leader and how to run meetings effectively. Last semester I taught the course to students taking computer science, software engineering and information systems management degrees, 153 students in total. These students tend to be reluctant to become involved in anything that they do not see as directly relevant to computing. They also tend to split into their own particular course groups (Computer Studies, Software Engineering & Information Systems Management). This can make it difficult when trying to teach them group working skills.

## Setting up Groups

The first thing I do in this module is put the students into groups of five people. I select the student groups so that, where possible, there is at least one woman in the group. I also ensure that the groups consist of people who do not know each other. My method is to make all the people born in January stand up, see where they are sitting and pick people who are sitting furthest away from each other. This carries on for all the months of the year until I have my groups. My justification for this is that, in a work situation, teams of experts are often put together to tackle projects. These teams may consist of people who may or may not know each other, and even, in some cases dislike each other, but who need to work together in order to complete the work on schedule.

## Team-Building and Team Guidelines

The groups consist of five to six students and they do some team-building exercises over the first fortnight designed to help them discover the talents and abilities of their group members. The exercises consist of a variety of problems, both mathematical and logic problems. They also have discovery problems where they have a limited amount of time to find certain information from the library or elsewhere. I also insist that they choose a team leader or spokesperson by the end of the second week. This is to ensure that group project information comes to me from one source only. Since there are 153 students, it would be impossible to have all of them coming to me for every handout, or every piece of information. The spokesperson/team leader is the only one authorised to come and see me in my office, though other group members may e-mail me if, for some reason, the spokesperson is not available. Only on one occasion was there a request from a group to change their spokesperson/leader and this was due to illness on the part of the leader. An alternative leader was then chosen from the remaining group members. The reason for their having to choose their spokesperson by the end of the second week is because they start their group project in the third week.

## The Cybercafe

The group project consists of them coming up with full details, costings and a financial plan for a cyber cafe. They are told where the site is, (one of the most expensive parts of Liverpool), and they are told that their project report should be good enough to convince a bank manager to lend them the money. They should, therefore, include reasonable forecasts for future income and plans to repay the loan within five years.

They are not given any of the costings, nor told what details they may need to include, but they are able to request sources of information. If a group leader comes to me to ask where they can obtain the costs of tables and chairs, for example, I will point them in the right direction. As far as health and safety regulations are concerned, they are told to contact the council for information. They are also told that they must put in some of their own capital, since the bank would not consider lending them the entire cost of setting up the cafe. Most of the students suggested that they could contribute fifteen thousand pounds, since this was the equivalent of three one-thousand pound student loans each, one per year, for the five group members. One enterprising student said that he would re-mortgage his house, and one foreign student told me that his parents would fund him since it would be no more expensive than keeping him at university!

The project lasts for three weeks, which is a very tight schedule. However, they do have one week when I do not give them a lecture, but run a drop-in session for any who need help. The students have to be able to apportion the workload between them, and have regular meetings to collate the work if they are to complete it in time. There is a coursework allowance of 15 hours for this project, which may not seem much, but there are five or six in a group, so this is quite a considerable resource for the students.

The students tackle the project in a variety of ways. Some groups undertake surveys, others spend hours drinking coffee in the internet cafe in Liverpool, others use forecasting software obtained from various sources. Many of them visited their own banks and talked to the small business advisor. They are then able to decide on the size of the site they are looking for, the number of computers they are going to need, and the likely numbers of customers and customer expenditure they can expect.

## Cost-Effectiveness

Out of the thirty groups who took part in this project, only one group said that the specified site would not be cost-effective, so they had chosen an alternative site. Other groups solved this problem in a number of different ways. Some of them proposed live music evenings, some of them proposed having a liquor licence, and others proposed special game evenings using some of the latest and/or most popular games available. They also proposed such things as e-mail accounts, giving courses on how to use the internet, the e-mail, or any of the software on the computers, and selling the software and other computer peripherals.

One group came up with such an innovative idea that I am convinced that not only would it work, but also that it could be a viable future prospect for them should they wish to go into business on their own after they graduate. Another group also thought that they had come up with a viable future business prospect and even stated that they had every intention of following it up after they had graduated. Unfortunately for them, though, I had to point out a number of deficiencies in their plan, which would have caused it to make quite big losses over their five-year time scale.

# Assessment

The project report is marked as a group effort, so all the students named on the report obtain an equal mark. Any information they have obtained from small business advisors, banks, companies and so on is put in their appendices. This information is a useful resource for them should they require any future financial advice. It is also useful for me to see where they obtained their information from and how extensive their research had been. They also find it useful if they are considering purchasing a computer or any other computing equipment. Since they have already investigated what would be the best value for money, they are in a better position to make a good purchase.

After they have completed the project, they then have to do a presentation in front of their tutorial groups. They are told that the presentation should be treated as a formal presentation to the bank manager, the bank manager having already received a copy of their report. The groups are given a fortnights notice of when they will be doing their presentation and, in the interim weeks, they are given advice on how best to prepare for it. They are shown a copy of the mark sheet for the presentation and are told that they are not being marked on the content of their presentation, but on how they perform. This means that they are marked on such things as appearance, clarity of speech, irritating gestures, eye contact and other non-verbal communication. They are also marked on whether or not they introduce themselves and on how well they kept to their time limit. Since there are so many groups, they only have fifteen minutes, three minutes each, in which to do their presentation, and there are five minutes at the end for questions.

The group members are marked individually by the member of staff and by the other groups in their tutorial group. This means that each presentation is marked by one member of staff and eight groups. The average of the group marks is added to the staff mark to give the overall presentation mark. This enables those who are good at presentation to receive a higher mark than those who do badly. This is good practice for the future when, as final year students, they will need to undertake a project and do a presentation on their own.

# Conclusions

This was the first time that I have set this project and run this course, so I was particularly interested in how the students reacted to it. I was also interested to see the standard of work that they would produce. As I said before, the computing students are generally reluctant, especially in their first semester, to tackle anything that doesn't mean sitting at a keyboard all day and this has caused difficulties in the past with attendance and submission of coursework.

I found that, with very few exceptions, the students tackled the project with enthusiasm. Their imaginations seem to have been fired by the idea of running a cyber cafe and, consequently, some of them put considerably more time and effort in to it than they needed to. The standard of reports received were quite exceptional, with only one or two being of a poor standard. The students had gone into such incredible detail, even looking at the costs of different types of electrical wiring, and the cost of providing headphones for those who wished to play noisy games. I have even heard from the careers department, who give them a talk in place of one of my lectures, that a small number of the students have been to see them regarding setting up their own business after they graduate. I'm not saying that they all intend to set up cyber cafes, but some of them are now considering the possibility of setting up their own business after graduation, as an alternative to other graduate employment.

# STUDENT POSTERS

# A Window on Group Formation Factors

Katherine Thorn

University of Kent

United Kingdom

## Introduction

Although many scholars have studied groups from many different perspectives, such as psychologists considering various aspects of within-group and between-group processes and structure, the sphere of 'group formation' has been largely ignored. This means that, although, within both the academic and the business worlds, groups are an increasingly important feature, how groups are formed remains largely a mystery. However if, as some have suggested, the way in which a group is formed and it's productivity are correlated then 'group formation' should be an area of research of interest to anyone who works with groups, as all within this category would rather work with more effective groups. In 'Group Processes and Productivity' Steiner (1972) argues that group productivity depends upon three types of variables: *task demands, resources* (human and material) and *processes*. Group formation may be irrelevant to task demands, but what resources are available is largely dependent upon how the group is formed. (If a software engineering group is created, with no consideration to the kinds of skills needed, then the group may find itself lacking vital resources needed to complete their task well.) Furthermore psychologists such as Moreno (1953, cited from Hare, 1982) have argued that what processes occur within a group will be affected by how the group was formed.

Moreno believed that in order to create more effective problem-solving groups one should place together individuals who like one another and who want to work together, rather than by simply engaging in more training. He argued that groups formed on the basis of interpersonal preference do not have to expend so much energy on socio-emotional processes (needed to alleviate interpersonal problems) and so can release more energy through the fulfilling of task-orientated processes (allowing for the group goals to be more rapidly fulfilled). Moreno sought to find correlates between group productivity and whether or not the group was formed on the basis of preference (which he ascertained through measures of the strength of interpersonal liking between individuals). In summarising the empirical evidence, from studies by both Moreno and of others who adopted his methodological approach, Shaw (1976) comments that the evidence is moderately consistent, with groups formed on the basis of preference both learning and achieving more (so long as the members were motivated to learn and achieve). There is also some evidence that this effect may operate more strongly for groups with more capable members.

In a similar vein Stanley Wasserman (1991) developed statistical models which allow study of the structure of social networks. He uses one and two mode matrices to look at the nature of relations between one and two groups of individuals, respectively. Like Moreno his matrices allow one to consider the strength of relationship between individuals, although he applies his models to many more varied types of relational ties than liking and preference.

Within this study 10 large groups (7 to 13 members in size) of 106 software engineering undergraduates, already engaged in computing group work, known as the 'Killer Robot' project, were studied. These students' course required that, at the end of the 'Killer Robot' project, from each of these initial 'Killer Robot' groups, two interdependent sub-groups were formed. These sub-groups participated in a 'Mail System' software engineering project, in which one sub-group was responsible for the mail system user interface, whilst the other undertook the creation of the underlying message handling code. These two sub-groups, like the initial 'Killer Robot' groups were self-selected. The goal of the study was to discover what factors determine this formation of the smaller software engineering groups from the initial group. Wasserman-type matrices were used to model the relations between the group members of the initial, larger group. These allowed predictions to be made regarding the optimum group divisions and enabled the construction of distributions (which showed all the possible group division outcomes and which outcomes are liable to be due to chance) against which the actual group formation decisions could be compared.

Six different factors were used to model the relationships between the group members:

• a balance of *skills* across the two sub-groups (which reflected whether the coverage of necessary software engineering skills have been optimised for each group)

• how industrious members are perceived to be (that is how much *effort* is seen to be expended by each member)

• how *competent* (or capable) members are perceived to be by others in the group.

• *liking* between members

• *meta-contrasts* (a consideration of how distinct the groups are from one another, which involves the consideration of prototypicality, that investigates to what extent each member maximises the meta-contrast.)

• *intention*. (Fishbein and Azjen in their theory of reasoned action (1974, cited from Eiser, 1986) state that intention is the best predictor of actual behaviour, though it must be noted that within this study the intentions of the individual members of each group were taken together to predict each group's behaviour, so different rules may apply.). How each member intends the groups to form should be based upon one, some or all of the other factors, depending upon which factors are of importance to them. For example, if a given member thinks that liking is the only important consideration then their liking and intention ratings should be very closely correlated.

Each of the factors was considered at both the individual group and global level (where the effect of each factor across all the groups was considered). Therefore, the study results reveal which factors were determinants of the formation of each of the pairs of sub-groups and which factor was the most important determinant for the groups overall. For the purpose of this article only three of the six aforementioned factors will be considered. These will exemplify the issue of whether rational (task-orientated) factors or interpersonal (socio-emotional) factors are of greater importance in determining intention (the postulated best predictor of the sub-group formation). Therefore, as well as *intention,* the factors of *competence* (task-orientated) and *liking* (socio-emotional) will be examined.

# Method

Information regarding all of the factors was gathered through the use of two questionnaires, one administered at the end of the 'killer robot' project and the other during the course of the 'mail system' project work. The data being referred to in this article was elicited by the first questionnaire alone, as the second was more concerned with meta-contrasts and the balance of skills factors.

## The Liking Model (L value)

Liking was considered using a one mode matrix, where the relations between individuals are not considered to be reflexive. The relevant question on the first questionnaire asks (referring to the initial 'killer robot' groups):

• How much do you like (as a person) each member of your group?

| 1 | 2 | 3 | 4 | 5 |
|---|---|---|---|---|
| I have no liking for this person | Average Liking (i.e. liking as for an average student) | | | I like them as a good friend |

These ratings were placed in the matrix such that the liking relationship flows from all the group members as placed on the horizontal i-axis to all the group members as placed on the vertical j-axis. The group members were not asked to provide a measure of how much they like themselves and so consequently there is a diagonal of zeros across the matrix where ratings of the liking of each member for himself would otherwise be placed. These zeros were excluded from the equations used to produce the L (liking) value. For any position in the matrix, bar for those where $i = j$, it can be stated that:

$$X_{ij} = k \text{ if group member i likes group member j at strength k}$$

The matrix was then divided into four quadrants (see figure 1) based on the division of the members into two approximately evenly sized groups (exactly even when the initial group size is even, but with group A having one less member than group B when the initial group size is odd). This is shown on the matrix by the first mail system sub-group (A) being placed in the first five members positions on both axes (five members if, for example, we are referring to an initial group of size 10). The second sub-group would then be placed in the last 5 positions on both axes (again using the example of an initial group of 10). This now means that two of the four quadrants contain the within-group liking scores for the two sub-groups (quadrants labelled A1 and B1), whereas the two other quadrants reveal the between-group liking scores (quadrants labelled A2 and B2). Therefore an equation could be used to calculate the L value, which indicated the difference between the liking within the two sub-groups and the liking-between these two groups.

$$L\ (L{:}{-}8,8) = (A1 + B2) - (A2 + B2)$$

**Figure 1**

Liking Received (j)

| Group Member | | 1 | 2 | 3 | 4 | 5 | 6 | 7 | 8 | 9 | 10 |
|---|---|---|---|---|---|---|---|---|---|---|---|
| | | | | Gp A | | | | | Gp B | | |
| | | | | **A1** | | | | | **B2** | | |
| Gp A | 1 | 0 | 3 | 3 | 5 | 2 | 5 | 3 | 3 | 5 | 5 |
| | 2 | 4 | 0 | 3 | 5 | 3 | 5 | 4 | 3 | 5 | 5 |
| | 3 | 4 | 4 | 0 | 4 | 3 | 4 | 2 | 5 | 2 | 2 |
| | 4 | 3 | 4 | 2 | 0 | 3 | 5 | 5 | 2 | 3 | 5 |
| Liking Given (i) | 5 | 2 | 3 | 3 | 4 | 0 | 4 | 4 | 4 | 2 | 2 |
| | 6 | 2 | 3 | 3 | 2 | 4 | 0 | 5 | 2 | 3 | 3 |
| Gp B | 7 | 4 | 4 | 2 | 5 | 5 | 5 | 0 | 3 | 5 | 5 |
| | 8 | 3 | 2 | 5 | 3 | 4 | 4 | 2 | 0 | 2 | 2 |
| | 9 | 2 | 5 | 2 | 4 | 2 | 4 | 4 | 2 | 0 | 4 |
| | 10 | 3 | 4 | 2 | 5 | 3 | 5 | 5 | 2 | 4 | 0 |
| | | | | **A2** | | | | | **B1** | | |

A random frequency distribution of L for the individual groups was calculated by the initial group being split exhaustively into all the different possible group combinations, with L being calculated for each different combination. If, for example, there are 10 members of the group then the exhaustive number of different possible splits is 252. This is calculated using a simple equation derived from Bernoulli's Law (Levy & Preidel, 1944). The calculation used, where n is the size of the original 'Killer Robot' group and r is the size of one of the smaller 'Mail System' sub-groups, is:

$$\text{No. of possible different divisions} = \frac{n!}{r!(n-r)!}$$

If liking was a determinant of the formation of the 'mail system' groups then the L value would be at the extreme positive end of the generated random distribution. Such a value, that is high and positive, would indicate that the within-group liking (A1 + B1) had been maximised and that the between-group liking (A2 + B2) had been minimised. As the direction of the outcome that would lead to the null hypothesis being rejected is known, the experimental hypothesis that 'liking affects group formation' is 1 tailed.

# The Intention Model (I value)

This factor data was treated in the same way as the liking data, having been elicited by the question:

• Would you like to work again in a coursework group with the various members of your group?

The students responded, regarding each of their other group members, using a 5 point scale (graded from 'I would not like this' to 'I would like this very much', with average intention being reflected by point two). As the I values should approximate most closely to how the sub-groups are actually formed the different intention ratings for each individual in each group were correlated with the other factor ratings. High correlations, therefore, indicate which of the 5 factors are most important in determining the intention to work in a group with another individual. As with liking, the intention experimental hypothesis 'intention predicts group formation' is also 1 tailed.

# The Perceived Competence Model (C value)

The Competence data was treated in a similar manner to the liking data and was gained by the question:

• How capable/competent do you think each member of your group is at academic coursework?

Again students responded using a 5 point scale, with point two reflecting average competence. Unlike the liking matrix there is no diagonal of zeros across the competence matrix, as each member additionally rates their own capability. Also in manipulating the competence factor data an equation different from the liking equation is used. This equation calculates the difference between group A's effort or competence (as perceived by both group A and group B) and group B's effort or competence (as perceived by both group B and A). The equation is:                                C (C:-8,+8)

$$= (A1 + A2) - (B1 + B2)$$

The influence of the perceived competence factor's outcome is less clear than that for the liking factor. If the actual values are at either extreme of the distribution this would indicate that the more competent individuals have clustered together in one of the sub-groups. (At which end of the distribution the actual values fall is determined by which of the two sub-groups gained the more able members.) Therefore, the experimental hypothesis that 'competence affects group formation' is 2 tailed. With this distribution even C values falling very close to the mean could suggest that perceived competence was a factor that influenced the sub-group formation, as this would point to there being a balance of competencies between the two groups. Such a result would still be uncertain, as C values around the distribution mean are also more likely to be due to chance, if the distribution is at all normal is shape. Further investigation would be required to further study this balance of competence influence.

# Results

The 'killer robot' group 6 was eliminated from the results analysis because by the 'mail system' component of the course the group had been disbanded by the lecturer concerned, due to it being "dysfunctional". Therefore, the results analysis involved the data pertaining to the 9 remaining groups (all of sizes 9 to 13), causing a decline in subjects from 106 to 99. The data was manipulated so that each of the factors could be considered at both the individual group and global level. In order to examine the former, that is which factors were the most important determinants of the formation of each of the pairs of sub-groups, it was necessary to generate random distributions, for each factor, for each group, to indicate which 'Mail System' group formation outcomes were likely to occur by chance (as explained in the Liking Model sub-section). Then actual scores for each factor for the individual groups (that is those corresponding to the actual group formation outcomes) were compared against the appropriate distributions in order to ascertain whether these real scores were from a different, non-random distribution. When the scores were found to be significantly unlikely to be from the random distribution this provided evidence that the factor in question was of importance in determining the group in question's formation decision.

The group by group results (see Figure 3 in appendix) indicated that both liking and intention were very good predictors of group formation for groups 5 to 10 (bar for group 6). This suggested that in these groups liking had influenced both intention and, in turn, the actual group formation decision process. For these groups the liking and intention null hypotheses could be rejected at the 1% level of significance. It is important to note that although highly significant intention was not always a better predictor than liking. For example with group 7 the liking factor predicted the correct group formation out the 462 possible options, whereas the intention factor placed the correct formation as the forth most likely outcome. On the other hand groups 8 and 9 exemplified almost perfect results, with the intention factor predicting accurately the correct formation outcome and the liking factor placing the actual outcome as the second most likely option, out of a possible 462 and 262 options respectively. At even the 10% level the competence null hypothesis could only be rejected by group 4, although for group 4 the null hypothesis could actually be rejected at the 1% level. In other words. competence only seemed to influence the formation of the sub-groups of group 4 and barely seemed to influence the other groups. Pearson correlations showed that liking was more highly correlated with intention than competence for each one of the groups, again suggesting that liking rather than competence determined intention.

In order to consider which factor was the most important determinant for the groups overall, for each factor all the distributions of all the groups were standardised (so that each distribution had a mean of 0 and a standard deviation of 1). Then the mean of the sample (the sample of the 9 actual factor scores for each of the groups, now standardised) could be calculated and compared against each factor's standardised, random distribution mean (which is equal to 0), using a T-test. T-tests reveal whether a sample (in this case the 9 true factor scores) is from a different distribution (in this case the random, standardised distribution). This method revealed the influence of each factor at this global level of analysis. (See Figure 2 below.)

## Figure 2: T-Test Results

| Factor | Intention | Liking | Competence |
|---|---|---|---|
| Sample Means | 2.52 | 2.69 | 0.5 |
| T Statistic | 7.56 | 8.08 | 1.51 |
| Critical Value at 1% level | 2.896 | 2.896 | 3.355 |
| Significant at 1% level | * | * | |
| Critical Value at 10% level | 1.397 | 1.397 | 1.86 |
| Significant at 10% level | * | * | |

These results show that when the groups were taken together the liking and intention factor means were significantly different from their random distributions. The null hypothesis that the mean (from all the groups) for liking and intention are from the random population can be rejected at the 1% level of significance. The competence null hypothesis is rejected at the 10% level of significance.

## Conclusion

The results clearly reveal that for the groups in this study and of the three factors considered, liking and intention were good predictors of the group formation patterns, whereas competence was not a good predictor overall, although it was successful in predicting the group formation outcome of one of the nine groups. Liking, rather than intention, was the best predictor of group formation patterns overall. There is some concern that this finding may actually be caused by the position of the intention factor in the first questionnaire. The intention question was the last out of 15 questions, so it may be that this finding reflects more upon the increase in boredom and carelessness of the students as they filled out the questionnaires, than upon liking being a truly better predictor. Further investigation alone would establish this. In terms of whether task-orientated or socio-emotional factors are more important in determining how groups form, this study of competence and liking factors would certainly suggest that socio-emotional factors were given higher consideration in the group formation process.

## References

Eiser, R.J. (1986) Social Psychology. Cambridge.

Hare, A.P. (1982) Creativity in Small Groups. Sage.

Levy, H. & Preidel, E. E. (1948) Elementary Statistics. Thomas Nelson & Sons.

Shaw, M.E. (1976) Group Dynamics: The Psychology of Small Group Behaviour. Mc-Graw-Hill.

Steiner, I.D. (1972) Group Process and Productivity. Academic Press.

Wasserman, S. (1990) Social Networks and Two Sets of Actors. Psycholmetrika, 55(4), 707-720.

# Appendix

## Figure 3: Group by Group Significance Levels for Three Factors

*S Ivalue= Standardardised Intention values
*CF=Cumulative Frequency

(One Tailed Hypotheses)

| Intention | Ivalue | *S Ivalue | Position | Out of. | *CF | Significant at * Level 20% | 10% | 5% | 1% |
|---|---|---|---|---|---|---|---|---|---|
| Gp1 | -0.43 | 0.41 | 79 | 252 | 68.40% | | | | |
| Gp2 | 0.09 | 1.26 | 173 | 1716 | 90.00% | * | * | | |
| Gp3 | 0.15 | 1.45 | 27 | 252 | 89.70% | * | | | |
| Gp4 | 0.63 | 2.1 | 13 | 462 | 49.60% | | | | |
| Gp5 | 0.76 | 2.63 | 2 | 126 | 99.20% | * | * | * | * |
| Gp7 | 0.94 | 2.96 | 4 | 462 | 99.40% | * | * | * | * |
| Gp8 | 1.39 | 4.23 | 1 | 462 | 100% | * | * | * | * |
| Gp9 | 0.33 | 3.68 | 1 | 252 | 100% | * | * | * | * |
| Gp10 | 0.99 | 3.77 | 8 | 1716 | 99.70% | * | * | * | * |

| Liking | Lvalue | S Lvalue | Position | Out of. | CF | Significant at * Level 20% | 10% | 5% | 1% |
|---|---|---|---|---|---|---|---|---|---|
| Gp1 | -0.33 | 0.6 | 53 | 252 | 79.40% | | | | |
| Gp2 | -0.21 | 0.85 | 331 | 1716 | 80.95% | * | | | |
| Gp3 | 0.16 | 1.42 | 25 | 252 | 90.50% | * | * | | |
| Gp4 | 0.42 | 1.57 | 29 | 462 | 93.80% | * | * | | |
| Gp5 | 1.32 | 2.91 | 3 | 126 | 98.20% | * | * | * | * |
| Gp7 | 1.54 | 3.67 | 1 | 462 | 100% | * | * | * | * |
| Gp8 | 1.47 | 4.36 | 2 | 462 | 99.80% | * | * | * | * |
| Gp9 | 0.39 | 3.15 | 2 | 252 | 99.60% | * | * | * | * |
| Gp10 | 2.16 | 5.72 | 2 | 1716 | 99.90% | * | * | * | * |

(Two Tailed Hypothesis)

| Competence | Cvalue | S Cvalue | Position | Out of. | CF | Significant at * Level 20% | 10% | 5% | 1% |
|---|---|---|---|---|---|---|---|---|---|
| Gp1 | 0.2 | 0.43 | 80 | 252 | 71% | | | | |
| Gp2 | 1.13 | 1.14 | 241 | 1716 | 86.10% | | | | |
| Gp3 | 0.72 | 1.22 | 27 | 252 | 89.70% | | | | |
| Gp4 | 1.19 | 2.36 | 4 | 462 | 99.40% | * | * | * | |
| Gp5 | -0.9 | -1.73 | 122 | 126 | 38.90% | | | | |
| Gp7 | 0.02 | -0.22 | 266 | 462 | 42.60% | | | | |
| Gp8 | -0.14 | -0.57 | 334 | 462 | 29.20% | | | | |
| Gp9 | 0.89 | 1.32 | 24 | 252 | 90.90% | * | | | |
| Gp10 | 0.33 | 0.6 | 495 | 1716 | 54.30% | * | | | |

# Project '98

# Poster Summary

# VICI

## University of Sheffield

**Grant Bardsley**

**Simon Cadd**

**Dan East**

**Adam Howitt**

**Dan Khan**

**Paul Todd**

# Database Project

## Database Requirements

- Available over the Internet.

- Consultants over Britain and Europe to be able to store information about new and existing child patients over the Internet.

- This information must be secure.

- Search the database for trends between patients, giving researchers a powerful tool.

- Supporting pages to maintain an accurate database of contact details.

- A discussion page to encourage communication between members.

## Development process

- Met with the client to establish project requirements.

- Produced an informal outline of what we understood to be his needs.

- Formally documented his requirements to form a contract between us.

- Used a prototyping strategy to develop the database.

- Database is now in form to be converted for Internet use.

## Deliverables

- Completed database.

- Help pages to assist users of the database on the Internet.

- Full documentation of the design of the database for maintenance.

# BPIIDG Web Site

A WWW based project for the BPIIDG to replace their current static web site with a new dynamic and interactive site. The original site was not really of much interest to their membership. The new site is designed for the members in mind.

## Website: Public Area

The aim of the public area of the site is to increase the profile of the group and allow interested parties to contact them.

- Introduction to Group including meetings and subscriptions

- Committee Contact Details

## Website: Private Area

A password protected area for members' use only. The aim of this area of the site is to enable easy communication between members.

- Full Member Details available on pages

- Users can change their own details

- Possible to send email to all members

- Announcement Boards

- Discussion Boards

- Links Pages

- Web Administration Kit

## Technologies employed

- Perl

- Apache

- CGI

- HTML

# Intelligent Web Browsers

## Introduction

- Our client approached us with the initial proposal of finding out they could utilise the World Wide Web more effectively.

- At present they have only a handful of employees who use the World Wide Web for information retrieval and extraction.

- Our contact, within the company has set up numerous meetings involving himself, his colleagues and representatives of VICI.

## Requirements

- Due to unfamiliarity with the Internet, our client requires VICI to provide a very basic Web browsing facility that will only search for the required information within a pre-defined list of Web pages.

- The client has given VICI a list of Web Pages that he already uses to find information. We must now find additional web pages for our client that he and his colleagues will find useful.

- The client must check that each of these Web pages will be useful before they are added to the Web Page list as expert knowledge is required.

## Work Done

- Obtained various Web Pages that may of interest to the client, and may be added to the Web Page list if we are instructed to do so by the client.

- Performed critical evaluation of a number of options that we have outlined to the client.

## Work Still To Be Completed

- Carry out interviews with a member of each group, so to provide us with a complete understanding of what each group's ideal solution would be.

- Provide a working solution to their problem that fits all the groups requirements as much as possible, whilst still providing a solution to the original problem.

# Internet Project

- VICI Training is the branch of the company responsible for any training projects that the company may receive.

- All members of the company have a number of different skills and have been exposed to a large number of computer products, packages and programming languages. This is an ideal basis for a training branch to the company.

## Project Brief

- We are currently undertaking a project for a local engineering company who have just installed a Worldwide Area Network.

- An initial meeting with the client to capture requirements determined that the company wanted us to train a number of their technical staff on using the Internet, Email and Netscape Communicator.

- The client also requested a self-contained training package on the same topics.

## Processes

- The requirements were researched to determine viability, and then more in depth research was undertaken.

- A choice of delivery options was given to the client including a paper copy, electronic copy or a combination of both.

- The client chose to have the self-contained package delivered as a set of HTML web pages.

- The content was written and passed through quality control where two group members not directly involved with the project checked it.

- We decided to present the training course using a set of slides and an interactive presentation.

# AUTHOR INDEX